TEACH YOURSELF BOOKS

NORWEGIAN

NORWEGIAN

A book on Self-instruction in the
Norwegian Bokmål

Alf Sommerfelt

Completely revised and enlarged by
Ingvald Marm

TEACH YOURSELF BOOKS

Long-renowned as the authoritative source for self-guided learning – with more than 30 million copies sold worldwide – the *Teach Yourself* series includes over 200 titles in the fields of languages, crafts, hobbies, sports, and other leisure activities.

Library of Congress Catalog Card Number: 92-82509

First published in UK 1943 by Hodder Headline Plc, 338 Euston Road, London NW1 3BH

First published in US 1993 by NTC Publishing Group, 4255 West Touhy Avenue, Lincolnwood (Chicago), Illinois 60646 – 1975 U.S.A.

Printed in England by Cox & Wyman Ltd, Reading, Berkshire.

New Edition 1967
Reissued 1992

Impression number	35	34	33	32	31	30	29	28	27	26
Year	1999	1998	1997	1996	1995	1994				

CONTENTS

PART III

INTRODUCTION

Norwegian is a Teutonic language closely related to the other Scandinavian languages: in fact educated Norwegians, Swedes and Danes usually understand each other without much difficulty. Among the Teutonic languages Scandinavian is closest to English and Dutch; the tribes who brought the English language to England came from those parts of North Germany which border upon Denmark. In Viking times Norsemen and Englishmen learnt to understand each other fairly easily and Norse and Danish words penetrated in large numbers into English.

Even now an Englishman will not find it very difficult to acquire a reading knowledge of modern Norwegian. Norwegian grammar is very simple, English and Norwegian having developed along parallel lines. But the correct use of the spoken and written word in Norway is beset with some special difficulties not usually met with in the same degree in other European languages. In order to understand these difficulties some knowledge of Norwegian linguistic history is required.

The Viking Age brought the Latin alphabet and literature to Norway from England. Old Norse, the language of Norwegian and Icelandic administration, became towards the end of the medieval period more and more different from spoken Norwegian. It had therefore to be kept up by scribal tradition.

In 1319 the Norwegian royal house became extinct and a Swedish king succeeded to the throne; towards the end of the century Norway was united to Denmark under one king, a union which lasted to 1814.

Norway had suffered terribly from the Black Death and the subsequent epidemics and also from the German Hansa which fleeced the country. A large number of low German words penetrated into the three Scandinavian countries at this time. The literary life of Norway declined and the distance between the old literary language and the spoken dialect which developed along the same lines as Danish, Swedish and Middle English became so great that Old Norse

was almost incomprehensible to the Norwegians of the six-
teenth century. The country had no powerful centre, the
language of which could impose itself. No wonder, therefore,
that Danish, which was not so very different from Norwegian,
became the written idiom of Norway. The king and the
central administration were in Copenhagen and Denmark
was then a much richer and more populous country than
Norway.

After the Lutheran reformation Norway again got the
beginnings of a literature; the Norwegian authors wrote
Danish but they used a number of Norwegian words and also
some Norwegian grammatical forms. Danish, however, did
not become the spoken language in Norway. Danish-born
officials, of whom there were a certain number, spoke Danish,
but their children used Norwegian.

In the eighteenth century, perhaps already in the seventeenth, a common form of speech arose in the south-east
which tended to spread, a form from which the one of the
present two Norwegian languages, called the *Riksmål*, is
descended.

The language of the townspeople of the south-east was
composed of three main layers. On solemn occasions, e.g. in
the pulpit, almost pure Danish was used. It was pronounced
according to the Norwegian phonetic system, with occasional
Norwegian grammatical forms and with a good number of
Norwegian words. It was called *høitidssproget*, 'the solemn
language'. The people spoke a local vernacular. The
bourgeoisie used the so-called 'intermediate' or middle-class
language with a mixed grammar and many more Norwegian
words than the 'solemn language'. But there was no sharp
division between these different standards. All classes of
society knew the vernacular and used it or at least forms,
words and expressions from it.

When Norway and Denmark separated, the influence of
the Danish written language became stronger for a short
time on account of the improvement of the schools which
used Danish grammars. But soon there was a reaction. The
poet Wergeland initiated a programme of norwegianizing the
written language. The Norwegian folk-tales by Asbjørnsen
and Moe in the 1840's used the Danish orthography and in
most cases also the Danish grammatical forms, but they

kept as close as possible to the original and retained very many Norwegian words. The result was a simple, vigorous style recalling that of the old Norse Sagas.

Some people were, however, not content with a slow norwegianizing of the written standard. A philologist and author, Ivar Aasen, created in the middle of the century a wholly Norwegian literary language, which he built mainly on the more conservative western dialects and which he termed *Landsmål*. This literary language gained official recognition in the 1880's and several famous Norwegian authors have made use of it. The 'solemn language' and the middle-class language merged in the south-east, in the course of the century, into a spoken mixed Dano-Norwegian idiom, which was continually norwegianized. In other parts of the country the language of the *bourgeoisie* had a more local character, in certain respects less influenced by the written norm, in others more, e.g. in Bergen. But the official orthography was not changed. In many cases Norwegian word-forms and also grammatical forms were used when reading aloud the Danish written form. Danish has in many cases *b*, *d*, *g* in intervocalic positions where Norwegian has retained the old *p*, *t*, *k*. One therefore wrote *flyde* 'to run, to float', *kage* 'cake', *gabe* 'to yawn', but pronounced *flyte*, *kake*, *gape*. There were numerous alternating forms as the written norm influenced the pronunciation of forms which had a more or less literary character; many of the abstract terms were also Danish. Thus, for instance, one said *flydende* 'fluent' (from *flyte*), *bog* [bɔːg¹] 'book', but plural [bøːkər]. One also wrote *heste* 'horses', *kastede* 'threw', but pronounced *hester*, *kastet*.

Several Norwegian authors, among them Bjørnstjerne Bjørnson, adopted an orthography closer to the pronunciation, and in 1907 the first reform of the official literary standard was carried through. Now intervocalic *p*, *t*, *k* were introduced according to the spoken language and many Norwegian grammatical forms were adopted, e.g. the plural ending in *-er* instead of *-e*, and the preterite in *-et* instead of *-ede*. The reform was based on the usage among educated people in the south-east. The language of this class is called *Riksmål*, a term which was initiated by Bjørnson about 1890,

---

[1] Probably from *Bogen* (the Book), i.e. the Bible.

and which means 'state-language'. Now the official names of the two languages are *Nynorsk*, 'Neo-Norwegian' for *Landsmål* and *Bokmål* 'the book-language' for *Riksmål*.

In 1917 a new reform of the written *Bokmål* was passed. This went much further than that of 1907 and adopted the main orthographic principles on which written *Nynorsk* is based. The use of the vowels *æ* and *e* was regulated on historical principles, so that *e* was introduced in many cases where *æ* had been the rule, the Danish *nd*, *ld* were replaced by *nn*, *ll* according to the pronunciation, and *nd*, *ld* were retained only in cases where Old Norse had the *d*. Short vowels in stressed syllables were indicated by the writing of a double consonant, e.g. *natt* 'night' instead of the older *nat*. The Swedish *å* was adopted instead of *aa*. Many diphthongs were allowed, especially in optional forms, and there were numerous minor changes in grammatical forms. At the same time the written standard of the *Nynorsk* was changed on some points in order to approximate it to the dialects of the east and to the *Bokmål*.

A third change was resolved upon in 1938 with the deliberate aim of preparing the amalgamation of the two languages. The orthographical changes in the *Bokmål* were not important, mainly *øy* for older *øi*, *meg*, *deg*, *seg* (the reflexive pronoun) for the previous *mig*, *dig*, *sig*, the dropping of the *h* before *v* in words of alien origin, e.g. *verve* 'enlist', the writing of *ll*, *nn* in a few cases for older *ld*, *nd*, e.g. *snill* 'kind', *funn* 'find', the doubling of *p* in the adverb *opp* 'up'. But in many cases diphthongs which previously had been optional now became compulsory. Some word-forms or grammatical forms which are not common among educated people in the south-east were introduced, some compulsory, e.g. *sju*, *sjuende* for *syv*, *syvende* 'seven', 'seventh', others as optional forms, e.g. *kem* for *hvem* 'who', *kval* for *hval* 'whale'. In *Nynorsk* more forms from the east were made compulsory or optional.

Many foreign words, especially the numerous international terms of Greco-Latin, French or English origin, have been adapted to the new rules, e.g. *sensor*, *sensur* for the earlier *censor*, *censur*, *sjåfør* for *chauffeur*. Already in 1917 a number of these adaptations had taken place and a step still further was taken in the subsequent reform of 1938.

At present the two languages have equal status. In the school the pupils have to learn to read and write both languages, while local school-boards have to determine which of the two is to be the chief language. The *Nynorsk* is mostly used in the west and the centre and the *Bokmål* in the south-east and the north. Both languages have rich literatures and much of both literatures has a strong regional character. Many *Bokmål* writers use dialect words and forms, especially in the dialogue.

Place-names, of which formerly the general elements were written according to the forms of the Dano-Norwegian and later the *Bokmål* standard, are now subjected to special rules which usually coincide with those of the *Nynorsk*, though some local variations are used in order not to make the written form too different from the local pronunciation. Therefore names on older maps ending in *-ø* 'island', now have *-øy* (with the article *-øya* or *øyi* for older *-øen*); other examples are: *-fjeld* 'mountain', now *-fjell*; *bæk* 'small river, stream', now *-bekk*; *åen* 'the river', now *-åa* or *-åi*; *-vand, -vann* 'lake', now *-vatn*; *-gaard, -gård* 'farm', now *-gard*.

The spoken language of the south-east exercises a powerful influence all over the country, though it has not got the same social *prestige* as Southern English or Parisian French. It is the language of the capital and the richest and most populous part of the country. All the main papers use the *Bokmål* and through the radio it penetrates everywhere, though the *Nynorsk* is, of course, also broadcast.

The development of the *Bokmål* from being a mixed Dano-Norwegian language into a really Norwegian one which is now taking place has created a curiously fluctuating standard which entails many pitfalls for the foreign learner. A diphthong, the use of the feminine or of certain verbal forms indicate *nuances* of style and sentiment which cannot be used correctly without a really thorough knowledge of the language. A foreigner ought, therefore, to be careful in using them and should to begin with adopt a rather conservative attitude.

In 1951 Parliament instituted a special body to serve as consultants to the Government on linguistic questions, a Norwegian linguistic commission (*Norsk språknemnd*). In this work the Commission is to further an amalgamation of the two languages. It is composed of 30 members, 15 for each of the two languages, representing linguists, authors, journalists, teachers of Norwegian, and the Norwegian State Broadcasting System. In 1959 a set of rules for the written forms to be used in the schools was issued by the Commission. From a strictly orthographic point of view there are few changes from the rules of 1938, the rules dealing mainly with a regulation of the grammatical forms. The fact that the Commission is to further the amalgamation of the two languages brought on an exacerbation of the linguistic fight.

Then in 1964 the Government charged a new commission with a report on the whole linguistic situation of the country in the hope of finding means of reducing the conflict which has serious consequences, especially for the schools, as most newspapers and authors do not observe the new rules. The Commission's report was submitted in Spring 1966, but was not debated by the Norwegian Parliament until 1970, and the issues are still being awaited at the time of going to press.

This book has tried to keep as near the 1938 Spelling Reform as is considered convenient from a pedagogical point of view. The phonetic description is based upon the pronunciation of educated people in Oslo and the south-east, but the main differences between this standard and the pronunciation used by speakers of *Bokmål* from other parts of the country are indicated. In Bergen educated speech differs in many ways from that of Oslo, not only in pronunciation, but also in grammar. Many forms which are now obsolete in the south-east are still in use there.

PUBLISHER'S NOTE TO THE 1967 EDITION

The Introduction was written by the late Dr Sommerfelt and the rest of this new edition by Mr Marm. The phonetic transcription is intended to serve above all a practical purpose, and specialists will therefore see at once on examining the book that the system adopted is not strictly phonological.

PART I

CHAPTER I

THE SOUNDS IN NORWEGIAN

The Norwegian Alphabet

1. The following twenty-nine letters are used in Norwegian. The phonetic transcription of the pronunciation of these letters is given in square brackets.

Capitals	Small letters	Pronunciation	Capitals	Small letters	Pronunciation
A ..	a ..	[aː]	P ..	p ..	[peː]
B ..	b ..	[beː]	Q ..	q ..	[kuː]
C ..	c ..	[seː]	R ..	r ..	[ærr]
D ..	d ..	[deː]	S ..	s ..	[ess]
E ..	e ..	[eː]	T ..	t ..	[teː]
F ..	f ..	[eff]	U ..	u ..	[uː]
G ..	g ..	[geː]	V ..	v ..	[veː]
H ..	h ..	[hɔ]	W ..	w	[ˈdɔbbəltveː]
I ..	i ..	[iː]	X ..	x ..	[eks]
J ..	j ..	[jɔdd]	Y ..	y ..	[yː]
K ..	k ..	[kɔ]	Z ..	z ..	[sett]
L ..	l ..	[ell]	Æ ..	æ ..	[æː]
M ..	m ..	[emm]	Ø, Ö ..	ø, ö ..	[øː]
N ..	n ..	[enn]	Å ..	å ..	[ɔː]
O ..	o ..	[oː]			

PRONUNCIATION

2. There is far less disagreement between spelling and pronunciation in Norwegian than in English. With a fair chance of success one should therefore be able to read the correct pronunciation out of the spelling after a short survey of the sounds. Words that do not comply with the ordinary rules for the pronunciation of written Norwegian will be specially marked in phonetics.

The Vowels—Length

3.   Norwegian long vowels are pure as in French and Italian and not diphthongized as in English. Norwegians also make a clear distinction between long and short vowels and consonants. A long vowel is expressed in the phonetic transcription used here by the sign **:** after the vowel. As a general rule stressed vowels are long in open syllables, e.g. *la* let, or followed by a short (single) consonant, e.g. *mat* food,—short in closed syllables, i.e. before double consonants or a consonant group, e.g. *katt* cat, *elg* elk. In other words, if the consonant is short (single), the vowel is long; if on the other hand the vowel is short, the consonant must be long (double).

Examine carefully these pairs:

long vowel:	short vowel:
pen pretty	*penn* pen
tak roof	*takk* thanks

Exception:

m is never written double when final, although the preceding vowel is usually short: *lam* lamb or lame, *hjem* home, *rom* room.

4.   **a** when long is pronounced almost like the English **a** in the word **father,** Norwegian *far*. Other examples: *ja* yes, *rar* funny, strange, *male* to paint. A word of warning! The long vowels must not be clipped off, make them really long!

a when short has no real counterpart in English, e.g. *katt* cat. The Norwegian **a** in *katt* comes very near the sound of English **u** in **cut** and the American **o** in **college** and **cotton.** That information may be of help to the beginner.

Practise on these words:

Long **a** in open syllables *far* father, *bare* only, *rar* funny, strange. Note the **r** must be clearly pronounced in these words. Further: *tale* to speak, *sak* matter, *sa* said.

Short **a** in closed syllables: *mann* man, *land* [lann] country, *katt*, or *takke* to thank, *vaske* to wash.

5. **e** has almost the same quality as English **e** in **let.** When long it is somewhat tenser, more like **e** in the French word for summer, **été.** Special care should be taken not to diphthongize it—keep the same sound all through **e—e,** not **e—i.**

Long **e** is found in: *se* see, *le* laugh, *pen* pretty, *del* part, *det* [de:] it.

Note: before **r** short **e** usually gets a much more open pronunciation, almost like the **a** in English **bad,** in phonetic transcription [æ], examples: *sterk* [stærk] strong, *herre* [ˇhærrə] gentleman, *verre* [ˈværrə] worse.

Long in: *her* [hæːr] here, *der* [dæːr] there, *er* [æːr] is *hver* [væ-r] each.

6. In unstressed syllables **e** is pronounced as [ə].

gate [ˇgaːtə] street, *nese* [ˇneːsə] nose. It is a lowered and retracted **e** corresponding fairly well to English [ə] in **effort** [effət].

We have already met it in some words above: *herre, verre, male,* to paint, *tale* to speak. The infinitive ending of most Norwegian verbs is **e** pronounced [ə].

7. **i** when long is tenser than its nearest English equivalent in words like **see, bee, tree.** The tongue is more raised and the corners of the lips are drawn well back.

Examples: *si* to say, *ti* ten, *smil* smile, *fin* fine, *rik* rich, *bris* breeze.

When short the position of the tongue is slightly lower: *litt* a little, *finne* to find, *drikke* to drink, *vill* wild, *mild* [mill] mild, *snill* good, kind, *silke* silk.

8. **y** is not found in normal English. It is an **i** pronounced with rounded lips, approximately the French **u** in **lune.** Start with a long **i** sound, then round the lips gradually.

Long **y** in *by* town, *ny* new, *fy!* (interj.) fie! shame!, *sy* to sow, *lyn* lightning, *lys* light, short in *stygg* ugly, *tynn* thin, *lykke* happiness, luck.

9.   ø, ö. This vowel is not found in English. It is an **e** pronounced with rounded lips. To an English ear it sounds very much like the sound of [əː] in **word, heard, bird,** and this sound can be used when a stronger rounding of the lips is added to it. The German **ö** or French **eu** in **peur** can be substituted.

Examples: Long in *dør* door, *søt* sweet, short in *nøtt* nut, *høst* autumn.

10.   u. The Norwegian **u** is a difficult sound for foreigners because it is narrower and pronounced more to the front than is usual in most other languages. It corresponds fairly well to the English variety in **few.** The Englishman must take care not to use his **u** in words like **foot** or **full.**

Examples: Long in *ut* out, *lur* cunning, *mur* stone wall; short in *gutt* boy.

11.   o. Written **o** has two pronunciations in Norwegian, [o] or [ɔ].

(*a*) The first is [o] which is very narrow and pronounced with pursed lips—well rounded. Say **oo**—and then round the lips as much as you can.

Examples: *fot* foot, *bok* book, *tok* took, *god* [goː] good. The [o] sound is generally long. There are a number of exceptions, however, when it is short, especially in front of **-rt, -st, -m** and **-nd,** but no strict rules exist.

Examples: *bort* away, *port* gate, *ost* cheese, *rom* room, *lomme* pocket, *ond* [onn] bad, wicked.

In some cases this sound is also written **u,** viz. in front of **m, kk, nk** and especially **ng**:

dum stupid, *drukket* drunk, *munk* monk, *ung* [oŋŋ] young. Here the sound is always short.

(*b*) When the **o** is short its pronunciation reminds one of English **o** in **doll** or **Molly** although it is placed higher in the mouth.

Examples: *tolv* [tɔll] twelve, *holde* [hɔllə] hold, *kort* [kɔ^rt] short or card. In some rare cases it is pronounced long: *sove* [ˇsɔːvə] to sleep, *love* [ˇlɔːvə] to promise, *doven* [ˇdɔːvən] lazy.

12.   å comes very near to the last-mentioned sound which is named after it in the alphabet: the **å**-sound. It is usually long and its nearest equivalent in English is the vowel in **call** [kɔːl] although the Norwegian sound is slightly narrower.

Examples: *på* (prep.) on, *få* get, *hår* hair, *båt* boat.

13. æ corresponds fairly well to the English **a** in **cat**, only it is a little less open. It appears usually in front of **r**.
Long in: *lære* [ˇlæːrə] to learn, teach, *være* [ˇvæːrə] to be, *bær* [bæːr] berry.

Short in: *lærd* [lærd] learned.

Before other consonants it is pronounced [eː]: *fæl* [feːl] ugly, nasty, *hæl* [heːl] heel.

Diphthongs

There are three important native diphthongs in Norwegian, written:

ei   øy   au

14. **ei** is easy, as English has more or less the same sound in words like: **hate, say, vain.**

Examples: *vei* road, *stein* stone, *seig* tough, *reise* to travel.

15. **øy** on the other hand has no equivalent in English. It is composed of an ordinary [ø] followed by an [i] with faintly rounded lips. An Englishman is apt to render it **oi**. Keep the ø-sound distinct! Practise on: *øy* island, *øye* eye, *tøy* cloth, material, *høy* high, tall.

16. **au** is pronounced [øu].

Examples: *au!* interjection of pain, *haug* [høu] small hill, *sau* sheep, *tau* rope.

To start with an Englishman will quite naturally use his nearest native diphthong **ow** in **how** in such words.

Take therefore extra care to pronounce the ø element quite distinctly.

The Consonants

17. When talking or reading Norwegian an Englishman can use most of his native consonant sounds such as **b, d, f,** his hard **g, h, k, m, n, p, t, v.** (The letters **c, q, w,** and **z** are found in the alphabet but are used only in foreign words.)

Examples: *bade* bathe, *fot* foot, *gate* street, *ha* have, *kake* cake, *mann* man, *nå* now, *Venus* Venus.

18. However, for the voiced **s** in **is,** the **j** sound in **joke** or the **th** sounds in **thin** and **this** he will not find any counterpart.

19. On the other hand there are a few consonant sounds which an Englishman lacks or which are not represented by any specific letter, first of all the one written **kj,** in phonetics written [ç]. This sound will need special attention. If he has some smattering of German he is well off, as **kj** is pronounced like the German **ch** sound in the pronoun **ich.** A similar sound may be observed in English in the beginning of words like **hue, human, huge.**

Advice: Start from such words, making the initial sound much tenser.

Note: When **k** precedes **i** and **y** we get as a result the same sound [ç].

Drill: *kjær* dear   *kjøre* drive
       kirke church   *kinn* cheek
       kyss kiss   *kyst* coast

20. **j** corresponds to English **y** in **yes, young, year.** A few letter combinations result in the same sound: **gj, hj, lj** (only very few occurrences).

Examples: *ja,* yes, *gjemme* to hide, *hjem* home, *hjul* wheel, *ljome* echo.

21. **g.** In front of **i, y,** or **ei** (very few examples) the **g** is made 'soft' and is pronounced as [j], e.g. *gi* give, *gift* married, *begynne* [bə'jynnə] begin, *geit* [jeit] goat.

In other positions the **g** is just like the English **g** in **gate, get, goat.**

ng, however, is pronounced [ŋ] as in many English words, e.g. *ring*, *long*-Norw. *ring*, *lang*. But whereas the English pronounce the **g** in words like *finger*, *longer* the Norwegians do not [fiŋŋər, leŋŋər].

22. 1. Take care to use the l in **letter** and not the sort called 'bottle' l exemplified in **full, bill.**

Note: In eastern Norway (and also in some northern parts of the country) there is another variant of l, the 'thick' l used in the dialects and very colloquial speech, but it is avoided in more guarded language.

23. r requires special attention. In the eastern part of Norway the r is trilled, but not so strongly trilled as in those parts of the British Isles that still retain the trilled r, for instance Scotland.

Note: People of south-western Norway use a uvular r similar to that which is heard in Parisian French.

Examples: *rar* funny, strange, *ring* ring, *hår* hair, *larm* big noise. Before a voiceless consonant the r tends to become voiceless, e.g. *skarp* sharp.

The Combinations **rt, rd, rl, rn**

24. In such positions the r loses its trill and is assimilated with the **t, l, n** and sometimes **d**. At the same time these dentals are retracted and pronounced just behind the upper teeth-ridge. They are therefore in phonetic terminology called *retroflex*, which is indicated by a dot underneath them: [ṭ, ḍ, ḷ, ṇ].

The r in this case is similar to, but not identical with, the American one before dentals.

Different degrees of assimilation of the two sounds may be heard in more careful speech, the r sometimes remains as an untrilled sound, here written [r], sometimes the assimilation is complete.

Examples:

kart [kaʳṭ] map
fart [faʳṭ] speed
bort [boʳṭ] away

ferdig [ˇfæḍḍi, ˇfæʳḍi], ready, finished

Before ʳḷ and ʳṇ the vowel is always long.

Karl [kaːʳḷ] Charles   *barn* [baːʳṇ] child
ærlig [ˇæːʳḷi] honest   *korn* [koːʳṇ] grain
sørlig [ˇsøːʳḷi] southerly   *ørn* [øːʳṇ] eagle

As already indicated ḍ is less frequent than ḷ and ṇ. The pronunciation [rd] is common in words of a more or less literary character such as:

lærd [lærd] learned   *mord* [mord] murder

Note: South and West Norway does not use retroflex sounds.

The Combinations sj, skj = *English* sh-*sound*

25.   The sign used in the phonetic alphabet is [ʃ].

Examples:

sjø [ʃøː] sea   *skjev* [ʃeːv] oblique
sjel [ʃeːl] soul   *skjorte* [ˇʃoʳțə] shirt
sjelden [ˇʃeldṇ] seldom   *skjære* [ˇʃæːrə] to cut, shear

The symbol ṇ in [ˇʃeldṇ] indicates that the consonant n here functions as a syllable.

26.   sk before **i, y,** and the diphthong **øy** also gives **sh** [ʃ] as a result.

ski [ʃiː] ski, *sky* [ʃyː] cloud, *skøyter* [ˇʃøytər] skates.

Other instances of sh-sound

27.   (1) After **r, s** is, as a rule, pronounced [ʃ] in the east, the **r** disappearing or being reduced as before **t, l, n.**

norsk [nɔʃk] Norwegian   *verst* [væʃt] worst
vers [væʃʃ] verse   *person* [pæˈʃoːn] person
Lars (Christian name) [laːʃ]

Also in juxtaposition as in **for sent** pronounced [fɔˈ ʃeːnt] = too late.

(2)   In the combination **sl** at the beginning of a word the **s** becomes [ʃ] in the east and the **l** > [ḷ].

Examples: *slank* [ʃlaŋk] slim, *slik* [ʃliːk] such, *slå* [ʃlɔː] beat.

If the **s** and **l** belongs to different syllables 'thick' **sl** is the rule in popular speech, while educated speech would prefer 'thin' **sl.**

rusle [ˇruslə] loiter, *Oslo* [ˇoslo], vulgar [ˇoʃlo].

Mute Consonants

28. **g** is mute in adjectives and adverbs ending in **-ig** and **-lig**.

stadig [ˇstaːdi] constantly, *ærlig* [ˇæːʳli] honest, *deilig* [ˇdeili] delicious.

29. **d** is mute at the end of a word after **r**, at the same time lengthening the vowel.

gård [goːr] farm, building, *hard* [haːr] hard, *jord* [joːr] earth, *bord* [boːr] table.

Very often after a long vowel. *god* [goː] good, *rød* [røː] red, *stod* [stoː] stood.

30. **ld** and **nd** are usually assimilated into **ll** and **nn** in the spoken language.

holde [ˇhɔllə] hold, keep, *land* [lann] land.

31. **t** is mute in the definite form of the neuter nouns: *huset* [ˈhuːsə] the house, and in the neuter pronoun *det* [deː] it.

32. **h** is silent before **j** and **v**.

hjem [jemm] home, *hvem* [vemm] who (interrogative), *hjelpe* [ˇjelpə] help, *hvor* [vorr] where.

33. **v** is silent in a few words:

selv [sell] *self* (but inflected [ˇselvə]), *halv* [hall] half, *tolv* [tɔll] twelve, *sølv* [søll] silver.

Stress

34. The stress signs used in this book are [ˈ] (in the case of 'single tone') and [ˇ] (in the case of 'double tone') before the stressed syllables. For the two 'tones' see paragraphs 36–41.

As in English the stress in Norwegian lies normally on the first syllable of a word. But the student will find a lot of exceptions to this rule, especially in connection with foreign words and words with certain prefixes. First of all those of German origin. Ex. **be, ge, er** [ær], and to a certain extent **for** [fɔr].

Ex. *betale* [bə'taːlə] to pay, *begynne* [bə'jynnə] to begin, *gevær* [gə'væːr] rifle, *erfare* [ær'faːrə] to experience, *forandre* [fɔr'andrə] to change, *forklare* [fɔ'klaːrə] explain.

However, it would take too long to list all the exceptions here, so the student is referred to the vocabulary, where words spelt in the ordinary way are sometimes given stress marks.

35. Special attention should be paid to words of Romance and Greek origin the majority of which are, in opposition to English, stressed on the last syllable, e.g. those ending in:

-sjon [ʃoːn]	*stasjon* station, *nasjon* nation
-al [aːl]	*sosial* social, *kapital* capital
-ell [ell]	*hotell* [ho'tell] hotel, *modell* [mo'dell] model
-ant [ant or aŋŋ]	*interessant* [int(ə)rə'saŋŋ] interesting *restaurant* [rəstu'raŋŋ] restaurant
-ent [ent]	*student* [stu'dent] student *korrespondent* [kɔrəspɔn'dent] correspondent
-ment [ment or maŋŋ]	*regiment* [regi'ment] regiment. With French pronunciation, e.g.: *departement* [depaᵣtə'maŋŋ] ministry, *kompliment* [kɔmpli'maŋŋ] compliment
-inne [ˇinne]	*lærerinne* [lærərˇinnə] schoolmistress, *venninne* [venˇinnə] friend (female)
-eri [ə'riː]	*bakeri* [bakə'riː] bakery, *meieri* [meiə'riː] dairy
-ere ['eːrə]	in a great number of verbs: *konferere* confer, *levere* deliver, hand
-log [lɔːg]	*teolog* theologian, *psykolog* psychologist
-ist [ist]	*sosialist* socialist, *artist* artist (in circus)
-ikk [ikk]	*teknikk* [tek'nikk] technics, *politikk* [poli'tikk] politics, and a host of others with various foreign endings:
-(t)itt	*appetitt* appetite
-anse [áŋsə]	*balanse* balance

-fon and -graf [fo:n, gra:f]	telefon, telegraf telephone, telegraph
-tur [tu:r]	kultur, natur, temperatur culture, nature, temperature
-ør [ø:r]	direktør director
-(t)i [(t)i:]	demokrati democracy
-tet ['te:t]	universitet university, kvalitet quality

Intonation

The two 'tones'

36. A most peculiar and interesting feature about the Norwegian language is the existence of two various types of speech melody—the two 'tones', the Single Tone and the Double Tone, which it has in common with the Swedish language alone. The tones are used in combination with stress.

37. *The single tone* starts rather low, then rises to a high note towards the end of the word, diagrammatically represented as:

['se:] see   ['vakkər] beautiful

The single tone is first of all used in words of one syllable, but is also found in a great many words of several syllables, especially those ending in -el, -en, -er, like *middel* ['midl] means, remedy; *verden* ['værdn] world, and the example above: *'vakker*. However, the so-called nomina agentis in -er indicating a profession, take the double tone, e.g. *baker* baker. Single tone occurs also in most loanwords, e.g. *'kaffe* coffee and certain compounds in which the first element is a single syllable noun ending in a vowel, e.g. *skitur* ['ʃi:tu:r] skiing trip.

38. *The double tone*, which is chiefly found in words of two or more syllables, starts on a higher note than the single tone, falls about three tones, then rises again to a higher pitch than the start, something like:

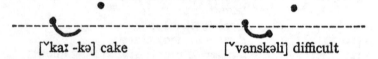

[ˇkaː -kə] cake   [ˇvanskəli] difficult

39. The marking signs for tones are [ˊ] for single tone and [ˇ] for double tone placed at the beginning of the syllable in question. As tone and stress accompany each other the same signs are used for both purposes. See para. 34.

40. Sometimes words which otherwise sound identical may be distinguished by the two tones, the classical example being:

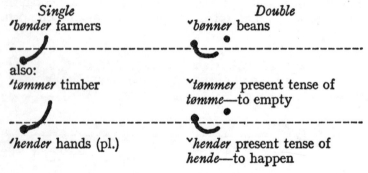

Single	*Double*
ˊ*bønder* farmers	ˇ*bønner* beans

also:

ˊ*tømmer* timber	ˇ*tømmer* present tense of *tømme*—to empty

ˊ*hender* hands (pl.)	ˇ*hender* present tense of *hende*—to happen

41. A foreigner will need a good bit of ear-training to notice clearly the different cadences and considerable practice to master them. So to start with you ought not to bother too much about such fine technicalities. But do listen to Norwegian broadcasts to get used to the speech melody.

As the two tones are also linked up with grammatical points you will find more about this subject under the various sections of grammar.

PART II
GRAMMAR

CHAPTER II

THE NOUN—GENDERS

42. Before the last major spelling reform there were only two genders in written Norwegian (as in Swedish and Danish), called 'the common gender' (comprising both the old masculine and feminine genders) and 'the neuter' gender, from now on abbreviated as c. and n.

The new spelling reform, however, also gave a certain room for the feminine gender on account of its existence in all Norwegian dialects except that of Bergen.

It is compulsory first of all in words describing Norwegian country life and scenery.

The student, however, had better assume only two genders: the common gender and the neuter gender, as he will meet these in most books and papers and, apart from a few nouns, in the speech of most '*Bokmål*-speaking' people. Only a few feminine forms will be used in this book.

The Articles

The different genders are shown by the articles, the definite and the indefinite article.

The Indefinite Article

43.

Masculine	Feminine	Neuter
en	**ei (en)**	**et**

Examples: *en stol* a chair, *ei (en) mark* a field, *et hus* a house.

The Definite Article

44. This article, in Norwegian, is suffixed to the noun, in striking contrast to most other European languages. In the masculine and neuter forms it is identical with the indefinite article.

Masculine	Feminine	Neuter
stol-en the chair	*mark-a* the field	*hus-et* the house
kake-n the cake	*høn-a* the hen	*eple-t* the apple

45. As no satisfactory rules can be formulated with regard to gender, the student should learn the words by heart, as he has to do with German and French nouns. He should therefore take care never to say: house = *hus*, but 'a house' or 'the house' = resp. *et hus* and *huset*. In other words he should associate the noun with one of its articles.

Naturally male beings such as *gutt* boy, *mann* man, *lærer* teacher, *snekker* joiner, *konge* king, and *prins* prince, and female beings like *dronning* queen, *pike* girl, *kvinne* woman, are of common gender (which as we know comprises masc. and fem.).

46. In a compound word the last element determines the gender of the noun. Thus *et pikenavn* a girl's name; *pike* is common g. and *navn* neuter g.

CHAPTER III

PLURAL OF NOUNS

The plural endings should not cause the foreigner too much difficulty. The following rough and ready rule may be set up initially:

The Indefinite Plural

47. (1) Nouns of the common gender (and also feminine gender) take **-er** (or only **-r** after unstressed **e**) in the indefinite plural. Examples: *stol-er* chairs, *kake-r* cakes, *mark-er* fields, *høne-r* hens; but **-er** in *skje-er* spoons, *idé-er* ideas, because the **e** is stressed.

(2) In the neuter nouns there are two possible plural forms, largely dependent upon the number of syllables in the word.

(a) Most neuters consisting of two or more syllables follow the same rule as the common gender, especially those ending in an unstressed **-e**, e.g. *eple-r* apples.

(b) Nearly all neuters consisting of one syllable, on the other hand, take no ending in the plural, for example *hus*, pl. *hus* (cf. old English neuters **sheep, deer** with no ending in the plural).

The Definite Plural

48. The definite plural is the same for all genders, **-ene** or **-ne** in words ending in an unstressed **-e**. Examples: *stol-ene* the chairs, *kake-ne* the cakes, *mark-ene* the fields, *skje-ene* the spoons, *idé-ene* the ideas, *høne-ne* the hens, *hus-ene* the houses, *eple-ne* the apples.

The complete paradigm will then give this picture:

c. gender	*en stol*	*stolen*	*stoler*	*stolene*
	en skje	*skjeen*	*skjeer*	*skjeene*
	en kake	*kaken*	*kaker*	*kakene*
f. gender	*ei/en mark*	*marka*	*marker*	*markene*
n. gender	*et hus*	*huset*	*hus*	*husene*
	et eple	*eplet*	*epler*	*eplene*

Note: Nouns ending in **m** double this final consonant in the plural besides the definite form singular, e.g.

en dam	pond *dammen*	*dammer*	*dammene*
et rom	room *rommet*	*rom*	*rommene*

Intonation: One-syllable nouns have single tone in all forms in the singular, the definite article having no influence on the intonation. In the plural, however, they usually change into double tone.

One-syllable neuters are more unstable in this respect than are the common gender nouns, *dyrene* the animals, *benene* the legs, take single tone while *husene* the houses, *landene* the countries, take the double.

Exercise 1

(a) *Decline the following nouns:*

en sjø a sea, *et dyr* an animal, *en gate* a street, *en vei* a road, *en gutt* a boy, *en by* a town, *et belte* a belt.

Numbers from 1 to 7

en, n. ett	= one
to	= two
tre	= three
fire	= four
fem	= five
seks	= six
sju	= seven

(b) *Translate the following words:*

two boys, four girls, seven apples, two loaves, five fishes.

  a loaf = *et brød* [brøː]   a fish = *en fisk*

Irregular Plurals

These details may conveniently be studied during the revision.

49. (1) *Contractions in the plural.*

If nouns end in **-el** or **-er** the **e** is dropped when the plural ending is added. At the same time a double consonant will be reduced to single.

en 'regel a rule	*regelen*	*regler*	*reglene*
en 'sykkel a bicycle	*sykkelen*	*sykler*	*syklene*
et 'middel a means	*mid(de)let*	*midler*	*midlene*
et ek'sempel an example	*eksemp(e)let*	*eksempler*	*eksemplene*
en ˇsommer	*sommeren*	*somrer*	*somrene*
en 'vinter a winter	*vinteren*	*vintrer*	*vintrene*
en 'finger a finger	*fingeren*	*fingrer*	*fingrene*
en 'åker a cornfield	*åkeren*	*åkrer*	*åkrene*
et te'ater a theatre	*teat(e)ret*	*teatre, teater*	*teatrene*
et or'kester an orchestra	*orkest(e)ret*	*orkestre, orkester*	*orkestrene*

      As for intonation see para. 37.

(2) *Shift of stress*

Words of foreign origin ending in **-or** or **-tor** change the stress in the plural, e.g.

motor ['moːtor], but *motorer* [moˈtoːrər] *motorene*
professor [proˈfessor], but *professorer* [profəˈsoːrər] *profess-orene*

Change of Vowel in the Plural

50. (*a*) A number of words mostly monosyllabic modify their root vowel in the plural, at the same time keeping the single tone all the way (because they had monosyllabic plurals in Old Norse), except *kraft* strength and *stad* city, and those mentioned under c. The commonest of these are:

and f. duck	*ender*	*endene*
bok book	*bøker*	*bøkene*
bot f. fine; patch	*bøter*	*bøtene*
fot foot	*føtter*	*føttene*
hånd hand, also *hand*	*hender*	*hendene*
kraft strength, power	*krefter*	*kreftene* (d. tone)
natt night	*netter*	*nettene*
rand edge, border	*render*	*rendene*
stad [staːd], lit. and arch. city, *hovedstad* capital	*steder*	*stedene* (d. tone)
stand profession, class	*stender*	*stendene*
stang pole, bar	*stenger*	*stengene*
strand f. beach	*strender*	*strendene*
tann f. tooth	*tenner*	*tennene*
tang f. tongs, pliers	*tenger*	*tengene*

One two-syllabic:

bonde [ˇbonnə] farmer	*bønder*	*bøndene*

No ending in the indefinite plural:

gås f. goose	*gjess* [jess]	*gjessene*
mann c. man	*menn*	*mennene*

en nordmann ['normann] a Norwegian, *nordmennene* the Norwegians.

(*b*) The following monosyllables, ending in a stressed vowel, take only **-r** and **-ne** with modification in the plural.

glo f. ember	*glør*	*glørne*
ku f. cow	*kyr* or ˇ*kuer*	'*kyrne* or ˇ*kuene*

rå f. naut. yard	*rær*	*rærne*
tå f. toe	*tær*	*tærne*

(*c*) Some nouns denoting family relations have **-e** in the indefinite plural, e.g.:

far father	*fedre*	*fedrene*
mor mother	*mødre*	*mødrene*
bror brother	*brødre*	*brødrene*
datter daughter	*'døtre* (s. tone)	*'døtrene*
also		
søster sister	*søstre*	*søstrene*

Intonation: In spite of being monosyllabic **far, mor, bror** take double tone in the definite form singular, **faren, moren, broren.** The reason is that they were two-syllabic in the older language—**faderen, moderen, broderen,**
On the other hand **døtre** daughters, take single tone in the plural being one-syllabic in old Norse.

(*d*) Some nouns denoting persons belonging to a profession, trade or nationality, which in the singular end in **-er** also take **-e** in the indefinite plural. In the definite plural, however, they add only **-ne**. These nouns are usually derived from verbs, as are the corresponding formations in English.

lærer teacher	*lærere*	*lærerne*
baker baker	*bakere*	*bakerne*
ameri'kaner	*ameri'kanere*	*amerikanerne*
American		

51. Finally some words which take no ending at all in the plural deserve mention.

sild f. herring	*mus* f. mouse
feil c. error	*lus* f. louse
ting c. thing, orig. neuter	*ski* f. ski
gender	*sko* c. shoe, also *skor* in the plural

The lack of an ending is particularly frequent with words of measurement, e.g. *fem fot, to meter* ['me:tər] c., *tusen kilometer* ['çilometər], c., *ti (ten) mil* f., *tre liter* ['li:tər] c. 20 *mann* (instead of **menn**), *Alle mann om bord!* all aboard!, 50 *øre*

(Norw. coin) but *krone* (= 100 øre) has ordinary plural,
10 *kroner*.

52. (1) A few neuters have a slightly irregular plural, e.g.:

tre tree	*treet*	*trær*	*trærne*
kne knee	*kneet*	*knær*	*knærne*
barn child	*barnet*	*barn*	*barna*
øye eye	*øyet*	*øyne, øyer*	*øynene, øyene*
klede cloth	*kledet*	*klær* clothes	*klærne*
			the clothes

In compounds the singular form is just **-kle**, e.g. *forkle*
apron, *håndkle* towel, but in the plural *forklær*, *håndklær*.

(2) A few monosyllabic neuters take **-er** in the plural, e.g.:

kinn cheek	*kinnet*	*'kinner*	*'kinnene*
lem limb	*lemmet*	*lemmer*	*lemmene*
verk literary work	*verket*	*verker*	*verkene*
punkt [poŋt] point	*punkte*	*punkter*	*punktene*
sted [steː(d)] place	*stedet*	*steder* [ˇsteːdər]	*stedene*

(3) In colloquial speech plural forms such as **brever,
karter** (maps) are very familiar and have also found their
way into writing.

(4) Clearly foreign neuters ending in **-ium/-eum** take **-er**
in the plural, while the **-um** is dropped.

et mu'seum museum	*museet*	*mu'seer*	*museene*
et studium study course	*studiet*	*studier*	*studiene*

A few neuters appear with foreign endings in the plural,
e.g.:

et faktum fact	*faktumet*	*fakta*	*fakta*
et leksikon dictionary	*leksikonet*	*leksika*	*leksika*

et sentrum   *sentret*   *sentra/senter*   *sentra/sentrene*
  centre

They take single tone in all forms.

The Auxiliaries:

53. *å være* (to be)   *å ha* (to have)

Present tense

jeg [jei]	*er* [æːr]	I am	*jeg*	*har* [haːr]	I have
du	„	you are	*du*	„	you have
han [hann]	„	he is	*han*	„	he has
hun [hunn]	„	she is	*hun*	„	she has
vi	„	we are	*vi*	„	we have
dere [ˇdeːrə]	„	you are	*dere*	„	you have
de [diː]	„	they are	*de*	„	they have

(**det er** [deː æːr] = it is and there is/are)

Past tense

jeg var, du var etc. I was, you were etc.
jeg hadde, du hadde etc. I had, you had etc.

Past participle: *vært* [væʳt] (been)   *hatt* (had)

The perfect: *jeg* etc. *har vært*   I have been
                jeg etc. *har hatt*   I have had

The pluperfect: *jeg* etc. *hadde vært*   I had been
                jeg etc. *hadde hatt*   I had had

Vocabulary

'eller conj. or
men [menn] conj. but
og [ɔː] conj. and
år n. year
nei no
fra from

til to, till
Norge [ˇnɔrgə] Norway
ja yes
bare only
mange [ˇmaŋŋə] many
venn c. friend

Exercise 2a

Read and translate:

Er han engelskmann eller nordmann? Han er nordmann, men moren er engelsk og faren amerikaner. Han har en søster. Hun er seks år. Har du en søster? Nei, men jeg har to brødre, Arne og Olaf. Arne har fem barn—to gutter og tre piker. Olaf har to piker. De er fra Drammen. Det er

fem (norske] mil fra Oslo til Drammen. Har du vært i
Norge? Ja, men bare i Oslo. Jeg har mange venner i Oslo.

Exercise 2b

i in **hvor** [vorr] where **nå** now

Translate into Norwegian:

My (*min*) father has two brothers and four sisters. Olaf is
my brother and Marit my sister. We are from Norway, but
we have many friends in England. Have you (sing.) been in
England? Yes, but only in London. Has your (*din*) sister
many children? She has four children. Where are the
children now? They are in London.

arm c. arm **skog** c. forest **ben** n. leg

We have two arms, two hands, two legs and two feet, but
we have ten fingers and ten toes. The forest has many trees.
My (*min*) town has three bakers, but only one teacher.

The Pronouns den, det—de, dem
54.

Singular		Plural	
Common	**den** [denn] $\Big\}$ it	Subject form	**de** [diː] = they
Neuter	**det** [deː]	Object form	**dem** [demm] = them

Whenever you refer to a common gender noun directly
the pronoun **den** [denn] must be used, but in the case of a
neuter, **det** [deː] is the correct form. English uses 'it' in
both cases.

The plural forms are the same for all genders.

Examples: *båten* the boat *den er norsk*
eplet the apple *det er norsk*
båtene $\Big\}$ *de er norske*
eplene

55. Exception: If—and only if—a noun follows the expression **it is**, the neuter form **det** for the English **it** is always
used, no matter what gender or number.

e.g.   *Det er en norsk båt* (*common*) but *den er norsk*
        Det er et norsk eple (*neuter*) ,, *det er norsk*

Plural: *Det er norske båter, epler,* but *de er norske.*

Pattern: *Det er* + **noun** (sg. or pl.).

CHAPTER IV

THE S-GENITIVE

56. The s-genitive is formed by adding **-s** without any apostrophe to all forms in the singular and plural of the nouns.

a man's	the man's	men's	the men's
en manns	*mannens*	*menns*	*mennenes*
en stols	*stolens*	*stolers*	*stolenes*
a chair's			
et barns	*barnets*	*barns*	*barnenes*
a child's	(*t* sounded)		
et ords ['oːʃ]	*ordets* ['oːrəts]	*ords*	*ordenes* ['oːrənəs]
a word's			

The second and third examples show that the s-genitive is used more freely in Norwegian than in English as it is used without any restrictions with inanimate objects as well.

57. (1) But in natural everyday language there is a general tendency to employ expressions with a preposition, first of all **til** (= belonging to) showing clear ownership, here corresponding to English 'of'. Example: *barnets mor = moren til barnet* the mother of the child. *Min brors hus = huset til min bror* the house of my brother.

Other prepositions that are often used are:

på on, *i* in, *av* of.

gatens navn	= *navnet på gaten*	the name of the street.
husets farge	= *fargen på huset*	the colour of the house.
havens trær	= *trærne i haven*	the trees in the garden.
bokens innhold	= *innholdet av boken*	the contents of the book.
bilens eier	= *eieren av bilen*	the owner of the car.

(2) Very often a compound word is used where English has s-genitive or construction with 'of', e.g. *en dameveske* a lady's bag, *et bordben* a leg of a table *or* a table leg, *bileieren* the owner of the car *or* the car owner.

58. The genitive can stand quite alone in Norwegian in sentences like: *Mitt hus er ikke så stort som naboens.* Corresponding to English: My house is not so big as that of my neighbour. On the other hand Norwegian has no equivalent to genitive expressions like: **to go to the chemist's, the baker's,** etc. Here a Norwegian would say: *å gå på* (= on) *apoteket* [apo'te:kə], *til bakeren osv...* (= *og så videre*).

59. After the preposition *til* (to) many nouns still retain the old genitive *-s* in certain expressions, e.g.:

til skogs [skoks] into the wood   *til lands* on land
til sjøs [ʃøss] at sea, to sea   *gå til sengs* go to bed

Exercise 3

Translate into Norwegian: using (*a*) the s-genitive:

redsel c. horror   **åker** c. field (ploughed)
herr [hærr] Mr   **hund** [hunn] c. dog

The man's hat, the farmer's field, the horrors of war, Mr Hansen's dog, the King's clothes (popular name of the military uniform).

(*b*) using a prepositional phrase:

kone f. wife

The name of the town, the son of the teacher, the men's wives, the children's mother.

Note: if we translated **Churchill's letter** as **brevet til Churchill** it would be ambiguous, as *til* indicates not only ownership, but also direction. We had therefore better keep the genitive or use the preposition **fra = from** in this particular case.

CHAPTER V

THE VERB

60. The infinitive of Norwegian verbs end in **-e**: *stoppe* stop, *kaste* throw, cast, *komme* come. This **-e** is lacking in monosyllabic verbs ending in a stressed vowel, e.g. *bo* live, i.e. reside, *ha* have. The infinitive mark is **å** corresponding to English **to.** Examples: *å bo* to live, *å være* to be.

The Present Tense—the Imperative

61. If we delete the ending **-e** of the infinitive, we get what is generally called the stem; thus the infinitive **stoppe**, the stem being **stopp**. This stem happens to serve as the imperative form in Norwegian: **stopp!** stop! **kast!** throw! **kom!** (double **m** is reduced to single) come!

62. The various inflexional endings are tagged on to the stem. The present tense is formed by adding **-er** (or **-r**) to the stem in all persons singular and plural: *stopper* stops, *kaster* throws, *kommer* comes, *bor* lives.

Paradigm:

Singular:	*jeg* [jei] I	*stopper* stop, *bor* live
	du you	,, ,,
	han, hun, den, det [deː],,	,,
	he, she, it	
Plural:	*vi* we	,, ,,
	dere you	,, ,,
	de [diː] they	,, ,,

Note: *Jeg bor* renders in English: I live and I am living.

Comments on personal pronouns:

Besides *du* (object form *deg* [dei] we have a more polite form *De* [diː] (written with a capital **D**), which has an object form *Dem*. Further details about this in para. 178.

The Conjugation of Weak Verbs

63. In written English practically all weak verbs have the same ending in the past and perfect tenses, e.g. **stopped, smiled, tried, lived.** In Norwegian, however, it is not quite so simple.

The corresponding words would, in Norwegian, represent four different classes, each with their specific endings:

(1) *stoppe* stop   *stop**pet***   *stop**pet***
(2) *smile* smile   *smi**lte***   *smi**lt***

These two are the most numerous ones. Then there are:

(3) *prøve* try   *prø**vde***   *prø**vd***
(4) *bo* live   *bo**dde***   *bo**dd***

You would naturally ask: How am I to decide which class a certain weak verb belongs to? Well, in spite of the fact that we have tried to set up some rules to make matters easier, there are quite a number of cases where the different inflections simply must be learned by heart and inculcated by drill, as is done with the genders. There is one good thing, however, the forms of all verbs in all tenses are identical in all persons singular and plural.

64. Class I, the **-et** class, includes verbs whose stems end in two or more consonants, e.g.:

(a) *våkne* awake, *kaste* throw, *miste* lose, *koste* cost, *huske* remember, *merke* notice, *snakke* talk, *hoppe* jump;
(b) also most verbs whose stems end in a single **d** or **g**: *lage* make, *våge* dare, risk, *jage* chase, *bade* bathe and bath.

Paradigm:

Inf.	Present	Past	The Perfect Tenses
stoppe	*jeg stopper*	*jeg stoppet*	*jeg har (hadde) stoppet*

Jeg stoppet expresses both: I stopped and I was stopping.

The perfect tenses:

Jeg har stoppet = both: I have stopped and I have been
stopping
Jeg hadde stoppet = both: I had stopped and I had been
stopping.

Note 1 : The older past tense form, used by the poets and dramatists
of the nineteenth century, was *stoppede*, but such forms are now
obsolete.

Note 2 : It should be noted that according to the latest Norwegian
spelling reform of 1938 a great many much-used verbs of this class
may also take the ending -a (adopted from the dialects) in the
past tense and the past participle, e.g. *kasta* instead of *kastet*. This
ending, however, is little used in writing.

Vocabulary

tidlig [ˇtiːli] early
i dag today
frokost c. [ˈfroːkɔst] breakfast
herlig [ˇhæːˈrli] glorious
ikke not
i går yesterday
vann n. water
bare only
grad [graːd] c. degree

skaffe (-et) provide, get
ham pron. him
min bror my brother
vente (-et) wait, *also* expect
brev n. letter
meg [mei] me
meget [ˇmeːgət] much
men [menn] conj. but
penn c. pen

Exercise 4a

Translate into English:

Jeg våknet tidlig i dag, hadde frokost ute i det fri, og
hoppet så (*then*) ut i sjøen. Det var herlig. Jeg badet ikke i
går. Vannet var for (*too*) kaldt, bare femten (15) grader
Celsius, men min kone badet.

Min bror har skaffet meg en bok av Ibsen. Jeg husket min
lærer snakket meget om (*about*) ham på skolen. Min bror
venter et brev fra meg, men jeg har mistet pennen jeg
hadde.

Vocabulary

redde (-et) save
kunne ikke could not
stein c. stone
ut i into
bort away

seng f. bed
børste (-et) brush
mitt hår my hair
vente på wait for
bil c. car

Exercise 4b

Translate into Norwegian:

They saved him. He had bathed in the sea and could not swim (*svømme*). The boys threw stones into the water and chased the ducks away. He awakes early and jumps out of the bed. I had not brushed my hair. She was waiting for me in the car.

65. Class II, the **-te** class, is characterized by the ending **-te** in the past and **-t** in the past participle.

(*a*) Long vowel (or diphthong) as root vowel.

Paradigm:

Inf.	Present	Past	The Perfect Tenses
smile	*jeg smiler*	*jeg smilte*	*jeg har (hadde) smilt*

The verbs of this type are those whose stems end in **l, n, s** or **r.**

Examples: *dele* divide, share, *føle* feel, *låne* borrow (also lend), *høre* hear, *kjøre* drive, *lære* learn (also teach), *lese* read, *reise* travel, *spise* eat, *vise* show. To this class also belong those numerous foreign verbs in **-ere**, e.g. *levére* deliver, *sitére* quote.

Vocabulary

kake c. cake
mellom between
oss [ɔss] us
kulde c. cold
garasje [ga'ra:ʃə] c. garage
låne av borrow from
henne pron. her

smile av smile at
student [stu'dent] c. student
spare (-te) save
penger c. pl. money
til utlandet abroad
vei c. way, road

Exercise 5a

Read aloud and translate:

Vi delte kaken mellom oss. Jeg følte kulden. Jeg hørte hva du sa. Han kjørte bilen inn i garasjen. Hun leste en bok om (*about*) Norge. Jeg lånte boken av henne. Jeg har studert norsk i over to år. De smilte av meg. Studenten sparte penger og reiste til utlandet. Han viste oss veien. Du har spist opp kaken.

Vocabulary

svare answer   *avis* [a'viːs] c. newspaper   *hver* [væːr] every

Exercise 5b

Fill in the blanks with the correct forms in the past and present ·perfect tense of these verbs:

låne	Jeg	————————	en bok av ham
lese	Hun	————————	avisen hver dag
kjøre	Far	————————	bilen inn i garasjen
høre	Barna	————————	barnetimen i radio
svare	Hun	————————	nei
vise	Du	————————	meg huset til din bror

(*b*) In a few verbs the long root vowel is shortened in the past tense and past participle:

bruke use	*brukte*	*brukt*
møte meet	*møtte*	*møtt*
kjøpe buy	*kjøpte*	*kjøpt*
rope shout	*ropte*	*ropt*
tape lose	*tapte*	*tapt*

Vocabulary

foran in front of
rådhus n. town (city) hall
klokka to at two o'clock
ti over ten past
blomst c. flower
'fødselsdag c. birthday
Gratulerer! Congratulations!

takk thank you, thanks
gave c. gift
i fjor last year
hvem who (interrog. pr.)
avisgutt newspaper boy
fotballkamp c. soccer match
mot against, versus

Exercise 6a

Translate into English:

Har du møtt min far? Nei. Det var rart (*strange*). Jeg skulle (*was to*) møte ham her foran Rådhuset klokka to, og nå er den ti over. Men der ser jeg ham. Han har kjøpt blomster til mor. Hun har fødselsdag i dag. Gratulerer! Takk. Jeg har også kjøpt en gave til henne som jeg håper hun vil like. Hun likte den jeg kjøpte i fjor. Hvem ropte? Å, det var bare avisgutten. Norge har tapt fotballkampen mot Danmark.

Vocabulary

musikk [mu'sikk] music
min søster my sister
mange many
grammofon [gramo'fo:n]
  gramophone
plate c. here = record

av glede c. for joy
på stasjonen at the station
pipe c. pipe
butikk [bu'tikk] c. shop
hvor where

Exercise 6b

Translate into Norwegian:

I like to read books. I read about Nansen yesterday. My sister likes to hear music, and has bought many records. She did not like the hat she bought yesterday. (Translate: She liked not, etc.) I have bought a pipe. Show me the shop where you bought it.

(c) Verbs whose stems terminate in **mm, nn** and **ll** usually belong to this class. N.B.—The double consonants are reduced to single when the verb is conjugated.

Infinitive	Present	Past Tense	The Perfect Tenses
glemme forget	*Jeg glemmer*	*Jeg glemte*	*Jeg har (hadde) glemt*

Other examples are:

drømme dream
dømme sentence, judge
gjemme hide
kalle call
kjenne know people (*also:* feel)

skille separate, distinguish
skjønne understand
spille play, e.g. piano, organized games

Vocabulary

i natt last night
Temsen the Thames
tyv c. thief
bak behind
tosk c. fool

som [sɔmm] rel. pron. who, which
arbeide (-et) work
piano n. piano
godt adv. well
ingenting nothing

Exercise 7a

Translate into English:

Jeg drømte i natt at jeg badet i Temsen. Tyven hadde gjemt (seg) bak et tre. Hvor har du gjemt pengene? Gjemt er ikke glemt (*a common saying*). Hva kaller du en mann som bor i Norge? Jeg kaller ham en nordmann. Hun kalte meg en tosk. Mannen og konen arbeidet bestandig og skilte ikke mellom natt og dag. Gutten spilte piano hele dagen. Jeg skjønte godt hva han snakket om. Min bror skjønte ingenting.

66. Notes on **spille—leke (-te)**; both = play.

As already mentioned, **spille** is used for playing an instrument and organized games. *Du kan spille piano og du kan spille tennis*: but if you want to say that the children were playing in the garden you have to use **leke**. *Barna lekte i haven.*

Idioms: *Han spilte en stor rolle i politikken.* He played a great role in politics.
Det spiller ingen rolle. It is of no importance.

67. Notes on **kjenne—vite**; both = know.

(1) *Kjenne* means:

  1. to know, be acquainted with people, countries, etc. (French **connaître**)
    Jeg kjente ham godt. Jeg kjente ham igjen. I recognized him.
  2. feel, be conscious of, notice.
    Han brakk benet, men kjente (følte) ingen smerte. He broke his leg, but felt no pain.

(2) *vite* (irr.) = to know, have knowledge of (French **savoir**).

present *vet*, past *visste*, p.p. *visst.*

Jeg vet ikke. I don't know.
Jeg visste det var galt [ga:lt]. I knew it was wrong.

  The double **s** merely serves to avoid any confusion with *viste*, *vist* (past tense and past participle of the verb *vise* show), in which the **i** is long.

Vocabulary

mene (-te) mean, but not signify	**tenke (-te)** think

Exercise 7b

Translate into Norwegian:

The mother understood that (*at*) the boy was dreaming.
She forgot to answer. They called him Gudmund. She had
hidden away the flowers she had bought. The boy understood what they meant. He had known her for (*i*) many
years. I learned to drive (a) car last year. I know what you
mean. I thought so (*det*).

Irregular Weak Verbs with different Vowels in the Past Tense and Past Participle

68. Some twenty verbs mainly of Class II change the infinitive vowel (which is generally **e** or **ø**) in the past tense
and the past participle (to resp. **a** and **u** (**o**)). The verbs
marked with an asterisk take single tone in the present tense.

Infinitive	Past Tense	Past Participle
kvele choke	*kvalte*	*kvalt*
*sette set, place, put	*satte*	*satt*
telle count	*talte* (also reg. *telte*)	*tált* (*telt*)
*fortélle relate	*fortálte*	*fortált*
*rekke hand, pass	*rakte*	*rakt*
*strekke stretch	*strakte*	*strakt*
vekke arouse	*vakte*	*vakt*
	but *vekte* awoke	*vekt* awoke
bringe bring	*brakte*	*brakt*
velge choose, elect	*valgte* [ˇvalte]	*valgt* [valt]
*selge [ˇsellə] sell	*solgte* [ˇsɔltə]	*solgt* [sɔlt]
følge [ˇføllə] follow (also accompany)	*fulgte* [ˇfultə]	*fulgt* [fult]
smøre smear, grease	*smurte* [ˇsmuːʳtə]	*smurt* [smuːʳt]
spørre ask questions	*spurte* [ˇspuːʳtə]	*spurt* [spuːʳt]

Further:

*legge lay, put	*la* (old form *lagde*)	*lagt*
si say, tell	*sa* (old form *sagde*)	*sagt*
gjøre do	*gjorde* [ˇjoːrə]	*gjort* [joʳt]

Note: The verbs *spørre* and *gjøre* have shortened forms in the present tense, resp. *spør* and *gjør* (instead of the forms to be expected: *spørrer* and *gjører*); *si* has *sier* [ˇsiːər] in the present tense from the older form *siger*.

'Hva du gjør, gjør fullt og helt og ikke stykkevis¹ og delt' (Ibsen).

Vocabulary

røk c. smoke
duk c. cloth
på on
bord [boːr] n. table
egg n. egg
stol c. chair
hjørne [jˇøːˈɳə] n. corner
hundre hundred
eventyr [ˇeːvəntyːr] n. fairy tale
ulv c. wolf
skade c. harm

om morgenen [ɔmm ˇmɔːˈɳ] in the morning
stor great
interésse c. interest
konge e. king
mitt råd [rɔːd] my advice
mine sko c. pl. my shoes
bonde c. farmer
smør [smørr] n. butter
sánnhet c. truth
gode nýheter c. pl. good news, sing. **nýhet** a piece of news

Exercise 8

Translate the following sentences, then change them into the past tense and the two perfect tenses.

1. Røken kveler ham. 2. Hun legger duken på bordet. 3. Høna legger egg. 4. Han setter stolen i hjørnet. 5. Dere teller til hundre. 6. Mor forteller eventyr. 7. Far rekker meg et eple. 8. Jeg strekker meg om morgenen. 9. Det vekker stor interesse. 10. Mor vekker meg tidlig om morgenen. 11. De velger en konge. 12. Følger du mitt råd? 13. Hva spør du om? 14. Jeg smører mine sko. 15. Bonden selger smør. 16. Du sier ikke sannheten. 17. Hun bringer gode nyheter. 18. Ulven gjør stor skade.

69. Class III, the **-de** class, consists of verbs with **-de** in the past tense and **-d** in the past participle. Formerly these verbs went like Class I, and there are still a great many people who persistently use the older forms. But the **-de** ending is constantly gaining ground, both in the written and spoken language.

The long vowel in the infinitive is generally shortened in the past tense and the past participle.

¹piecemeal.

Paradigm:

Inf.	Present	Past	The Perfect Tenses
prøve try	*Jeg prøver*	*Jeg prøvde*	*Jeg har (hadde) prøvd*

In this class we find verbs whose stems mostly end in a **v** or in the diphthongs **ei** and **øy**.

Examples: *behøve* need, require, *leve* live (not reside), *streve* strive, work hard, *sveve* float, glide (in the air), *øve* practise, train.

An exception forms the useful verb *love* [ˈlɔːvə] promise which follows class II conjugation with *lovte* in the past and *lovt* in the past participle. With diphthongs: *eie* own, have, *bøye* bend, *greie* manage, be able to, *pleie* be in the habit of.

70. Expressions with *pleie*. The present tense: *Jeg pleier å gjøre det* is in English best rendered by: I generally do that, and past tense *pleide å* with: used to.

Example: *Vi pleide å spille tennis om ettermiddagen.* We used to play tennis in the afternoon. *Pleie* can also alternate with *bruke* in this sense. *Jeg brukte å gjøre det.* I used to do it.

Vocabulary

adrésse c. address
lå past tense of **ligge** = lie
drosje c. taxi
andre other pl.
folk n. people
fattig poor
lomme f. pocket
få few
setning c. sentence
de fleste most people
hjelpe irr. help
Å, ja da Oh yes
lett easy (also light)

gå feil go wrong, miss it
dreie (-de) turn
til venstre to the left
til høyre to the right
fortsette (conj. like
sette) continue
rett fram straight on
til slutt in the end
furutre fir tree
nesten almost
tak n. roof (also ceiling)
sannelig indeed

Exercise 8a

Read and translate:

Sent en kveld kom jeg til byen hvor min venn bodde. Jeg hadde hans adrésse, men var ikke kjent i byen og visste ikke hvor huset hans lå. Det beste hadde vært å ta en drosje—det pleier andre folk å gjøre—men jeg var en fattig student og eide ikke en øre. De få kroner jeg hadde i lom-

ma da jeg startet, var brukt opp. Jeg øvde på setningen:
Kan De si meg veien til ... Kan De si meg veien til ...

De fleste skjønte hva jeg sa og prøvde å hjelpe meg, 'Tror
De jeg greier å finne huset?' spurte jeg, 'Å ja da,' svarte de
'Det er så lett, så. De kan ikke gå feil.' Men det var akkurat
det jeg gjorde. Det begynte å bli mørkt også. Jeg dreide til
venstre, og jeg dreide til høyre—fortsatte så (then) rett fram,
slik de hadde fortalt meg, men huset, hvor var huset? Var
det brent ned? Til slutt greide jeg å finne det. To store
furutrær gjemte det nesten helt. Jeg var reddet. Jeg hadde
fått tak over hodet, men sannelig hadde jeg strevd hardt.

Vocabulary

sanger c. singer	**både** both
daglig daily	**dag** c. day
hardt [haᵗ] adv. hard	**natt** c. night
lite little	**fiolin** [fio′liːn] c. violin
ørn c. eagle	**en gang** once
høyt oppe high up	**helt** completely
luft c. air	**nå** now
elev (eleːv) c. pupil	**jeg tør ikke** I dare not
dikt n. poem	**igjen** [i′jenn] again
utenat by heart	**musikalsk** [musi′kaːlsk]
betále (-te) pay	musical
meget, svært very	**glad** [glaː] i fond of

Exercise 8b

Change the verbs in the following sentences into the past
tense and the perfect. Then translate the piece, as it stands,
into English:

1. Sangeren øver daglig. 2. Jeg strever hardt, men lærer
lite. 3. Ørnen svever høyt oppe i luften. 4. Eleven prøver
å lære diktet utenat. 5. Du behøver ikke å betale.

Exercise 8c

Translate into Norwegian:

She plays very well. She practises both day and night. I
used to play (the) violin once, but I have forgotten it
completely now and I dare not try again. I am not very
musical, but I like to hear music. I am very fond of Grieg.

71. Class IV, the **-dde** class, is made up of verbs which in
the infinitive end in a stressed vowel.

Paradigm:

Inf.	Present	Past	The Perfect Tenses
bo live	*Jeg bor*	*Jeg bodde*	*Jeg har (hadde) bodd*

Examples: one syllable: *tro* believe, think, *ro* row, *snu* turn, *gro* grow, *skje* happen, occur, *strø* strew, *spå* prophesy.

With two syllables: *be'ty* mean (i.e. signify), *be'ro på* depend on.

72. In this class we may also include the auxiliary **ha** (have) in spite of its somewhat anomalous past participle form **hatt.**

Inf.	Present	Past	The Perfect Tenses
ha	*Jeg har*	*Jeg hadde*	*Jeg har (hadde) hatt*

73. *tenke, tro, mene, synes.*

The above synonyms will give the student of Norwegian a little trouble. To a very large extent they can be rendered by the single verb 'think' in English. In other words, the various meanings and nuances of 'think' represent at least four separate words in Norwegian.

tenke (-te)
   1 = to think, i.e. use the brain. *Piken satt og tenkte.* The girl sat thinking.
   2 = think used in a more vague sense = presume, suppose = *Kommer han snart?* Will he soon be here? *Ja, jeg tenker det.* Yes, I think so.

tro (-dde)
   1 = believe (trust) in its original and full meaning. *Jeg tror deg.* I believe you. *Faren trodde ikke et ord av det gutten sa.* The father did not believe a word of what the boy said.
   2   used in a loose sense = believe, think, and is in this capacity a little more frequent than *tenke* (2).

mene (-te)
   does not always correspond to its namesake in English 'mean'.

Instances where it does correspond are:

1   to express the contents of one's thoughts. *Jeg mener hva jeg sier*. I mean what I say. *Han mente det ikke slik*. He did not mean it like that.

2 = refer to, Norw. 'sikte til'. *Mener du meg?* Do you mean me? *Si hvem du mener*. Tell whom you mean.

3 = intend. *Min bror mener å reise i morgen*. My brother means to leave tomorrow.

Instances where 'mene' does not correspond to 'mean'.

1   *Mene* in Norwegian can never mean: to signify. For this use **bety** (**-dde**) is the right word. *Eleven visste ikke hva ordet betydde*. The student did not know what the word meant. *Hva skal dette bety?* What does this mean?

2 = maintain, hold, be of the opinion, think. In a discussion: *Jeg mener at Norge ikke kan være nøytralt*. In my opinion Norway cannot be neutral. *Ja, men jeg mener det motsatte*. But I hold the opposite view. *Hva mener de andre?* What do the others think?

3   Like *tenke* and *tro*, *mene* can also have a weakened meaning = suppose. *Soldaten mener han vil få permisjon*. The soldier thinks he will get leave. *Turisten mente Bergen var hovedstaden i Norge*. The tourist thought that Bergen was the capital of Norway.

synes, syntes, synes. This originally reflexive verb has a very high frequency in Norwegian. It is used to express one's private opinion, how one feels about a certain matter. It corresponds to 'think' in most cases, but also to find, feel.

(a) *Jeg synes det er kaldt her*. I think it is cold here. *Hva synes du?* What do you think? *Jeg synes at piken er ganske pen*. I think that the girl is quite pretty. *Det synes ikke jeg*. I don't think so. *synes om* = think of. *Hva synes du om det bildet?* What do you think of that picture?

(b) seem to, have a feeling (you are not quite certain). *Jeg syntes så tydelig at jeg hørte noe*. I clearly seemed to hear something.

Exercise 9

Sentences for practice (main verbs only to be translated).

forstyrre [fɔ'ʃtyrrə] (**-et**) disturb

1. Do you think he will come?
2. I think she is one of the sweetest girls I have seen.
3. Has he gone? No, I don't think so.
4. Don't disturb him. He is thinking.
5. I think we had better go.
6. We think you ought to-come, or what do you think yourself?
7. I thought I saw a man in the room.
8. She thought I was fifty. I am only forty.
9. This is rather strange, I think.
10. This is difficult to believe.
11. That[1] means war (krig c.).
12. I don't believe in miracles (miracle = *mirakel* [mi-'raːkəl] n.).

The Relative Pronoun

som = who, which

74.   The most common relative pronoun in Norwegian is **som**, which may refer to both persons and things.

Example: *Mannen som* . . . the man who; *Boken som* . . . the book which . . .

Preliminary Notes on Word Order

75.   Although there is great similarity between Norwegian and English word order there are two special points where the two languages differ substantially:

(1) *The use of inversion*, i.e. when the subject and the main verb of the sentence change places. There are examples of this phenomenon in English, too, of the type: *Hardly had he* . . . *Here comes the bride*, but they are far less frequent than in Norwegian. Here the rule is: When an adverb, or any other element of the sentence for that matter, apart

---

[1] *Det* (stressed).

from conjunctions, precedes the subject, subject and verb change places. Examples:

Det er for sent nå, but *Nå er det for sent*. In English: It is too late now—Now it is too late.

This rule also applies when a subordinate clause precedes a principal clause. *Hvis det begynte å blåse, snudde vi.* English: If the wind started to blow, we turned.

(2) *The position of adverbs.*

Watch these sentences:

(*a*) *Vi rodde* **ofte**. We **often** rowed. *Vi nådde* **alltid**. We **always** reached. *Vi tapte* **aldri**. We **never** *lost*.

(*b*) *Jeg har* **alltid** *vært*. I have **always** been.

Rule: The position of the adverbs (e.g. **ofte, alltid, aldri**) is, unlike English, after the verb (**rodde ofte**) in the simple tenses (present and past tenses), but after the auxiliary in the compound tenses, like English. Remember that the rule only applies to the principal clauses.

Vocabulary

familie [famí:lie] c. family
feriére (-te) spend one's holiday
koselig [ˇko:səli] cosy
hytte f. hut, cottage
foreldre [fɔrˈeldrə] pl. parents
leie (-de) hire, rent
øy f. island
samle (-et) collect
skjell n. shell
langs along
blåse (-te) blow
hjémover homewards
'alltid always
aldri never
ulykke c. accident. mishap
heldigvis fortunately
selv om ['sellɔm] conj. although

hende (-dte) happen, occur
en vakker dag one fine day
nesten almost
hun fikk rett she was right
sky c. cloud
ingen [iŋŋən] no, no one
vind c. wind
bølge c. wave
torsk [tɔʃk] c. cod
om ettermiddagen in the afternoon
det blåser a wind is blowing
redd frightened
åre c. oar
vifte (-et) med wave
av alle krefter of all one's might
hvis [viss] conj. if
da conj. when

Exercise 10a

Min familie er meget glad i sjøen og ferierte hver sommer på Sørlandet. Vi bodde i en liten koselig hytte som mine foreldre leide. *Vi rodde ofte* ut til en øy for å bade, fiske og samle skjell, som lå strødd langs stranden. Hvis det begynte å *blåse*, snudde vi og rodde hjemover igjen. *Vi nådde alltid* land, og *det skjedde aldri* noen ulykke, selv om mor spådde at noe ville hende en vakker dag. Hun fikk nesten (*almost*) rett. Vi rodde ut en morgen i fint, stille vær—ikke en sky på himmelen, ingen vind, ingen bølge. Vi skulle fiske torsk. Om ettermiddagen begynte det å blåse, og min bror som rodde, ble så redd at han mistet en åre. Det var bare én ting å gjøre—rope om (*for*) hjelp. Vi viftet med armene og ropte Hjelp! Hjelp! Far hørte oss heldigvis. Han sprang i en båt, og rodde av alle krefter for å nå oss. Han greide det fint. Vi var reddet, men det kunne lett ha skjedd en ulykke hvis ingen på stranden hadde hørt oss da vi ropte.

Ordspråk: Når enden er god, er allting godt.

Vocabulary

på fjellet in the mountains (lit. on the)
luft c. air
riktig right, correct
natúr c. nature, scenery
det dem. pron. n. that

turist [tu'rist] c. tourist
propagánda c. propaganda
du vil you will
lyve irr. lie, be lying
skuffe (-et) disappoint

Exercise 10b

Are you fond of the sea? No, I like to spend my holidays in the mountains. I have a cosy little cottage, not far (*langt*) from Lillehammer. Is Lillehammer a big (*stor*) town? No, fortunately not. I do not like (trans. I like not, etc.) big (*store*) towns. I cannot live there. I have heard that the air at (trans. *på*, lit. *on*) Lillehammer is so fine. Yes, that is right—and the scenery! I call that tourist propaganda. Call it what you will. It is true (*sant*). Come and see if you think I am lying. You will not be (=*bli*) disappointed.

Vocabulary

klokka syv at seven o'clock
seng f. bed
inn i into
bad n. bath, bathroom
pusse (-et) brush
etterpå afterwards
tørke (-et) dry
håndkle n. towel
kle (-dde) dress
fart [faᵲtt] c. speed
i en fart in a hurry
først [føʃt] first
undertøy n. underwear
skjorte [ᵛʃoᵲtə] f. shirt

bukse [ᵛboksə] f. pair of trousers
strømpe c. stocking
så then = afterwards
slips n. tie
til slutt at last, finally
jakke f. coat
fullt adv. fully
påkledd dressed (på—on)
med [meː] prep. with
glupende (pres. part.) ravenous
appetitt c. appetite
álltid always
avis (aʹviːs) c. newspaper
mens conj. while

Exercise 11a

En ny dag begynner.

Jeg våkner hver morgen klokka syv (7), strekker meg og hopper ut av senga og inn i badet, pusser tennene og vasker meg. Etterpå tørker jeg meg med et håndkle, kler på meg i en fart—først undertøy, skjorte og bukse, strømper og sko, så slips og til slutt en jakke.

Jeg er nå fullt påkledd og spiser min frokost med glupende appetitt. Jeg leser alltid avisen mens jeg spiser.

Having translated the exercise, rewrite it in the past tense.

Vocabulary

norsk Norwegian
venn c. friend
om sommeren in the summer
neste vår next spring
ti lo
språk n. language
flere (ʹfleːrə) several
ord n. word

allerede (aləᵛreːdə) already
veldig morsomt great fun
på engelsk in English
svare (-te) til correspond to
besøke (-te) visit
gang c. here: time (occasion)
over (ʹɔːvər) across
elv f. river

Exercise 11b

You said you had a Norwegian friend. Yes, that is true (*sant*). He lived in Oslo, but used to go (*reise*) to England in the summer. He said he could (*kunne*) not live there, but liked to travel in England.

I shall (*skal*) go to Norway next spring. I have bought a Norwegian book which cost 10 shillings. I am learning to read and speak the language. I have learnt several words already. It is great fun. I can say: *God morgen*. That means good morning in English, and *God aften*, which corresponds to: good evening.

My friend likes rowing and fishing. I have visited him several times. We rowed across the river.

Special Note: My friend likes rowing and fishing is best rendered in Norwegian: *Min venn liker å ro og fiske.*

Rule: The English verbal nouns here—rowing and fishing— are in Norwegian generally replaced by the ordinary infinitive, although here you could say: *roing og fisking.*

Strong or Irregular Verbs

76. (1) In striking contrast to the weak or regular verbs, the strong or irregular verbs take no ending in the past tense. Notice also that the infinitive vowel almost invariably changes in the past tense and past participle.

	Infinitive	Past	Past Participle
English:	sing	sang	sung
Norwegian:	*synge*	*sang*	*sunget*

It should be noted that a great many of those verbs which are strong in English are also strong in Norwegian.

In the course of time, however, these verbs have undergone great changes, being constantly influenced by the weak classes. Therefore many analogous forms have sprung into existence. Some verbs have gone to the weak classes, others have weak forms besides the strong ones. (Similar developments are found in English. Cf.: show, showed, shown, knit or knitted in the past tense.)

(2) Throughout there has been a marked tendency to introduce the infinitive vowel into the past participle.

The strong verbs in Norwegian today give one a rather confused impression, and to facilitate the task of the student they have therefore been arranged alphabetically in a list at the end of the book.

In spite of this apparent confusion, however, one may discern certain fixed patterns, as will be seen in the list below. Repeat therefore the verbs in the three main forms over and over again so as to impress the general run of the vowel variations on the ear.

77. *Intonation.* It is interesting to observe that whereas the forms in the infinitive and the past participle of two-syllable verbs have double tone (as might be expected) the forms in the present tense have *single*—the reason being that the latter were monosyllabic in Old Norse (*syngr, bitr*).

Inf. [ˈbiːtə]   Pres. [ˈbiːtər]

Take care not to clip off the vowel in words like bite, and the long consonant sound in *synge, finne* (find), etc.

78. (1) *iː*   *eː*   *e/i*

skrive write	*skrev*	*skrevet*

Further examples:

gripe seize	*grep*	*grepet*
skrike cry, scream	*skrek*	*skreket*
bite bite	*bet*	*bitt*
bli get, become	*ble*	*blitt*

Exercise 12

Translate:

(*a*) Jeg grep gutten i armen. Sønnen skrev brev hjem hver uke. Min bror har skrevet en bok om Ibsen. Hunden (*the dog*) bet gutten i benet, og gutten skrek.

79. (2) *yː*   *øː*   *ø/u*

krype creep	*krøp*	*krøpet*

Further examples:

bryte break	*brøt*	*brutt*
skyte shoot	*skjøt*	*skutt*
fryse freeze	*frøs*	*frosset*

gjerde n. [ˈjæːrə] fence

Translate:

(b) Tyven krøp lange gjerdet. Du har brutt ditt løfte (løfte n. = promise). Jegeren (= the sportsman) har skutt en elg og en rev (= fox). Vannet har frosset til is.

80. (3) *i/e*   *a*   *u/i*

drikke drink	*drakk*	*drukket* [ˇdrokkət]

Further examples:

stikke put, pierce	*stakk*	*stukket* [ˇstokkət]
finne find	*fant*	*funnet*
hjelpe help	*hjalp*	*hjulpet* [ˇjolpət]

Translate:

(c) Han drakk bare to glass. Har du funnet ringen? Jeg fant den da jeg stakk hånden i lommen (lomme c. = pocket). Gutten hjalp piken med kåpen (kåpe c. = coat).

81. (4) *æ:/e:*   *a:*   *å:*

bære bear, carry	*bar*	*båret*

Further examples:

skjære cut	*skar*	*skåret*
stjele steal	*stjal*	*stjålet*

Translate:

(d) Han bar henne over bekken (bekk c. = brook). Jeg har skåret meg i fingeren. Han stjal fra de rike og ga til de fattige (fattig = poor).

82. (5) *e/i*   *a:/å:*   *i/e*

gi [ji:] give	*ga(v)*	*gitt* [jitt]

Further examples:

be ask one to, request	*ba*	*bedt*
se see, look	*så*	*sett*
ligge lie	*lå*	*ligget*

Translate:

(e) Eva ga Adam et eple. Adam hadde ikke bedt om det. Ingen (no one) har sett ham. Piken så på (= at) meg med store øyne. Min søster har ligget syk i tre dager.

83. (6) *a:/â:*   *o:*   *a/â*
 ta take   *tok*   *tatt*

Further examples:

 dra pull; depart   *dro(g)* *dratt*
 la let   *lot*   *latt*

84. By itself:

 slâ strike, beat   *slo*   *slâtt*
 stâ stand   *sto(d)* *stâtt*
 le laugh   *lo*   *ledd*

Translate:

(*f*) Jeg tok min hatt og sa farvel. De lot meg gå. Klokka i tårnet (*târn* n. = tower) slo akkurat tolv [tɔll] (12). Vi dro til England [éŋlann] med fly. Vi lo og sang hele veien. Hun sa hun stod opp klokka åtte (8) hver dag. Den som ler sist, ler best (*a common saying*).

85. (7) The same vowel all through:

 komme come   *kom*   *kommet*

Further examples:

 holde hold, keep *holdt* *holdt*
 løpe run   *løp*   *løpt*
 sove [ˇsɔːvə] sleep *sov*   *sovet*

By itself:

 gâ go, walk *gikk [jikk]* *gâtt*
 fâ get, receive *fikk*   *fâtt*

Note: *Gâ* in Norwegian never means 'travel', which is *reise*. *Fâ* is often used as an auxiliary and in many idiomatic combinations which we shall deal with later.

Translate:

(*g*) Flyet kom til Fornebu flyplass i går. Jeg fikk ikke sove i natt. Stormen holdt meg våken (*awake*). Jeg stod opp og gikk (meg) en lang tur. Min venn gikk til London i går. Nei, det gjorde han ikke. Han *reiste* til London.

86. When prefixed the strong verbs maintain the same conjugation:

'tilgi forgive	tilga	tilgitt
'gjenta repeat	gjentok	gjentatt
'ankomme arrive	ankom	ankommet

Rendering of the English Continuous Tenses

87. Right from the start we saw that there were no equivalent forms to the so-called continuous tenses in English, like: He is coming. He was coming. In translation these forms have been rendered by ordinary simple tenses, corresponding to English: He comes. He came. (See note, para. 62.)

In order to stress that the action is taking place at this very moment the following idiomatic expressions could be employed: *'holde på (med)'* or: *'drive på med'* (keep on with).

Examples: *Hva holder du på med?* What are you doing? *Jeg holder på (med) å skrive et brev.* I am (occupied with) writing a letter.

Note conjugation of *holde* and *drive*:

| holde | holdt | holdt |
| drive | drev | drevet |

Vocabulary

meget [ˇmeːgət] very
lærd [lærd] learned
sine reflex. pron. pl. his
når [nɔrr] conj. when
om morgenen in the morning
derfor ['dærfɔrr] therefore
universitet [univæʃiˈteːt] n. university
'unngå irr. avoid

klesplagg n. piece of clothing
om kvelden ['kvell(ə)n] in th evening
stolrygg c. back of a chair
slokke [ˇʃlokkə] (-te) put out
lys n. light
våkne (-et) awaken
gripe irr. seize, grasp
den gangen that time

Exercise 13a

Professoren i senga

En meget lærd professor, la oss kalle ham N.N., fant aldri (igjen) klærne sine når han skulle kle på seg om morgenen. Han kom derfor alltid for sent til universitetet. For å unngå dette skrev han opp hvor han hadde lagt hvert klesplagg om kvelden.

Han satt i senga og skrev:

Strømpene på skoene, skoene under senga, skjorte, slips og jakke over stolryggen, undertøyet på stolen. Til slutt skrev

·han: Professoren i senga. Så slokte han lyset, og ikke lenge
etter sov han som en stein.

Da han våknet neste morgen, grep han listen og fant alle
klærne der de skulle være. Men—professoren i senga fant
han ikke. Han kom for sent den gangen også.

Exercise 13b

Translate:

He drank a glass of beer before (*før*) he went to bed in the
evening. The man always[1] rode alone. He offered me only
ten pounds for the car. The girl never[1] forgave him. Arsenal
have won again. They always[1] win. He always[1] seized the
chance when he saw it. I have not found her. What did
Cæsar say?[2] He said: 'I came, I saw, I conquered (= won).'

CHAPTER VI

HOW TO FORM QUESTIONS
IN NORWEGIAN

First we need to get acquainted with the main question words.
They are:

88. (*a*) The interrogative pronouns (cf. page 123) *hvem*
[vemm] = who, whom (used about persons only).

hvilken ['vilkən] c. *hvilket* ['vilkət] n. '*hvilke* pl. =which (used
about persons and things).

hva [vɑ:] = what (used about things).

(*b*) The interrogative adverbs:

når = when. *Når er du født?* When were you born?

hvor [vorr] + adj. = how. *Hvor gammel er du?* How old are
you?

hvordan ['voʳdann] } how *hvorledes* ['voʳledəs]	*Hvordan var været?* How was the weather?
	Hvordan vet du det? How do you know?
hvorfor ['vorfɔrr] = why	*Hvorfor ler du?* Why are you laughing?

---

[1] For correct position of adverb see pages 42 and 166.
[2] Translate 'What said Caesar?'

89. In some special cases English and Norwegian form questions exactly in the same way, viz.

(1) When dealing with auxiliary verbs (be, have, can, shall, will, etc.).

(2) When an interrogative pronoun is the **subject** of the sentence.

(3) When an interrogative pronoun or adverb (i.e. *hvor* + adj.) is **part of the subject.**

Examples:

(1) Are you hungry? *Er du sulten?*
   Have you seen him? *Har du sett ham?*
   Can you tell me? *Kan du fortelle meg?*

(2) Who knows? *Hvem vet?*
   What comes next? *Hva kommer så?*

(3) What train is he coming by? *Hvilket tog kommer han med?*
   How many Norwegians live in America? *Hvor mange nordmenn bor i Amerika?*·

90. Otherwise the congruity does not exist any longer, as Norwegian has no equivalent to constructions with 'to do', but form questions in the same way as above (in 1), viz. by reversing the word order.

Do you know him? *Kjenner du ham?*
Did you see her? *Så du henne?*
What do I find here? *Hva finner jeg her?*

Shakespeare could write: What find I here? So when forming questions in Norwegian the student should apply the pattern 'have I' or 'can I'.

Progressive forms:
Present: Are you leaving today? *Reiser du i dag?*
Past: Were you listening to the radio? *Hørte du på radio?*

91. Note: Sometimes questions may be formed by using an ordinary affirmative sentence adding the expression 'ikke sant' (= is it not true?). *Du har spist, ikke sant?* You have eaten, haven't you? *Han hette Per, ikke sant?* He was called Per, wasn't he? *Oslo er hovedstaden i Norge, ikke sant?* Oslo is the capital of Norway, isn't it?

Vocabulary

teater [te'a:tər] n. theatre
ingen anelse [ˇa:n(ə)lsə] c. no idea
med'en gang at once
se'godt ut look well
pause c. interval
gå på konsert [kon'sæʳʈ] c. go to a concert

av og til now and then, occasionally
moderne [mo'dæ:ʳŋə] modern
klassisk ['klassisk] classical
foretrekke [ˇfɔ:rətrekkə] irr. (as trekke) prefer
instrument n. instrument
sannelig adv. indeed
hu'kommelse c. memory

Exercise 14a

Translate:

1. Traff du Per i går? Ja, jeg så ham i teatret.
Visste du at han var der? Nei, jeg hadde ingen anelse.
Kjente du ham igjen? Ja, med en gang.
Hvordan så han ut? Han så meget godt ut.
Snakket du mye med ham. Ja, i alle pausene.
Er du ofte i teatret? Jeg ser nesten alt *som går* (*which is on*).
Går du aldri på konserter? Jo, av og til.
Hva liker du best, moderne musikk eller klassisk? Jeg foretrekker det siste.
Spiller du noe instrument selv? Nei, dessverre, men du spiller piano, ikke sant?
Husker du det også? Du har sannelig en god hukommelse.

2. Make these sentences interrogative:

Du bor i Oslo. Han hører ofte på radio. Hun skrev brev til kjæresten (kjæreste *c. sweetheart*) sin hver dag. Han er soldat [sol'da:t]. Byen Narvik ligger i Nord-Norge. Bjørnson døde i Paris [pa'ri:s].

Deres (*your*) kone vil ha en kopp te til (= another cup of tea).

3. Translate the following sentences: (Oversett følgende setninger:)

She is writing a letter. You are studying Norwegian, aren't you? He is leaving tomorrow, isn't he? What are they doing? Are they playing bridge?

Vocabulary

få (tak i) irr. get (hold of)
billett [bi'lett] c. ticket
heldig lucky
klokka åtte at eight o'clock
spille kort [kɔʳʈ] play cards
jeg synes I think, find

kjedelig [ˇçe:d(ə)li] dull, boring
'tennis tennis
mer more
interessert [intrə'se:ʳʈ] interested
fotball c. soccer

Exercise 14b

Translate:

Did you get (hold of) tickets for (tr. *til*) the concert? Yes, I was lucky. When does the concert begin? It begins at eight o'clock. Do you like to play cards? No, I think it is boring. Does your brother play tennis? No, he is more interested in soccer.

CHAPTER VII

NEGATIVE SENTENCES

not = ikke

92. Here again we find similarities between the two languages as far as auxiliaries are concerned:

I have not (I haven't)	*Jeg har ikke*
He cannot (can't)	*Han kan ikke*
Questions: Haven't I?/Have I not?	*Har jeg ikke?*
Can't he?	*Kan han ikke?*

This is the pattern used in Norwegian for expressing negative statements, as constructions with 'to do' have no counterpart.

'I don't know' must therefore be translated as: *Jeg vet ikke.* (Cf. Shakespeare: I know not.)
I didn't know, as: *Jeg visste ikke.*

Questions: Doesn't he know? *Vet han ikke?*
　　　　　 Didn't he know? *Visste han ikke?*

Paradigm:

Inf.	Present	Past	Perfect Tenses
ikke å vite	*han vet ikke*	*han visste ikke*	*han har (hadde) ikke visst*
not to know	he doesn't know	he didn't know	he hasn't (hadn't) known

Negative questions:

Present	Past	Perfect
Vet han ikke?	*Visste han ikke?*	*Har (hadde) han ikke visst?*
Doesn't he know?	Didn't he know?	Hasn't (hadn't) he known?

English negative continuous forms are translated:

You are not writing.	*Du skriver ikke.*
Aren't you writing?	*Skriver du ikke?*
You were not writing.	*Du skrev ikke.*
Weren't you writing?	*Skrev du ikke?*

The imperative:

don't be afraid	*vær ikke redd!* or *ikke vær redd!*
don't do it	*gjør det ikke!* or *ikke gjør det!*
don't laugh	*le ikke!* or *ikke le!*

Reflexive:

don't strain yourself	*overanstreng deg ikke!* or *ikke overanstreng deg!*

Answering Words in Norwegian

93. These are: **ja** yes, but after a negative **jo**. (cf. German: *ja* and *doch*; French: *oui* and *si*.) **nei** = no.

Examples: *Heter du Per? Ja (jeg heter Per).*
Is your name Per? Yes (my name is Per).
but   *Heter du ikke Per? Jo (jeg heter Per).*
Isn't your name Per? Yes (my name is Per).
Er hun ikke søt? Jo.
Isn't she sweet? Yes.

94. Note also these answers where the pronoun 'det' (that) is added.

Have you a car? *Har du (en) bil?* Yes, I have. **Ja, det har jeg.**
Do you know him? *Kjenner du ham?* No, I don't. **Nei, det gjør jeg ikke.**
Did you get the tickets? *Fikk du billettene?* Yes, I did. **Ja, det gjorde jeg.**
Aren't you English? *Er De ikke engelsk?* Yes, I am. **Jo, det er jeg.**

Place of 'ikke' in Subordinate Clauses

95. In a subordinate clause **ikke** is normally placed before the verb. Note the divergence from English. This peculiarity also applies to other adverbs.

Examples: *Han sa at det* **ikke** *var sant.* He said that it was not true. *Du må skynde deg hvis du* **ikke** *skal komme for sent til toget.* You must hurry up if you are not to miss the train. *Da de* **ikke** *kom, måtte vi 'avlyse møtet.* As they did not come, we had to cancel the meeting. *Det er (fins) folk som* **ikke** *vil arbeide.* There are people who will not work.

For order of words in Norwegian (see page 165).

Vocabulary

å gå på ski to ski
så—som as—as
lett easy, -ly
stiv stiff
ordentlig ['ɔ'nṭli] properly
redd afraid
med godt humør n. good-
   humouredly

på én dag in one day
øvelse c. practice
méster c. master
det lønner seg [dəˈlønnəʃei] it
   pays
uforsiktig [ˈuːfɔʃikti] careless
naturligvis [naˈtuːˈlivi(ː)s] of
   course
tåpelig silly

Exercise 15a

Translation:

Å lære å gå på ski er ikke så lett som en tror. Har du prøvd? Nei, jeg tør ikke. Du må ikke være stiv. Glem ikke å binde skiene ordentlig på (deg). Vær ikke redd. Ta det med godt humør. Tro ikke at du kan lære det på en dag. Øvelse gjør mester. Brekker en ikke ofte benene? Nei, det hender ikke ofte. Det lønner seg ikke å være uforsiktig, naturligvis. Det er tåpelig.

Exercise 15b

tid [tiːd] c. time   divan [diˈvaːn] c. divan
ypperlig [ˈyppəˈli] splendid

Didn't you know that I was coming? (use simple past tense). No, you haven't written. I didn't get time. Don't you like to see me? Of course, but I don't know where I can find a bed for (*til*) you. I can sleep in a chair. I don't need a bed to sleep in. Don't be silly. You can sleep on a divan. Yes, many thanks, that[1] is splendid. I have done that[1] very often (transl. many times).

CHAPTER VIII

THE PASSIVE VOICE

96. The passive is expressed in two ways in Norwegian, first of all by the auxiliary **à bli -ble -blitt** (become, get) with the past participle of the main verb.

Inf.	Present	Past	Perfect
à bli rost	*han blir rost*	*han ble rost*	*han er (har) blitt rost*
to be praised	he is praised	he was praised	he has been praised

For 'he was caught' English can also say 'he got caught' and then comes very near the Norwegian construction.

97. But Norwegian like the other Scandinavian languages also has passive forms ending in **-s**.

Inf.	Present	Past
à rose	*han roses*	*han rostes*
to be praised	he is praised	he was praised

This **-s** is actually a remnant of the Old Norse reflexive **sik,** in modern Norwegian **seg** (see page III), which in course of time was reduced to **-s** when tacked on to the verb.

98. In most cases the **s**-forms can be changed into expressions with **bli,** *han kastes* (he is thrown) into *han blir kastet.*

Sometimes, however, there is a slight nuance between the two formations.

(*a*) The **s**-form has a more general meaning and is often used about customary and repeated actions. They are often met with in public notices and in announcements and advertisements.

[1] = **det** [de:] (stressed) dem. pron. n.

Eksamen (sg.) *holdes hvert år*. Examinations are held every year. *Publikum anmodes om ikke å røke*. The audience are requested not to smoke.

(*b*) Constructions with **bli** are often used to denote isolated and limited actions. *Huset blir bygd*.

99. But on the whole the s-forms have a rather restricted use. They are quite common in the present tense and in the passive infinitive after the so-called modal auxiliaries. (*See para. 161*.)

Examples:

Noe må gjøres. Something has to be done. *Det kan ikke beskrives, det må oppleves*. It cannot be described, it must be experienced. *Det kan lett se(e)s* [ˇseːəs, ˈseːs]. It can easily be seen.

In the past tense it is rare, let alone the perfect tenses: *kjøptes* was bought, *betaltes* was paid, but when it comes to verbs of the first conjugation (the **-et** class) we get such clumsy forms as *kastedes* which belong to a bygone period. You may find them in the works of Ibsen, Bjørnson, Lie and Kielland, etc.

The **s**-form is hardly ever used in the past tense of strong verbs either.

100. In forcible narrative style, which is closely related to everyday speech, the active voice is generally used in preference to the passive. Sentences like: *Det sies* [ˇsiːəs] can be rendered by: *Folk sier*, or *man sier*. One says.

Passive in English—Indicative in Norwegian

101. In some instances English uses the passive voice where Norwegian would employ the indicative, e.g. *Han druknet*. He was drowned, but: They drowned the cat in Norwegian is *De druknet katten*. *Huset brant ned*. The house was burnt down. *Han skal gifte seg*. He is going to be (get) married. *Du tar helt feil der*. You are quite mistaken there. *Hun var ingensteds å se (å finne)*. She was nowhere to be seen (to be found). *Det er å håpe*. It is to be hoped.

102. Sometimes a passive construction can be rendered by an active one in Norwegian with the indefinite pronouns **man, en** or **de** as subject, i.e. He was thought to be dead. *Man trodde at han var død.* It is believed that ... *Man tror at* ... It is said ... *Man sier* or *Det sies at* ... What is to be done? *Hva er å gjøre?* or better: *Hva skal man gjøre?*

Further Remarks on the s-Forms

103. It should be observed that the student will meet with several **s**-forms, in writing as well as in ordinary conversation, which have no strictly passive meaning at all, and which cannot therefore be replaced by the auxiliary *bli*. In some instances the **s**-form has a slightly different meaning from the original verb, as will be seen from the examples below. Most of them are not used in the perfect tenses.

høres = sound. *Det høres rart (ut).* It sounds strange. *Det høres (ut) som fiolinmusikk.* It sounds like violin music. *Det hørtes (ut) som om han hadde gitt opp alt håp.* It sounded as if he had given up all hope. But: *Dine ord hørtes (ble hørt).* Your words were heard.

kjennes = be noticed, be felt. *Det kjennes på farten når Grane (navnet på en hest) legger i vei. (Fra Ibsens: Peer Gynt.)* You can tell by the speed when Grane (the name of a horse) starts off. (From Ibsen's 'Peer Gynt'.) *Det kjentes (ut) som om hele hånden var frosset til is.* It was as if the whole hand was frozen to ice.

føles = be felt, means more or less the same as *kjennes.* *Hvordan føles (or kjennes) det å være fri?* What does it feel like to be free? Past tense: *Det føltes.*

merkes = be noticeable. *Det merkes når han har vært her.* You can (always) tell when he has been here. *Det merkes ikke.* Nobody will notice it. Past tense: *Det merktes ...*

behøves, trenges = be necessary. *Skal jeg hjelpe? Nei, takk, det behøves ikke.* Shall I help? No, thank you, it isn't necessary. Past tense: *det behøvdes (trengtes) ikke.*

undres = wonder, has reflexive meaning. *Jeg undres (på) om han kommer*. I wonder if he is coming?

synes = be apparent, noticeable. *Det synes ikke*. It doesn't show. *Det synes på deg at du har løpt*. One can see that you have been running. But to express personal opinion: *Jeg synes* = I think—an expression of very high frequency. *Jeg synes hun er vakker*. I think she is beautiful. *Det synes ikke jeg*. I don't think so. See page 40.

skilles = part. *De skiltes som gode venner*. They parted as good friends. *De skal skilles*. They are getting divorced.

104. A few other s-forms have reciprocal meanings:

Infinitive Present	Past Tense	Past Participle	
slåss	sloss [ʃɭoss]	slåss	fight each other

Spillerne sloss om ballen. The players fought for the ball.

Vi sees i morgen. We will see each other tomorrow. Past tense: *sdes*.

Further examples are: *møtes* or *treffes* meet each other. *Vi møttes første gang på en dans*. We met the first time at a dance.

105. Finally there are some verbs of this type which have not passive, but active meaning such as:

Lykkes succeed, which also has a past participle form (= inf.).

Infinitive Present	Past Tense	Past Participle
lykkes	lyktes	lykkes

Det lyktes meg ikke å stoppe ham. I did not succeed in stopping him.

Remember, never *Jeg lyktes*, but always *Det lyktes meg*.

Minnes remember, recall. *Jeg minnes min barndom*. I remember my childhood. Past tense: *mintes*. The plain verb *minne* means 'remind'.

Infinitive Present   Past Tense

Finnes (or *fins*) exist, be   *fantes*

Det fantes ikke mat i huset. There was no food in the house.

Infinitive Present   Past Tense

trives thrive, be comfortable, feel at home   *trivdes*

Han trivdes ikke i store byer. He did not feel at home in large cities.

Preposition 'av' = by

106. The preposition used in connection with the passive is **av** in Norwegian, corresponding to **by** in English. *De ble angrepet av fienden.* They were attacked by the enemy. *Maten lages av kokken.* The food is prepared by the cook.

Vocabulary

ro'man c. novel
helt c. hero
narre (-et) lure
drepe (-te) kill
forræder [fɔ're:dər] c. traitor
fange (-et) capture
straffe (-et) punish

om noen få dager in a few days
óppdage (-et) discover, detect
likevel [ˇli:kəvəl] nevertheless
ugjerning [ˇu:jæ:ᵊņiŋ] c. crime, evil deed
død [dø:d] c. death
føre (-te) lead, take

Exercise 16a

Translation:

Jeg leste i dag en roman. Helten narres ut i skogen, og drepes av en forræder. Ingen ser det. Men om noen få dager oppdages likevel ugjerningen. Forræderen fanges og straffes med døden (*by death*).

Rewrite the above sentences using the auxiliary **bli** instead of the **s**-form.

Vocabulary

historie [hi'sto:riə] c. story
prinsesse [prinˇsessə] princess
redde (-et) save
fattig [ˇfatti] poor
slott [ʃlɔtt] n. castle

be'lønne (-et) reward
gjøre til konge make someone king
lykkelig happily

Exercise 16b

Use the **s**-forms first and then the auxiliary **bli**.

The story is read by many children. The princess is saved by the hero, who is only a poor man. He is taken to the castle to be rewarded. He is made king, and they live happily ever after (*for resten av livet*).

Comments on Passive

107. An English-speaking person may be in doubt sometimes how to translate sentences like: The house was painted. He was punished. It is said, etc. Is he to translate: *Huset var* or *ble malt? Han var* or *ble straffet? Det er* or *blir sagt?* Similarly: He is loved—*han er* or *blir elsket?*

Rule: When **bli** is used the stress is laid on the action. When **være** is used stress is laid on the result attained. If the verb 'get' or the continuous form can be used then **bli** is the correct auxiliary. If **he was caught** is identical with **he got caught** then the correct translation is **Han ble fanget.**

Exercise 17

Insert the correct forms of **være** or **bli** in these sentences.

1. Hennes bror — drept i siste krig. Her brother was killed in the last war.

2. Jeg — så forbauset da jeg hørte det. I was so surprised when I heard it.

3. Da vi kom, — døren låst. When we arrived the door was locked.

4. Tele'grammet — sendt i går. The telegram was sent yesterday.

5. Vi — gift i går. We were married yesterday.

6. Jeg håper dere vil — lykkelige. I hope you will be happy.

7. Det tror jeg vi skal —. I think we shall.

8. Han — elsket av sine venner. He was loved by his friends.

9. Fant du pengene? Nei, de — stjålet. Did you find the money? No, it was stolen.

10. Det så ut som om han — — stukket av en veps. It looked as if he had been stung by a wasp.

Vocabulary

barber [bar'be:r] c. barber
hos bar'beren at the barber's
fri'sør c. hairdresser
bar'bersalong c. barber's shop
få (irr.) **av seg** get rid of
skjegg n. beard
kunde [ˇkundə] c. customer
tur c. here: turn
vær så god here: please
som vanlig as usual
klippe (-et) cut
bar'bere (-te) shave
stund c. while, time
svært [svæ:'t] adv. very
nærsynt [ˇnæ:ʃy:nt] short-
  sighted

tomat [to'ma:t] c. tomato
suppe c. soup
til middag c. for dinner
forbauset [fɔr'bøusət] astonished
fiskesuppe c. fish soup
biff c. beef
syltetøy n. jam
løk c. onion
pudding c. pudding
saus c. sauce
til dessert [də'sæ:r] c. for dessert
frukt c. fruit
salat [sa'la:t] c. salad
merkelig [ˇmærkəli] strange
likevel adv. after all

Exercise 18

Hos barberen/frisøren

En mann gikk inn i en barbersalong for å få av seg skjegget. Da (As) det var en fire-fem kunder før ham, måtte han vente på tur. Så roper barberen: 'Vær så god neste!' Vår mann setter seg opp i stolen, og barberen spør som vanlig: 'Klippes eller barberes—?' 'Barberes,' svarer mannen.

Etter en stund sier barberen, som er svært nærsynt: 'Har De spist tomatsuppe til middag i dag—?' 'Nei,' svarer kunden forbauset, 'jeg har spist fiskesuppe.' 'Og etterpå—?' 'Biff.' 'Med syltetøy til?' 'Nei, med løk.' 'Har De spist pudding med rød saus til dessert?' 'Nei, fruktsalat.' 'Det var merkelig! Da må jeg ha skåret Dem likevel.'

'det er' = it is, there is

108. *Det er* corresponds both to: (a) *it is*, and (b) *there is* (*are*), in English, since the old form *der* has been almost entirely superseded by *det*.

(a) *Det er ikke salt, det er sukker.* It is not salt, it is sugar. *Det er meget sannsynlig* [sann'sy:nli]. It is very likely. Note the difference in construction between Norwegian: *Det er sannsynlig at han kommer*, and English: He is likely to come.

(b) *Det var mange dengang som trodde at det var helt umulig* [u'mu:li]. There were many at that time who thought that it was absolutely impossible. *Er det noe blekk i blekkhuset* ['blekk(h)usə]? Is there any ink in the inkstand?

There is and *there was* can in a good many cases be rendered by: *Det finnes* (or *fins*) and *Det fantes*. See page 60.

Dengang fantes det ingen biler. There were no cars in those days.

(c) *Det* is further used in impersonal expressions like: *Det regner* [ˇreinər]. It is raining. *Det snør.* It is snowing, etc.

CHAPTER IX

THE ADJECTIVE

109. You will already have come across adjectives scattered here and there in the book. But you have not learned to decline them as yet. The declension of adjectives in Norwegian is not very complicated, but it requires some practice.

In English, where there are no genders in the nouns, the adjective remains unchanged. In Norwegian, however, as in French and German, the adjective agrees with the noun both in gender and number. There are two declensions which must be learned: (*a*) the Indefinite Declension and (*b*) the Definite Declension.

The Indefinite Declension

c.	n.	pl.
110. *stor* big	*stort*	*store*

Examples:

stor gutt big boy
stort hus big house
store gutter, hus big boys, houses

This type of declension is used when the adjective stands alone or isolated before the noun as in the examples above, or is preceded by the indefinite article **en, et,** or the indefinite adjectives. The latter you have not met yet, so you had better be introduced to them. Those in question are:

	c.	n.	pl.
111.	*noen* [ˈnoːən] some, any	*noe*	*noen*
	ingen no	*intet*	*ingen*
	(en)hver [væːr] every, each	*(et)hvert*	—

112. Note *ingen* is equivalent to *ikke noen* (not any), and *intet* (rarely used in everyday language) to *ikke noe*, and the plural *ingen* to *ikke noen*.

Examples:

en vakker dag, et langt brev, noen lange brev.
Han er ingen fin mann = ikke noen fin mann.
hver fri mann = every free man.
hvert grønt blad = every green leaf.

113. Note: The adjective also takes the same endings when used predicatively. *Gutten er stor, Huset er stort, Guttene, husene er store.*

Det blir mørkt. It is getting dark.
De må være røde. They must be red.
Vinduet er åpent. The window is open.
Vinduene er åpne. The windows are open.

Exercise 19

Insert the correct forms of *stor* (big) and the article, where required, in the following examples:

> *e- — bok.* *e- — barn.* *e- — båt.*
> *noen — skip.* *— epler.* *— menn.*

The adjective *lang* (long): *e- — vei. — film. e- — ord. — båter.*

Predicatively: *Veien er —. Ordet var —. Skoene var —.*

The adjective *høy* (high, tall); *e- — tre. — trær. ingen — fjell.*

Predicatively: *Mannen er —. Huset er —. Prisene er for* (too) *—. Trærne var blitt —.*

The Definite Declension

114. This declension is very easy to master, as the adjective here has the same ending throughout, viz. **-e**, i.e. the same ending as the indefinite declension in the plural.

c.	n.	pl.
store big	*store*	*store*

115. This pattern is used when the adjective is preceded by (*a*) **den** (c.), **det** (n.), pl. **de** (= English the), which in Norwegian grammar is termed the definite article of the adjective.

Examples:

Den store by(en) = The big town, *det store hus(et)*, plural: *de store byer* (or *byene*), *de store hus(ene)*.

(*b*) The demonstrative adjective:

c.	n.	pl.
denne this	*dette* this	*disse* these

Examples:

denne vakre park(en)	this beautiful park
dette grønne blad(et)	this green leaf
disse grønne trær(ne)	these green trees

The student will have observed from the parentheses that even the definite article of the noun can be used in these cases. We call that double definition (lit. the big the town, this green the leaf). This construction is very frequent in colloquial style.

(*c*) Possessive adjectives:

c.	n.	pl.		
min my	*mitt*	*mine*	*hans* his	
din your	*ditt*	*dine*	*hennes* her	
vår our	*vårt*	*våre*		

These are fully treated on page 113.

min nye hatt	my new hat
vårt lille hus	our little house
hans fine hund	his fine dog

In colloquial speech the possessive adjective is very often placed after the noun with the latter in the definite form, *den nye hatten min* (cf. English, the new hat of mine), *det lille huset vårt, den fine hunden hans.*

(*d*) the **s**-genitive.

Min kones nye hatt. My wife's new hat. *Desember er årets mørke måned.* December is the dark month of the year.

Note especially:

In some cases the definite declension is used without any preceding determinative, e.g.:

(*e*) When the adjective forms part of a proper name, adding to the characterization of the latter, e.g.: *Gamle Norge* old Norway, *vesle Hans* little Hans, *Vestre Aker* (district near Oslo), *Unge fru Pedersen* The young Mrs. P., *Lille Eyolf* (play by Ibsen). These often contract into one word: *Lillegutt* little boy (pet name), *gamlemor* grandma.

(*f*) In exclamations and expressions of address:

Store Gud, du store min, du store verden! (All meaning: Good gracious!) Further: *arme mann!* poor man! *Hallo, gamle venn!* Hallo, old friend! In letters: *Kjære venn!* Dear friend.

(*g*) In a number of expressions the definite article is omitted after a preposition; the definite declension is still retained.

Examples: *på rette måten* in the right manner, *i hele mitt liv* in all my life, *i hele dag* all day. Note: *hele dagen*; *hele huset*; *halve riket* half the kingdom; *midt på lyse dagen* in broad daylight.

As the definite form of the adjective is identical with the strong form in the plural, what is said in the following paragraphs about the latter also applies to the former.

Some Details on Adjectives (for later study)

116. 1. Double consonants are reduced to single before the ending **-t** in the neuter:

c.	n.	pl.
stygg ugly	*stygt*	*stygge*
grønn green	*grønt*	*grønne*
vill wild	*vilt*	*ville*

Exceptions: *full* full -*fullt*, *viss* certain -*visst*, to avoid confusion with other words with only one consonant in the common gender.

2. Adjectives ending in unstressed **-el, -en** or **-er** drop the **-e** in the plural and in the definite form. If this **-e** is preceded by a double consonant the latter will be reduced to single.

c.	n.	pl. and def. form
travel ['traːvəl] busy	*'travelt*	ˇ*travle*
sulten hungry	*sultent*	*sultne*
doven [ˇdɔːvən] lazy	*dovent*	*dovne*

With reduction of double consonant in the pl.

'bitter bitter	*'bittert*	ˇ*bitre*
'vakker pretty	*'vakkert*	ˇ*vakre*
gammel old	*gammelt*	*gamle*

Examples: *travle tider* busy times, *den sultne ulv* the hungry wolf, *vakre piker* beautiful girls, *i gamle dager* in olden days.

117. Special attention should be paid to the two adjectives *liten* little, small, and *egen* own.

c.	n.	pl.
liten	*lite*	*små*
en liten mann	*et lite hus*	*små menn, hus*

The definite form singular is *lille* (*den lille mann*) (coll. also *vesle*) pl. *små* (*de små menn*).

egen	*eget*	*egne*

This is the only adjective that keeps the indefinite form in the singular when preceded by a possessive.

sg.	pl.
min egen sønn my own son	But *mine egne sønner*
mitt eget barn my own child	*mine egne barn*

118.   Adjectives without -t in the neuter

(*a*) A number of adjectives do not add any *-t* before a neuter noun:

First of all, adjectives which already end in *-t*, preceded by a consonant, e.g. *svart* black, *lett* easy; *et svart hus*, *et lett arbeid* work. To this class belong the past participles of weak verbs: *et elsket barn*; *en elsket mor*. In the plural the participles of Class I change the *-t* into *-d* before the plural *-e*: *elskede fedre*. When used predicatively, participles remain unchanged: *Barna var elsket*.

(*b*) Adjectives ending in *-ig* and *-lig* (*g* not pronounced): *riktig* correct, *ferdig* finished, *lykkelig* happy.

Example: *et riktig svar*, plural *riktige svar*. *Huset er ferdig*. *ferdige hus*, *et ferdig arbeid*, *et lykkelig par* a happy pair, couple.

(*c*) Further, some words which end in *-sk*, often denoting nationality: *et norsk ord* [oːr], *et engelsk skip*, *et krigersk folk* a warlike people.

Exceptions: *fersk* [fæʃk] fresh, and *frisk* healthy, also fresh, *falsk* false, *rask* quick.

(*d*) Furthermore, some adjectives ending in *-d* such as: *glad* [glaː] glad, happy, and *redd* frightened, *solid* [soˈliːd] solid, strong, *fremmed* unfamiliar.

Example: *et glad barn*. *Barnet er redd*. *et solid hus*. *et fremmed ansikt* an unfamiliar face.

(*e*) Those ending in *-s*: *dagligdags* [ˇdaːglidaks] daily, every-day, *gammeldags* old-fashioned, *tilfreds* [tilˈfrets] contented.

Example: *et tilfreds folk* a contented people. Plural: *tilfredse borgere*[1] contented citizens, *et gammeldags hus*. Plural: *gammeldagse møbler* old-fashioned furniture.

Shortening of the vowel before the neuter -t

119. The following adjectives are affected by this shortening:

(*a*) Some adjectives ending in a stressed vowel.

The neuter *t* is doubled to show that the preceding vowel is short.

blå blue—neuter *blått*, *grå* grey—neuter *grått*, *rå* raw, also brutal—neuter *rått*, *fri* free—neuter *fritt*, *ny* new—neuter *nytt*, *stø* steady—neuter *støtt*. The *-e* in the plural is often lacking in some of these adjectives.

Examples: *blå himmel* blue sky—n. *blått hus*—plural: *blå(e) hus*; n. *grått hår* grey hair—plural: *grå hår*; *rå frukt*

[1] *borger* [ˇborgər] c. citizen.

fresh fruit—n. *rått klima* ['kliːma] raw climate, *et rått overfall* a brutal attack, plural: *rå(e) poteter* [po'teːtər] raw potatoes.

(*b*) Adjectives ending in a *-t* or a mute *-d* preceded by a long vowel.

Examples: *bløt* soft—n. *bløtt*, plural *bløte*. Further: *hvit* white—n. *hvitt*, plural *hvite*, *søt* sweet—n. *søtt*. *hvit snø*, *hvitt papir* [pa'piːr] white paper. Exceptions: *lat* lazy—n. *lat*; *kåt* wild, wanton—n. *kåt*.

With *d* (*mute*).

rød red—*rødt*, plural *røde*.

død dead—*dødt*, plural *døde* (*d* pronounced in solemn speech).

Note: god [goː] but n. *godt* [gɔtt], plural *gode* [ˇgoːə].

Indeclinable Adjectives

120. Adjectives of two or more syllables ending in an unstressed *-e* remain unchanged in every position. They are *indeclinable*.

stille quiet	*bange* frightened
øde desolate	*moderne* [mo'dæːrŋə] modern

These include the present participles of verbs: *spennende* exciting. (See page 136.)

The same thing applies to some monosyllables ending in *-a*, *-o* and *-u*, e.g.: *bra* fine, excellent, *sta* stubborn, *tro* faithful, *slu* cunning, *edru* [ˇeːdru] sober. To these can be added *kry* proud. But most of these may sometimes be seen with *-e* in the plural.

Finally the following adjectives with the ending *-s* are also indeclinable: *felles* common, *stakkars* poor, used in exclamations.

Exercise 20a

Fill in the blank spaces in the following examples:

The adjective: *lang* long, d. ... *veien*. d. ... *veiene*. d. ... *bordet*. d. ... *stykket*.

The adjective: *vakker*, d. ... *haven*. d ... *pikene*. d. ... *huset*.

Exercise 20b

Questions: What is the form of *denne* in the neuter and the plural? Insert the correct form of this pronoun as well as the correct form of the adjective in the above examples.

Using the Adjective as a Noun

121. In English the adjective can serve as a noun only when used in a general sense: **the good** meaning either (*a*) everything that is good, goodness = Norwegian *det gode*, or (*b*) the good people = Norwegian *de gode*; further examples: the dead *de døde*, the poor *de fattige*.

But if individual persons or things are meant, a noun must be added or the prop-word *one*: the old man, the sick person, the little one. This is not necessary in Norwegian owing to the genders, so we get *den gamle*, *den syke*, *den lille* (*vesle*), *de fire store* the four big ones.

Which apple do you prefer? I prefer the red one. In Norwegian: *Hvilket eple foretrekker du* (*vil du helst ha*)? *Jeg foretrekker* (*vil helst ha*) *det røde*.

Vi ga den fattige noen penger. We gave the poor man some money. *Det første jeg så, var en gris.* The first thing I saw was a pig. *Det eneste jeg husker, er at jeg var veldig redd.* The only thing I remember is that I was terribly frightened.

The adjectives used in this way may also take **-s** in the genitive: *De gamles juleaften.* The old people's Christmas Eve.

Vocabulary

den syttende [ˇsøtt(ə)nə] **mai** the seventeenth of May

nasjoˈnaldag c. independence day

glede c. joy

tog [toːg] n. train, here: procession

marsjere [maˈʃeːrə] (**-te**) march

gjennom [ˈjennəm] through

flagg n. flag

kledd i dressed in

klær pl. clothes

anledning [anˈleːdniŋ] c. occasion

særlig especially

drøy adj. here: long, or 'good'

time c. hour

se på look at

hver [væːr] every, each

musikk-korps n. band

marsj [maʃʃ] c. march

sang c. song

tone [ˇtoːnə] c. sound, tune

på avstand c. at a distance

nasjoˈnaldrakt c. national costume

fargerik richly coloured, picturesque

bue c. curve, bend
'avholdt past part. beloved, popular
al'tan c. balcony
hilse (-te) greet
juble (-et) cheer
hals c. neck, here: throat
'nedover down(wards)

så adv. then
mot towards
'munter adj. gay, cheerful
farge c. colour
over'alt everywhere
nord [no:r] north
sør south
'munterhet c. gaiety

Exercise 21a

Norges nasjonaldag

Den syttende mai er Norges nasjonaldag, og det er stor glede over hele landet den dagen. Det er en fest (*a delight*) å se det lange toget med alle de glade barna som marsjerer gjennom gatene. Alle bærer små, vakre norske flagg i hånden, og de er kledd i sine (*their*) beste klær for anledningen.

I Oslo er barnetoget særlig langt. Du kan stå i (*for*) to drøye timer og se på det.

Hver skole har sitt eget musikk-korps, som hele tiden spiller nasjonale marsjer og sanger. Du kan høre de friske tonene på lang avstand. Guttene er kledd i fine røde, hvite og blå drakter (here: *uniforms*), og småpikene i fine nasjonaldrakter. Det fargerike toget marsjerer så i en stor bue opp til det vakre slottet.

Nordmennenes avholdte konge, Olav den femte, står på altanen og hilser de små barna, og disse jubler av full hals (*for all they are worth, at the top of their voices*).

Toget går så videre (*on*) nedover mot den muntre byen. Du ser norske flagg og norske farger overalt, og du møter smilende ansikter og hører vennlige ord. Alle er i godt humør, det vi på (*in*) norsk kaller: 'perlehumør' (perle *c.* = *pearl*).

I alle Norges byer fra nord til sør finner vi den samme glede og munterhet.

Exercise 21b

1. Have you seen his new house? 2. He did not like to live in big cities. 3. We had no money. 4. Do you like *The Merry Widow*? (merry = *glad*, widow = *enke*). 5. Do you know the white lady? 6. Lillehammer is only a small town. 7. The little girl had no home to go to (= *til*). 8. That was a

nice little girl. **9.** These Norwegian apples are too small.
10. We bought some very fine strawberries in the town
(strawberry = *jordbær* ['jorbæ⁽ᵗ⁾r] n.). **11.** The weather was
fine. **12.** That was a fine word for it. **13.** This brown hat
was very expensive (expensive = *dyr*, cf. dear). **14.** She
wrote a long letter to her (= *sin*) father. **15.** The prices have
become too high (price = *pris* c.). **16.** I saw some big ships in
(tr. *på* = on) the harbour (harbour = *havn* c.). **17.** He gave
a foolish answer (foolish = *dum*, *tåpelig*). **18.** The big egg
was bad (here = *råtten*). **19.** I can't see any red house.
20. Is that clear?

CHAPTER X

COMPARISON OF ADJECTIVES

122.   Most Norwegian adjectives form the comparative by
adding **-ere** [-ərə] and the superlative by adding **-est** [-əst]
to the form of the positive.

Positive	Comparative	Superlative
(1) *rik* rich	ˇ*rik*ere	'*rik*est
(2) *dum* stupid	ˇ*dumm*ere	'*dumm*est
(3) *stille* still, quiet	ˇ*still*ere	'*still*est

(2) *m* is always doubled before **-ere** and **-est**.

(3) If the adjective ends in an unstressed **e** no new **e** is
added.

Intonation: Whereas the comparative takes double tone the
superlative takes the single, except when inflected, see
para. 128.

123.   When comparing we use the word **enn** corresponding to English than.

Han er rikere **enn** *kongen.* He is richer than the king.

124.   To emphasize the comparative, the adverb **mye** (or
meget) = English **much** is used. *Det er mye bedre.*

To emphasize the superlative, the adverb **aller** ['allər] is
used — *aller best* the very best, best of all.

Some Irregularities in the Comparison

125. (1) Adjectives ending in *-ig* (*-lig*), where the *g* is not pronounced except in the superlative, have *-ere* in the comparative, but only *-st* in the superlative.

Examples:

billig cheap	*billigere*	*'billigst*
lykkelig happy	*lykkeligere*	*'lykkeligst*

The same thing applies to adjectives in *-som*, where the *m* is doubled before the vowel in the comparative:

virksom active	*virksommere*	*virksomst*
langsom slow	*langsommere*	*langsomst*

(2) Adjectives ending in an unstressed *-el*, *-en* or *-er* drop the *-e*, as we should expect, before the comparative and superlative endings.

Example:

	d. tone	s. tone
'travel busy	*travlere*	*travlest*
doven [ˇdɔːvən] lazy	*dovnere*	*dovnest*
'sikker sure, safe	*sikrere*	*sikrest*
'tapper brave	*taprere*	*taprest*

(For the reduction of double consonants in the last two comparatives and superlatives, see page 67.)

(3) A group of adjectives which undergo 'mutation' in the comparative and superlative ($a > e$, $o > ø$, $u > y$, $å > æ$) take just *-re* in the comparative and *-st* in the superlative.

Note single tone throughout.

lang long	*'lengre*	*lengst*
ung young	*'yngre*	*yngst*
tung heavy	*'tyngre*, also regular	*tyngst*, also
	ˇ*tungere*	*'tungest*
stor big	*større*	*størst*

With *-est* in the superlative:

få few	*'færre*	*'færrest*

(4) The following adjectives form their comparatives and superlatives from an entirely different stem. English has the same peculiarity:

gammel old	*'eldre*	*eldst*
god good, fine	*'bedre*	*best*
ond, vond bad	*'verre*	*verst*
liten little	*'mindre*	*minst*

Besides:

mye or *meget* much	*mer*	*mest*
mange pl. many	*flere* ['fleːrə] more	*flest* most

(5) Finally there are a number of comparatives and superlatives with no corresponding form in the positive. We must replace the missing form by an adverb.

		Adverbs
bakre rear	*'bakerst* rearmost	*bak* behind
bortre farther	*'bortest* farthest	*bort* away
fremre 'anterior'	*fremst* foremost	*fram* forward
indre inner	*'innerst* inmost	*inne* within
ytre outer	*'ytterst* utmost	*ute* out
øvre upper	*'øverst* uppermost	*over* above
nedre lower	*'nederst* lowest	*nede* down
midtre centre	*'midterst* midmost	*midt* middle

126. The following are only used in the comparative:

nordre [ˇnordrə] northern of *nord* north, *søndre* or *søre* southern of *sør*, *syd* south, *østre* eastern of *øst* east, *vestre* western of *vest* west.

127. Only in the superlative:

nest next, *først* first, *sist* last, *forrest* ['fɔrrəst] foremost, *ypperst* ['yppəʃt] supreme, *mellomst* in the middle.

Note: *nær* near has the comparative: *nærmere*, the superlative: *'nærmest*.

Example: *I (den) ˇnærmeste fremtid.* In the near future.

128. Intonation: The superlatives usually change from single tone to double tone when they are inflected.

Examples: 'vakrest most beautiful, has single tone, but the inflected form den ˅vakreste double tone. 'forrest foremost, single tone, but den ˅forreste double tone.

Vocabulary

'Afrika Africa
besøk [bə'sø:k] n. visit
hjemland n. homeland
slektning c. relative
Idiom: Jeg ville gjerne[ˇjæːᵗŋə] vite I should like to know

hvordan ['voᵗdan] how
jo adv. here = well
fyre (-te) heat, burn
ovn [ɔvn] c. stove

Exercise 22a

Den grønne vinteren var verst

En mann fra Afrika hadde vært på besøk i Norge, og da han kom tilbake til sitt hjemland, ville hans slektninger og venner gjerne vite hvordan det var deroppe i det høye nord. 'Jo,' sa han, 'det var to vintrer, en grønn vinter og en hvit vinter. Men den grønne var verst, for da fyrte de ikke i ovnene.'

Exercise 22b

Write the complete answers to these questions in Norwegian:

1. What country was the man from?
2. What had he done in Norway?
3. What would his relatives and friends like to know?
4. What did he mean by (tr. med) green winter and white winter?
5. Why was the green winter worst?

En tvilsom kompliment [kɔmpli'maŋŋ] (A doubtful compliment)

like vakker som just as beautiful as
litt adv. a little, slightly

Hun: Er jeg ikke like vakker som den dagen vi ble gift? (got married).

Han: Jo da, kjæreste, men nå tar det bare litt lengre tid.

Idiomatic expression: Det er ikke så verst [væʃt]. It is not too bad.

Vocabulary

kanskje [ˇkanʃə] perhaps
kjekk nice, square
dyr expensive, dear
jo—'desto conj. the—the
tørst [tøʃt] thirsty
forsiktig [fɔ'ʃikti] careful

to'bakk c. tobacco
prøve (-de) try
høy tall
klasse c. class
flink clever

Exercise 22c

You are perhaps rich, but your father was richer. Sissel is the nicest girl in the whole town and the happiest too. Oslo is much bigger than Bergen, but much smaller than London. England has bigger towns than Norway. It is more expensive to live in a town than in (= *på*) the country. I am two years older than my brother. I was much stronger in my younger days. The more he drank, the thirstier he became. Be more careful next time (*gang* c.). That is the very best tobacco I have tried. Svein is the tallest boy in the class, but not the cleverest.

Comparison by 'mer' and 'mest'

129. Quite a few adjectives, especially of two or more syllables, form their comparative and superlative with the help of **mer** and **mest** (corresponding to English **more** and **most**) when for purely phonetic reasons it may sometimes be impossible or inconvenient to add any ending **-ere** or **-est.**

This is the case with:

(1) Adjectives of two or more syllables ending in:

(*a*) -(*i*)*sk*: '*krigersk* warlike, *mer krigersk*, *mest krigersk*.

Further examples are: *bar'barisk* barbaric, '*kritisk* critical, *hys'terisk* hysterical.

(*b*) -*et*(*e*) (= full of): *steinet* stony, *bakket* hilly.
(*c*) -*en*, generally derived from nouns: *ullen* woollen, *gyllen* golden, *våken* awake.

(2) The adjectives: *fremmed* unfamiliar, foreign, and *verdt* [væᵣt] or *verd* [værd] worth.

Verdt (*verd*) is only used predicatively: '*tomten* (the site) *er mer verdt enn huset.*

(3) Participles: The past participle and the present participle.

Example: *Han er mer fryktet* (feared) *enn elsket. Hans unge kone 'derimot* (on the other hand) *har et mer vinnende 'vesen* (a more charming nature).

Use of the Comparative and Superlative

130. The comparative form is indeclinable.

Example: *Hans hus er større enn mitt.*

The superlatives have *-e* in the definite declension and also in the plural of the indefinite declension, but otherwise they take no ending.

Hvem er størst av dere to? We could also say: *Hvem er den største av dere to*, the definite declension being required after *den*.

131. Sometimes the comparative can be used to express a fairly high degree without any idea of actual comparison:

e.g. *en eldre dame* an elderly lady
en yngre dame a youngish lady
en bedre middag quite a good dinner
en lengre tur a rather long walk (longish)
en større bestilling a considerable order
noen mindre de'taljer some minor details

Mindre can also be used as a negative understatement: *mindre bra* not so good.

Vocabulary

dyp deep
dal c. valley
stri persistent, swift-flowing (of rivers)
'sørover southward
munne (-et) ut i flow into
fa'brikk c. factory
fart [fa'ṭṭ] c. speed
den ene—den annen one—the other
foss c. waterfall
rik på rich in
tu'rist c. tourist

laks c. salmon
kyst c. cóast
helt til as far as
sjøfarende seafaring
nasjon [na'ʃoːn] c. nation
'handelsflåte c. merchant navy
verden ['værdn̩] c. world
'verdenshav n. ocean
vaie (-et) wave
havn c. harbour
fjord c. fjord
stykke n. (1) piece; (2) distance
utenlandsk foreign

beúndre (-et) admire
nordover ['no(ː)rɔvər] north-
wards
smal narrow
'kilometer (km.) kilometer
(about ⅝ of a mile)
grense c. border, frontier
svenskegrensen the Swedish
frontier
bred [breː] broad, wide
område n. area
fjellpar'ti n. (pl. **-er**) mountain
range, area

over 'havet above sea-level
likeså stor som as big as
om'trent almost, about
for ek'sempel n. (abbr. **f. eks.**)
for exámple
sjøfart c. shipping
sjøfartsby c. shipping town
hi'storie c. history
det samme gjelder the same
applies to, or can be said about
høre til belong to, be amongst

Exercise 23a

Norges geografi [geogra'fiː]

I Norge finner en høye fjell, dype daler og strie elver. Den lengste elva heter Glomma. Den kommer fra Aursundsjøen, og renner sørover og munner ut i havet ved byen Frédrikstad, en av de mest kjente fabrikkbyer i Norge.

De norske elvene har stor fart, og den ene store fossen følger etter den andre. De er også rike på fisk, og engelske turister fisker laks i mange av våre elver.

Norge har en lang kyst, og nordmennene begynte tidlig å seile på sjøen. De hadde da ikke så store skip som vi har nå. Dere har sikkert (*surely*) hørt om de vakre vikingskipene.

Med disse små skipene seilte de helt til England og Frankrike. I moderne tid er nordmennene velkjent som en sjøfarende nasjon. Landet har en meget stor handelsflåte, en av de største i verden, og en kan møte norske skip på alle verdenshav. Det norske flagget vaier i hver større havn.

Norge har mange dype og lange fjorder. Den lengste er den kjente Sognefjorden, som går et langt stykke inn i landet med høye fjell på begge (*both*) sider. Den er meget vakker, og de utenlandske turister beundrer den svært.

Etter hvert som (*as*) man kommer lengre nordover, blir landet[1] smalere og smalere. På det smaleste stedet, ved byen Narvik, er det bare omtrent 8 km til svenskegrensen. På det bredeste stedet er avstanden fra vestkysten til Sverige omtrent 450 km.

[1] For change of word order see pages 42 and 166.

I den midtre del av dette brede området ligger Norges høyeste fjellpartier: Jotunheimen og Rondane. Den aller høyeste fjelltoppen heter Galdhøpiggen. Den er 2468 meter over havet og ligger i det ville fjellpartiet Jotunheimen.

Norges hovedstad heter Oslo, og er den største byen i landet. Den er omtrent like så stor som den engelske kullbyen Newcastle. Andre større byer er f. eks. Bergen og Trondheim. Bergen er kjent som en livlig sjøfartsby med en interessant historie.

Det samme gjelder Trondheim. De hører begge til Norges aller eldste byer.

Vocabulary

sjøby c. seaside town
tre three
fire four
sju (syv) seven
lys here: fair
veldig exceedingly
hissig hot-tempered
hver gang c. every time
trette (-et) v. quarrel
bakke c. hill
utsikt c. view
under ['unnər] below
kai c. quay

passasjer [passa'fe:r] passenger
passasjerbåt liner
straks immediately
ukjent unknown
mennesker people, folk
svenske Swede
'tysker German
danske Dane
'engelskmann Englishman
vanskelig difficult
de fleste av dem most of them
stille quiet

Exercise 23b

Translate into Norwegian:

Life in a seaside town (tr. The life)

I have two brothers and three sisters. My eldest brother is called Per. He is three years older than I. My youngest brother is four years younger than I, but much taller. All my sisters are very young. The eldest is only seven years old. All have fair hair and are very pretty. They are exceedingly fond of playing. (See page 152.)

My two brothers are very strong and like to fight. They are both hot-tempered, but they quickly become good friends again every time they have quarrelled. Our house stands (lies) on the top of a hill, and we therefore have a fine view over the sea below. We can see all the big ships coming (which come) into (inn på) the harbour.

Some (*noen*) are white, others (*andre*) are red or black. It is very busy on the quay when a big liner comes in. The little town is immediately full of new, unknown people: Swedes, Danes, Germans and Englishmen. If you can speak foreign languages you can have many interesting conversations with these people. The Swedes and the Danes understand our own language. Next morning the fine boat has disappeared, and the town is as quiet as it was before.

CHAPTER XI

NUMERALS

Here and there we have already come across numerals, but now we must learn the whole list.

132. The numerals are divided into Cardinals (1, 2, 3, etc.) and Ordinals (first, second, third, etc.).

Cardinals	Ordinals
0 *null*	(*den, det*) *nulte*
1 *en* (*n. ett*)	„ *første*
2 *to*	*den annen* [ˇaɳ]
	det annet [ˇaɳt]
	pl. *andre*, see notes
3 *tre*	(*den, det*) *tredje*
4 *fire*	„ *fjerde* [ˇfjæːrə]
5 *fem*	„ *femte*
6 *seks*	„ *sjette*
7 ¹*sju* [ʃuː], *syv*	„ *sjuende, syvende*
8 *åtte*	„ *åttende*
9 *ni*	„ *niende*
10 *ti*	„ *tiende*
11 *elleve* [ˇelvə]	„ *ellevte* [ˇelləftə]
12 *tolv* [tɔll]	„ *tolvte* [ˇtɔltə]
13 *tretten*	„ *trettende*
14 *fjorten* [ˇfjoʳtn̩]	„ *fjortende*
15 *femten*	„ *femtende*
16 *seksten* [ˇseistn̩]	„ *sekstende* [ˇseistnə]

17	*sytten* [ˇsøttn̩]	(*den, det*)	*syttende*
18	*atten*	,,	*attende*
19	*nitten*	,,	*nittende*
20	[1]*tjue* [ˇçuːə], *tyve*	,,	*tjuende, tyvende*
21	[2]*tjueen, enogtjue* (*tyve*)	,,	*tjueførste, enogtyvende*
22	*tjueto, toogtjue*	,,	*tjueandre, toogtyvende*
30	*'tretti,* ˇ*tredve*	,,	*'trettiende, tredevte* [ˇtredəftə]
31	*tretti'en,* *'enogtredve*	,,	*tretti'første, 'enogtredevte*
40	*'førti*	,,	*førtiende*
41	*førti'en, 'enogförti*	,,	*førti'første, 'enogførtiende*
50	*'femti*	,,	*femtiende*
51	*femti'en, 'enogfemti*	,,	*femti'første, 'enogfemtiende*
60	*'seksti*	,,	*sekstiende*
61	*seksti'en, 'enogseksti*	,,	*seksti'første, 'enogsekstiende*
70	*sytti* ['søtti]	,,	*syttiende*
80	*'åtti*	,,	*åttiende*
90	*'nitti*	,,	*nittiende*
100	[3](*ett*) *hundre*	,,	*hundrede*
101	*hundreogen* (n. *ett*)	,,	*hundreog'første*
129	(*ett*) *hundreogtjue'ni, hundreogniogtyve*	,,	*hundreogtjue'niende, hundreogniogtyvende*
200	*to hundre*	,,	*tohundrede*
1,000	(*ett*) *'tusen*	,,	*tusende*
2,000	[3]*to tusen*	,,	*totusende*
500,000	*femhundre tusen en halv million*	,,	*femhundretusende*
1,000,000	*en million* [milli'oːn]	- ,,	*milli'onte*

1,579,365 *en million femhundreog syttinitusen trehundreog- • sekstifem*, or usual form: *en million femhundreogniogsyttitusen trehundreogfemogseksti*

Comments on the Cardinals

133. The cardinals remain unchanged except **en** which has **ett** in the neuter (double **t** so as to distinguish it from the indefinite article neuter). It has also a definite form **ene,**

e.g. **den ene** (the one), and even a superlative **eneste** single (the only one).

1. The forms *sju* [ʃuː] = 7 and *tjue* [çuːə] = 20 instead of *syv* and *tyve* were introduced in the spelling reform of 1938, but to many people they are still unfamiliar.

2. A new counting method was officially introduced in 1951. From 21 and upwards the 'tens' are mentioned before the units as in English. According to the older system which is still in full use, the units were mentioned first.

3. As will be seen *hundre* and *tusen* have no plural ending— 2500—*to tusenfemhundre*—but if they are used as nouns the ordinary plural ending **-er** is added:

Hundrer av båter hundreds of boats, *tusener av tilskuere* thousands of spectators. Alternatively the adverbs in **-vis** can be substituted: *hundrevis av*, *tusenvis av*, etc.

million and *milliard* on the other hand are pure nouns having always **-er** in the plural.

Intonation: The two-syllabic numerals from *tretti* (30) to *nitti* (90) inclusive have single tone, so has *tusen*, while *hundre* and the form *tredve* for 30 have double.

Comments on the Ordinals

134. The ordinals up to 6 inclusive are rather irregular, but from then on the ending **-(e)nde** prevails. A few have **-te**. Thus common to them all is the ending **-e.**

Intonation: What is said about the cardinals as regards 'tones' also applies to the ordinals.

135. The ordinals are treated as definite forms of an adjective, except **annen** which has an inflection of its own:

c.	n.	plural
$\left.{en \atop den}\right\}$ *annen*	$\left.{et \atop det}\right\}$ *annet*	*de andre*

The last form **andre** can be used throughout, but usually it means 'other' and **annen, annet** 'second'.

(den) annen mai. The second of May. *Dronning Elisabet den annen* Queen Elizabeth the Second.

første etasje   bottom floor
annen   „   first   „
tredje   „   second   „

Only the form *andre* can take double definition, *den andre gangen* the second time, or just *andre gangen* without the article.

Idioms: *for det første, for det annet*—firstly, secondly; *annen* etc. as indefinite pronoun, see para. 208.

Å, Matilde, du er min eneste (my only one).
Akk, kjære Adolf, du er min tjuefjerde (fireogtyvende).

Simple Sums

136.   3 + 3 = 6 *tre pluss (og) tre er seks*
         3 − 3 = 0 *tre minus (fra) tre er null*
         3 × 4 = 12 *tre ganger fire er tolv* or
                   tre multiplisert med fire er tolv
     64 : 8 = 8 *sekstifire dividert med (delt på) åtte er åtte*

Fru X: *I dag er min mann og jeg akkurat sytti år til sammen* (= together). *Kan De gjette* (= guess) *hvor mange år jeg er, og hvor mange år min mann er?*

Herr Y: *Det er lett. De er syv, og Deres mann er . . . null.*

137.   In Norway the decimal system is used.

1000 *gram*   = *et kilo(gram)* about two pounds
 100 *centimeter* = 1 *meter* about one yard 4 inches
1000 *meter*   = 1 *kilometer* = ⅝ of a mile
  10 *kilometer*   = *en norsk mil* about six English miles
  10 *deciliter*   = *en liter* about a quart

138.   Time—*(Tiden)*

time c. hour   **klokke** f. watch, clock
sekund [sə'kunn] n. second   **minutt** [mi'nutt] n. minute
Hvor mange (or mye) er klokka?   ⎫
Hva er klokka?   ⎬ What time is it?
Klokka er tolv   12.0   It is twelve o'clock
fem (minutter) over tolv 12.05 five past twelve

halv ett	12.30 half past twelve
ti over halv ett = tjue	
på ett	12.40 twenty to one
et kvarter [kva'ᴿţeːr] **(kvart)**	
på ett	12.45 a quarter to one
ti (minutter) på ett	12.50 ten to one
et kvarter (kvart) over ett	1.15 a quarter past one
presis [prə'siːs] **klokka åtte**	8.0 eight o'clock sharp

Officially the 24-hour system is used.

Note. **klokka fem**   At five o'clock

Vocabulary

navn n. **på** name of	**kulde** c. cold
måned [ˇmɔːənt] c. month	**slik som** such as
årstid [ˈåːʃtid] c. season	**mens** conj. while
vår c. spring	**unntågen** except
høst c. autumn	**skuddår** n. leap-year
vare (-te) last	**vanlig** usual(ly)
gjerne here: generally	**uke** c. week
slutt c. end	

Exercise 24a

Read aloud:

Navn på måneder og årstider

Året har tolv (12) måneder. Den første måned heter január, den andre február, den tredje mars, den fjerde a'pril, den femte mai, den sjette júni, den sjuende júli, den åttende au'gust, den niende sep'tember, den tiende oktober [ɔk'tɔːbər], den ellevte november [no'vembər], den tolvte de'sember, som er den siste måned i året.

Våren kommer i Norge i april og mai måned, og i juni og juli og august er det sommer. Høsten kommer i september og varer gjerne til slutten av november, da vinteren setter inn med kulde og snø. Noen måneder har 31 dager, slik som januar, mars, mai, juli, august, oktober og desember, mens april, juni, september og november har 30 dager, og februar har bare 28, unntagen hvert fjerde år, da den har 29. Det året heter skuddår. Ett år har vanlig 365 dager, men når det er skuddår, 366. Det er 52 uker i ett år. En uke har 7 dager.

Dagenes navn er: ' søndag, 'mandag, 'tirsdag, onsdag ['onsda], torsdag ['tɔːʃda], ' fredag, 'lørdag. (**g** mute as a rule in these words.)

139. Dates are indicated in the following way:

Jeg er *født den 28de september, 1910.* I was born on the 28th of September 1910. About persons no longer alive one usually says *ble født. Ibsen ble født den 20de mars, 1828.* In correspondence full stop is the best way: *den 1. mai, den 2. juni* (instead of *den 1ste mai* and *den 2nen juni*).

Vocabulary

far'vel, ad'jø good-bye
minst at least
med tog n. by train
hvilken dato what date?
det vil si (abbrev. dvs.) that is
med bil by car

for å (in order) to
nøy'aktig exact(ly)
flytte move
om fjorten dager in a fortnight
regne [reine] (—et) ut. work out

Exercise 24b

Write the figures in letters.

Can you tell me what time it is? It is 16 minutes past 11. Then (*Da*) I must say good-bye. My train leaves (tr. goes) at quarter to 12, and it takes at least 20 minutes to the station. What date is it today? It is the 19th of July. How far is it to Lillehammer? By train it is (tr. is it) 185 kilometres, that is about 116 English miles. By car it is 200 kilometres or 125 English miles. An English mile is about 1·6 kilometres, as (*som*) you know. How many hours will it take? 3 hours and 18 minutes to be exact. What is your address in Oslo?— Storgaten 14, but we shall move to Karl Johans gate 27 in a fortnight. How many children have you (got)?—Three sons. They are called Per, Hans, and Ole. How old are they? Ole was born on the 9th of July 1950. Hans was born on the 28th of September 1953. Per was born on the 5th of May 1957 and then you can work out yourself how old they are.

Note 1: House numbers come after the name of the street in Norway, e.g. Parkveien 17; Storgaten 25.

Note 2: Don't forget: When an adverb or any other element of the sentence apart from conjunctions precedes the subject, subject and verb change places (Inversion). Then 'must I' . . . By train 'is it' . . .

Vocabulary

gene'ral general
treffende apt
morsom ['moʃʃɔm] amusing
bemerkning c. [bə'mærkniŋ]
  remark
under prep. about time: during
mili'tær military
øvelse ['ø:vəlsə] c. exercise

'oppdage (-et) discover
motorsyk'list motor-cyclist
'tillatt p.p. allowed
'nettopp just
i timen per hour
'anta irr. suppose, think
ryste (-et) shake
om conj. whether

Exercise 25

En anekdote [anək˅do:tə]

Den norske general, Helset, var kjent for sine treffende og morsomme bemerkninger. Under en militærøvelse oppdaget han en dag en motorsyklist som kjørte mye fortere enn det var tillatt.

Han stoppet ham og spurte ham hvor gammel han var. 'Jeg er 21, herr general' svarte den unge mannen. 'Hvor fort kjørte du nettopp (*just now*)?' 'Å, ca. 95 km (i timen), antar jeg.' Generalen rystet på hodet og sa: 'Spørsmålet er nå, min venn, om du vil kjøre 95 og ikke bli mer enn 21 eller kjøre 21 og bli 95.'

Et godt råd: Bedre en fot på bremsen, enn tre fot under jorden.

et råd a piece of advice; brems c. brake

Fractions (brøker)

140. These were originally formed by adding the word del c. (or sometimes part [paʳʈ] c.) to the ordinals, e.g. $\frac{1}{3}$ *en tredjedel*, $\frac{2}{3}$ *to tredjedeler*, $\frac{1}{4}$ *en fjerdedel* [fjæːɽəde(ː)l] (also called *en kvart* [kvaʳʈ]), $\frac{1}{5}$ *en femtedel*, $\frac{5}{6}$ *fem sjettedeler*. This is still the usual way, although the new counting method of 1951 introduced cardinals in the denominator, e.g. $\frac{1}{3}$ *en tredel*, $\frac{2}{3}$ *to tredeler*, $\frac{1}{4}$ *en firedel*, $\frac{1}{5}$ *en femdel*, $\frac{5}{6}$ *fem seksdeler*. Officially the old way is optional in the case of numbers up to twelve.

Note especially: $\frac{1}{2}$ **en halv** [hall], $1\frac{1}{2}$ **en og en halv**, or very often **halvannen** [hal˅aːn̩]. When **halv** is treated as an adjective, it takes -t in the neuter, and -e in the plural and in the definite declension.

Examples: *en halv kopp te* half *a* cup of tea, *et halvt glass vann* (*øl*) half *a* glass of water (beer). Plural: *halve flasker* = *halvflasker* half bottles.

The definite article of the adjective is very often omitted. *Prinsessen og halve kongeriket.* The princess and half the kingdom.

Forming compounds: *halvveis* half way, *halvmåne* c. half moon, *halvsirkel* c. semicircle.

Halvdelen ⎫
Halvparten ⎭ the half.

Example: *Halvdelen av be'folkningen var' negrer.* Half of the population were Negroes.

kvart can also be used before neuter noun: **et kvart minutt.**

141. Collective Numbers

et par	a couple of, a few, a pair of.
Har du noen fyrstikker ['fyʃţikər]?	Have you any matches?
Ja, jeg har et par stykker	Yes, I have a few.
et snes	a score (generally used of eggs).
Jeg kjøpte tre snes egg på torget i dag	I bought three scores of eggs at the market today.
et dusin [du'siːn]	a dozen

dusin is oddly enough used mostly for counting buttons.

en pro'sent	one per cent.
Hva er rentefoten? ...	What is the rate of interest?
Den er 3% pro'anno ...	It is 3 per cent per annum.

Further Notes

142. Difference in number: *I det 19de og 20de århundre* (singular), compared with English: In the 19th and 20th centuries (plural). Further: *To og en halv måned* (singular). English: Two and a half months (plural). *Hvor gammel er du?* How old are you? *Jeg er en og tjue år* (*en* in spite of *år* being n.).

CHAPTER XII

THE ADVERB

The adverbs fall into two main categories:

A. Those formed from adjectives.
B. Independent adverbs.

A. Those formed from Adjectives

143. The neuter form of the adjective (ending in **-t**) serves as adverb as well. Refer back to para. 118, paying special attention to when the **-t** is omitted.

Adjectives	Adverbs
pen nice	*pent*
lang long, far	*langt*
stygg ugly, bad	*stygt* (see para. 116)
sen slow, late	*sent*
lykkelig happy	*lykkelig* (see para. 118 (b))

Examples:

Det var svært pent gjort. That was very nicely done. *Det var stygt gjort.* That was badly done. *Vi har gått langt i dag.* We have walked far today. *Du kommer sent som vanlig.* You are coming late as usual. *Hun var lykkelig gift.* She was happily married.

Vocabulary

nabo c. neighbour
gal wrong, incorrect

flue f. fly
sveive (-et) inn wind in

En hi' storie (story)

En dame som hadde vært på fisketur.sammen med sin mann, forteller naboen om turen: 'Jeg gjorde allting *galt*. Jeg snakket for *høyt*, jeg brukte gal flue, jeg sveivet inn for *fort*, og det verste av alt—jeg fikk mer fisk enn han.'

Comparison of Adverbs

144. Adverbs derived from adjectives form their comparative and superlative in the same way as the corresponding adjectives.

| *pent* nicely | *penere* | *penest* |

Per skriver pent, men søsteren skriver **enda** (still) *penere.*

| *stygt* badly | *styggere* | *styggest* |
| *lykkelig* happily | *lykkeligere* | *lykkeligst* |

Irregular:

| *godt, vel* well | *'bedre* | *best* |

opposite to:

vondt) painfully		
dårlig } badly, ill	*'verre*	*verst*
ille) badly		

| *langt*) far | | |
| *lenge*) long, long time | *'lenger* | *lengst* |

N.B.—The corresponding adjective has the form *'lengre* in the comparative (see para. 125 (3)).

145. A few adverbs that are not derived from adjectives can also have degrees of comparison.

| *ofte* [ˇɔftə] often | *oftere* oftener | *'oftest* oftenest |
| *gjerne* [ˇjæːʳɳə] willingly | *'heller* rather | *helst* preferably |

fort [foʳʈ] quick(ly), has the same form both as adjective and as adverb. It is compared *fort—fortere—fortest.*

Hos tannlegen. At the dentist

Idiom: *stort lenger*[1] = much longer.

Tannlegen: Gjør det vondt? Does it hurt?

Pasienten: Å ja, det gjør ikke noe godt akkurat. Well, it isn't exactly pleasant.

T. Hvordan er det nå? How is it now?

P. Ærlig talt, jeg syns det blir verre og verre jo lenger De holder på. Honestly, I feel it is getting worse and worse the longer you are carrying on.

T. Det skal ikke vare lenge nå. It won't last long now.

P. Varer det stort lenger, skriker jeg høyt. If it is going to làst much longer, I will shriek loudly.

T. De burde gå oftere til tannlegen. You ought to go more often to the dentist.

---

[1] After a negation and in if-clauses.

P. Ja, jeg vet det meget godt, men det er lettere sagt enn gjort.
Yes, I know it very well, but it is more easily said than
done.

B. Independent Adverbs

146. These form a large and varied group of words which
may be divided according to their different meanings. You
are not supposed to memorize them all at once. Pick out a
few which you actually need and then go back for more.

147. *Degree* —to express a fairly high degree the following
are used:

ganske quite, *ganske bra* quite good, *ganske riktig* quite
right.

temmelig rather, *temmelig kaldt* rather cold.

'nokså fairly, rather. *Hvordan har du det?* How is life? *Jo,
takk, nokså bra.* Not too bad, thank you.

riktig quite, almost very, and thus a little stronger than
the ones above. *Det var riktig fint.* That was quite fine.

To express a high degree:

for = too. *En er for liten og en er for stor.* One is too small
and one is too big. Still stronger:

'altfor = far too, much too; *altfor stor* far too big.

svært and **meget** = very. *Han er meget farlig.* He is very
dangerous. *Det blir svært vanskelig.* That will be very difficult. Higher still:

over'måte exceedingly, **ytterst, overordentlig** [ɔvər-
'ɔʳn̩t̩li] extremely, **used'vanlig** unusually. In colloquial
speech **veldig** is widely used. *Hun er overmåte popu'lær.* She
is extremely popular, common: *veldig popu'lær.*

Besides there are:

aldeles [al'deːləs], **helt, full'stendig** completely, entirely.
Er du aldeles (helt, fullstendig) gal? Are you completely mad?

Finally we have a lot of nonsensical intensifiers like:

for'ferdelig = awfully, **fryktelig** = frightfully, **skrekkelig** = terribly. *Hun er skrekkelig søt* (sweet), *forferdelig
pen, fryktelig stor,* etc.

148. *Time.* **da**—then. Here lurks a pitfall. 'Then' has two different meanings in English: (1) at that time, where it corresponds to Norwegian **da**; (2) after that, afterwards, subsequently, where it corresponds to Norwegian **så.**

Examples: *Jeg var meget ung da* (= *den gang*). I was very young then (= at that time). *Først spiste vi middag, og så gikk vi en tur.* First we had dinner and **then** (= afterwards) we went for a walk. Get this point quite clear:

> *Then,* i.e. at that time = **da.**
> *Then,* i.e. after that = **så.**

enda, ennå still, yet. *Han er ennå i byen.* He is still in town. *Jeg er ikke ferdig ennå.* I am not ready yet. **enda** is used to strengthen the comparative: *enda verre* still worse. *Han vil ha enda mer.* He wants still more. Cf. page 89.

før earlier, before. *Vi har ikke sett ham før.* We have not seen him before. *like før* just before, *ikke før—før* no sooner—than. *Ikke før hadde han sagt dette, før han falt død om.* No sooner had he said this than he fell to the ground dead.

først first. *Han kom først.* He came first. *Den som kommer først til mølla, får malt først* (*mølle* f.=mill, *male*=grind). Corresponding to English: First come first served.
Note specially: *Først i går fikk jeg vite at du var kommet.* Not till (only) yesterday did I hear that you had arrived.

'nettopp, akku'rat just, exactly. *Var det Hansen du stod og snakket med?* Was it Hansen you were talking with? *Ja, nettopp* (*akkurat*). Yes, exactly. *Min bror har nettopp vært i London.* My brother has just been to London. *Han er nettopp gått.* He has just gone.

straks at once. *Jeg kommer straks.* I am coming at once (directly, right away) = *med en gang* = *med det samme.*

plutselig, brått suddenly. *Det kommer så plutselig* (*brått*). It comes so suddenly.

ofte often. Like its English counterpart this adverb can be compared: comp. *oftere*, sup. *oftest.* The superlative can have the meaning of 'as a rule, usually'. *Oftest går jeg på kino.* As a rule I go to the cinema.

sjelden (comp. *sjeldnere*, sup. *sjeldnest*) seldom. *Jeg går meget sjelden på restaurant.* I very seldom go to a restaurant.

lenge long, a long time. *Vær ikke lenge!* Don't be long! *For lenge siden.* Long time ago, but *Det er lenge siden.* That is a long time ago. About distance the form **langt** is used = far. *Er det langt å gå?* Is it far to go?

siden later, since then (also conj., see pages 160 and 161). *Vent til siden!* Wait till later! *Har du hørt noe fra ham siden?* Have you heard from him since? *Vi fikk ett brev. Siden har vi ikke hørt noe.* Since then we haven't heard anything.

aldri never. *Du skal aldri si aldri.* You ought never to say never. *aldri i livet* never in my life, *aldri på en søndag* never on a Sunday.

under'tiden, stundom [ˇstundɔm], **somme tider, av og til** occasionally, sometimes. *Somme tider spiller vi kort.* Sometimes we play cards. *Røker De? Ja, av og til.* Do you smoke? Yes, occasionally.

etterpå afterwards, **så** then (see page 91), **deretter** after that, **derpå** thereupon: *Og så var det dans etterpå.* Afterwards there was dancing (a slangish saying). *Først kom Kongen, så Kronprinsen, derpå Statsministeren, og så en lang rekke (med) fine folk, og så til slutt (til sist) kom stakkars lille jeg.*

nå now. *Skal jeg gjøre det nå?* (see also para. 156(3)).

'alltid, be'standig, stødt (og stadig) always, constantly. *Han klager alltid (or bestandig, stødt).* He is always complaining.

alle'rede already.

nylig, nyss recently, lately.

snart soon. *Jeg kommer snart.* I am coming soon, I'll soon be there.

fremdeles [frem'deːləs] still. *Fremdeles ungkar* still a bachelor.

noensinne, noen gang ever. *Har du noensinne (noen gang) vært sjøsyk?* Have you ever been seasick?

igjen (1) again. *Kom igjen.* Come again. (2) left. *Jeg har ingenting igjen.* Nothing left.

imidlertid however, but. *Imidlertid kom taleren for sent.* However, the speaker came too late.

149. Uncertainty and supposition:

kanskje perhaps, **kan hende** maybe, **muligens** possibly, **sannsynligvis** probably, **visstnok** it is true, I dare say.

150. *Admission:*

riktignok it is true, I admit, admittedly. *Han er riktignok en god venn av meg, men likevel.* He is admittedly a good friend of mine, but all the same ...

151. *Manner:*

så so, **slik** such, **således** like that, **hvorledes** how, **annerledes** differently. In addition come all the adverbs derived from adjectives. *Han kjører langsomt.* He drives slowly.

152. *Negation:*

ikke, ei not. Ei is used only in a few fixed phrases: *enten du vil eller ei,* willy nilly.

neppe, knapt hardly, scarcely, *Jeg tror neppe han kommer.* I hardly believe he will come.

lite as a negative has no equivalent in English. *Han er lite interessert i saken.* He is **not very much** interested in the matter, while **litt** means a little. *litt interessert* a little interested.

153. *Place:*

her here, **der** there, **where** hvor, **'derfra** from there, whence, **herfra** from here, hence.

'herfra og dit from here to there.

unna away, in expressions like: *hold deg unna* keep away. *Tyven kom seg unna.* The thief escaped.

154. *Contrast:*

ellers [ˈelləʃ] otherwise, or else. ... *ellers har jeg det bra.* Otherwise I am all right. In threats: *Gjør som jeg sier, ellers.* Do as I tell you, or else. *Noe ellers?* Anything else? *Det samme som ellers.* The same as usual.

Adverbs with Double Forms

155. Some very common adverbs of place have two forms, a short one signifying direction (*ut, inn*), and one with a final *-e* (*ute, inne*) expressing rest.

hjem—hjemme

Jeg bilte hjem.	I motored home.
Det var ingen hjemme.	There was nobody at home.

bort—borte

Han er reist bort (= *bortreist*).	He has gone away.
Han er borte.	He is away.

ut—ute

Onkel har gått ut i haven.	Uncle has gone out into the garden.
Vi skal spise middag ute i dag.	We are dining out today.

inn—inne

Gjestene gikk inn i spisestuen.	The guests went into the dining-room.
Mor satt inne i stuen.	Mother was sitting in the drawing-room.
Er Per inne?	Is Per in?

opp—oppe

Han ble kastet høyt opp i luften.	He was thrown high up in the air.
Ørnen svevde høyt oppe i luften.	The eagle was soaring high up in the air.

ned—nede

Skipet gikk ned.	The ship went down.
Bonden bor nede i dalen.	The farmer lives down in the valley.

fram—framme

Vi kom fram (frem) til sist.	We got there in the end.
Er vi snart framme (= *fremme*).	Shall we soon be there?— viz., at our destination.

hen—henne

De gikk hen (or *bort*) *til ham.*	They went up to him.
Skapet står henne i hjørnet.	The cupboard stands over in the corner.

Instead of **hen—henne, bort—borte** is more common.

Note:

Kom hit! Come here! (to the speaker).
Gå dit! Go (over) there! (from the speaker).
Compare *hit og dit* with English 'hither and thither'.

Expressions: *Jeg har lett både oppe og nede.* I have searched both high and low. *Hva han sier, går inn av (ad) det ene øret og ut av det andre.* What he says goes in at one ear and out at the other. *Hun visste hverken ut eller inn.* Meaning: She was at her wits' end. *Borte er godt, men hjemme er best.*

Some Adverbs as Sentence Modifiers

156. Certain very common adverbs serve to modify a statement in various ways, and so have a meaning often very different from their original one. In these cases they are all unstressed.

The main ones are:

1. **da**, 2. **vel**, 3. **nå**, 4. **nok**, 5. **visst**, 6. **jo.**

(1) **da** almost = after all.

Han har da en del erfaring. After all he has some experience *Det var da rart.* That was indeed strange.

(2) (*a*) **vel** denotes hesitant supposition.

Det er vel ikke meg du sikter til? It is not me you are referring to, I suppose? *Du har vel tatt med deg nøkkelen?* You have taken the key with you, I hope?

(*b*) Also in cautious asking: *Jeg kunne vel ikke få låne sykkelen din?* Do you think I could borrow your bike?

(*c*) Both **vel** and **da** together: *Det er da vel ikke livet om å gjøre?* It is not a matter of life and death, surely?

(3) **nå** almost identical with **da**, with which it can be combined. *Han har nå en slags eksamen (da).* After all he has an examination of some sort. *Det er nå engang slik.* It is like that, you know.

(4) **nok** modifies a command or an assurance.

Du får nok gjøre som jeg sier. You had better do as I tell you. *Er det sant? Ja, det er nok det dessverre.* Is it true? Yes, it is, I am afraid. *Du forstår meg nok.* I am sure you understand me. *Det går nok bra.* That will come out all right, I am sure.

(5) **visst** = apparently, it seems . . .

Han er visst syk. He is ill apparently. *Vi har visst truffet hverandre før.* We have met before, I think.

(6) **jo** almost = as you know.

Klokka er jo alt fem. It is already five o'clock, you know.

For place of adverbs see page 166.

Inversion caused by Adverbs

157. When an adverb comes before the subject the result is inverted word order.

Examples: *Likevel líker jeg det.*

Still   I   like it.

Vocabulary

foreldre [fɔ'reldrə] parents
for-siden ago
dere [ˇdeːrə] you pl.
linje c. line
i all hast c. all in a hurry
især especially
kaffe ['kaffə] c. coffee
røke (-te) smoke
sigarett [siga'rett] c. cigarette

anta ['anta(ː)] suppose (conjugated as: **ta**)
hjertelig [ˇjært(ə)li] or [ˇjæʳtˌli] hearty, cordial
skuespill n. play
konsert (pl. **-er**) [kɔn'sæʳtˌ] c. concert
fottur c. walking tour
slutte (-et) close, end

Exercise 26a

Holmenkollen, den 28. juli, 1966.

Kjære foreldre!

Takk for brevet. Jeg fikk det akkurat for en time siden og sender dere noen få linjer i all hast. Jeg har det aldeles utmerket, især når det gjelder *(as regards)* mat og frisk luft.

I går *var hele familien* ute på Bygdøy og badet. Solen skinte som vanlig. Det regner visst aldri her.

Det var fullt av folk overalt, unge og gamle, som badet og lå i solen etterpå. Vannet var temmelig varmt. Ellers *ville* nok ikke *jeg* ha våget å gå uti *(in)*.

Etterpå *drakk vi* kaffe på stranden og røkte en sigarett eller to.

Jeg har ikke fått noe (*any*) brev fra Ola enda, men han skriver nok snart, *antar jeg.*

Hjertelig hilsen
Rolf.

Exercise 26b

Oslo, 25th August, 1966.

Dear friend,

Thank you for your last letter which I got exactly a week ago. I must tell you that this will be (*bli*) just a short letter. You ask me what I have seen in Oslo. I have seen many interesting things recently, several films and plays, and have also heard some good concerts. I can now tell you that next month *I am going* (translate: *skal jeg reise*) back to England again. Therefore, *I try* to see as much of Norway as I can.

I have also recently been on a long walking tour in the 'Nordmarka'. It was a little too long for me, so I was rather tired when I reached the town. But still *I liked* it. You get plenty of fresh air. You can hardly find anything (*noe*) which is better for you, can you? Well, I must close now.

Hope to see you again soon.

Best wishes,
Gunnar.

CHAPTER XIII

COMPOUND VERBS

158. There are in Norwegian a number of particles—mostly prepositions and adverbs—that are used to form the so-called *compound verbs*. The most important are:

av of, **'avta** decrease, abate; **etter** after, **etterligne** imitate; **fra** from, **'frata** take from, deprive of; **frem/fram** forward, **'frembringe** produce; **inn** in, **'innhente** catch up with (on the road); **ut** out, **'utgi** give out, edit, publish; **opp** up, **'oppstå** arise; **ned** down, **'nedlegge** close down; **om** about, **'omtale** mention; **med** with, **meddele** ['meːdeːlə] inform;

over [ˈɔːvər] over, ˇ**overta** take over; ʹ**under** under, ˇ**underholde** entertain; **til** to, ʹ**tilhøre** belong to.

Cf. English uphold, undertake, overtake, offset, etc.

Intonation: When the first element is one-syllabic the compound gets single tone´, see examples above.

159. A great many of the compound verbs may be split up without changing the meaning; e.g. ˇ*overta* = ˇ*ta over*, ʹ*oppgi* = ˇ*gi opp*, ʹ*avfyre* fire a shot = ˇ*fyre av*, ʹ*tilhøre* = ˇ*høre til. Jegeren avfyrte et skudd* or *Jegeren fyrte av et skudd.* The hunter fired (off) a shot. You may hear both: *Forfatteren utgav en roman,* and: *Forfatteren gav ut en roman.* The author published a novel. Others cannot be split up at all. The compound forms have generally a more formal or literary flavour than the split forms which are therefore gaining ground in everyday speech. This tendency can, however, lead to comic results at times.

In other instances there is a clear distinction between the separable and inseparable forms, the latter being often used in a more specific, figurative sense, the former in a more direct and concrete sense. Compare *Fienden er blitt avskåret.* The enemy has been cut off, with *Legen skar av benet* (or *benet av*). Lit. The surgeon cut the leg off.

Further examples:

Han stod opp tidlig [ˇtiːli].	He got up early.
but: *Det oppstod en trette.*	A quarrel arose.
Unnskyld at jeg avbrøt Dem.	Excuse my interrupting you.
but: *Hun brøt av en gren.*	She broke off a branch.
å oppdra barn	to bring up children
but: *å dra opp en fisk*	to pull up a fish
å oversette en bok	to translate a book
but: *å sette over en elv*	to cross a river
å innhente	to catch up with (on the road)
but: *å hente inn*	to fetch in
å opplyse (om)	to inform (of, about)
but: *å lyse opp*	to light up, illuminate

å utløpe (*om tid*)	to expire
but: *å løpe ut*	to run out
å avta (*om storm*)	to decrease, abate
but: *å ta av*	to lose weight
å nedkomme	to give birth to a child
but: *å komme ned*	to come down
å overdrive	to overdo, exaggerate
but: *å drive over* (*om skyer f. eks.*)	to pass, drift over (about clouds for instance).

Cf. English to overtake, but to take over.

160. Finally there is also a special group of compound verbs consisting of noun + verb and adjective + verb.

Examples: *delta* [ˇdeːlta] *i* partake in = *ta del i* take part in; *'fastspenne* strap = *spenne 'fast*.

Note: On the rare occasions where the past or present participles of the separable compounds are used as adjectives, they are not split: *de fastspente skiene* the strapped skis.

CHAPTER XIV

MODAL AUXILIARIES

The Future Tenses

161. In addition to the three well-known auxiliary verbs *være* (to be), *ha* (to have), and *bli* (to become, get), there are also the so-called *Modal Auxiliaries*, which have a rather irregular conjugation. Most of them have their counterparts in English, although expressing slightly different shades of meaning at times.

Of special interest are those which represent one way of expressing future in Norwegian.

162. In common with English the modal auxiliaries *skal* (shall) and *vil* (will) + the infinitive can be used. These two verbs have, however, complete inflected forms in Norwegian:

Inf.	Present	Past	Perfect
skulle	*skal*	*skulle*	*skullet*
ville	*vil*	*ville*	*villet*

skal/vil covers shall/will, but also other ways of expressing future in English, which can be graphically illustrated as follows:

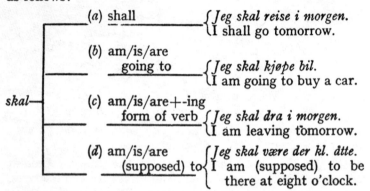

(a) shall { *Jeg skal reise i morgen.* { I shall go tomorrow.

(b) am/is/are going to { *Jeg skal kjøpe bil.* { I am going to buy a car.

skal—

(c) am/is/are + -ing form of verb { *Jeg skal dra i morgen.* { I am leaving tomorrow.

(d) am/is/are (supposed) to { *Jeg skal være der kl. åtte.* { I am (supposed) to be there at eight o'clock.

163. As in English there is a tendency to use **skal** in the first person and **vil** in the second and third, but there are no rigid rules. Apart from the future **skal** has also an element of determination and promise in it. *Jeg skal komme i morgen. Hun skal se 'Peer Gynt' i kveld.*

164. Vil is used to a great extent with non-personal subjects. *Det vil ta lang tid før han blir frisk igjen.* It will take a long time before he gets well again. *Det vil koste ham mange penger.* It will cost him a lot of money. *Det vil bli vanskelig for meg å få tid til det.* It will be difficult for me to find time for it. With personal subjects: *Du vil snart merke det.* You will soon notice that. *Gå forsiktig* [fɔˈʃikti] *over isen, ellers vil du falle igjennom.* Step carefully over the ice, or you will fall through. In these examples **vil** implies that something is likely to happen.

165. A peculiarity about the Scandinavian languages is that when the direction is sufficiently expressed by an adverb of place or a preposition, the verb of motion is often left out after the verbs *skulle, ville* and *måtte* (to have to).[1]

[1] Cf. Shakespeare: 'Wit, whither wilt?'

Examples: *Hvor skal du hen?* Where are you going? *Jeg skal på stasjonen.* I am going to the station. *Han vil ut.* He wants to get out. *Jeg må av sted.* I must be off. *Vi må hjem.* We must get home.

166. Present tense is often the best way of expressing future action in Norwegian, especially if an adverb of time clearly indicates future tense. Cf. English I leave tomorrow = Norwegian *Jeg reiser i morgen.*

Jeg kommer ⎫
    er ⎬ *snart tilbake.*   I will soon be back.

Det blir vanskelig.   That will be difficult.

167. Shall/will be correspond to **vil bli** or just **blir** when the expression points to the future. If you say **skal/vil være** the situation becomes static. Compare: *Vi skal bli lykkelige* (future) with *Vi skal være lykkelige* = We shall stay happy. We shall always be happy.

Exception: When **være** is identical with **be present.** *Når vil han være her?* When will he be here?

Note specially: When will he be coming? which in Norwegian translation will run: *Når vil han komme?* or *Når kommer han?*

168. Future can also be excellently indicated by the idiom **komme til å** (in the infinitive and present). Example: *Jeg kommer til å reise bort i morgen,* instead of *Jeg skal reise. Det kommer til å koste en god del.* It is going to cost a good deal. It is used even in combination with **vil.** *Det vil komme til å koste en god del.*

Future Perfect

skal/will ha lest   shall/will have read

169. *Jeg skal* (or *vil*) *ha lest boken når du kommer tilbake.* I shall have read the book by the time you are back. *Du vil ha glemt det når jeg har reist.* You will have forgotten it when I have left.

Future in thè Past

skulle/ville lese	should/would read
skulle/ville ha lest	should/would have read

170. *Han skulle (reise) til London.* He was going to London. In English **should** would have a widely different meaning here.

As shown by the parentheses, the verb of motion can be omitted.

In conditional sentences, however, English and Norwegian do correspond. *Hvis du skulle treffe ham, (så) hils ham fra meg, er du snill.* If you should see (meet) him, give him my best regards, please. *Det ville ha vært bedre om du hadde fortalt meg det på forhånd.* It would have been better if you had told me (it) beforehand. *Hadde jeg vinger, (så) ville jeg fly.* If I had wings I would have flown.

With subjunctive meaning, 'I wish I were you'—'*Jeg skulle ønske jeg var deg*'.

171. In colloquial speech *skulle/ville ha vært* is often shortened to *skulle/ville vært.*

Han skulle (ha) vært her allerede i går, men ble antakelig forhindret fra å komme. He should have been here already yesterday, but was probably prevented from coming. *Det ville (ha) vært bedre om du kunne ha kommet i morgen.* It would have been better if you could have come tomorrow.

172. When two events synchronize, the expression used is: **skulle til å** be about to, going to. *Jeg skulle nettopp til å legge meg da telefonen ringte.* I was just about to go to bed when the telephone rang.

More on 'skal/skulle', 'vil/ville'

173. Besides denoting future these two auxiliaries also express other meanings and nuances.

skal often expresses:

(1) A command: *Du skal ikke stjele.* Thou shalt not steal. *Du skal ikke spise med kniven.* Do not eat with the knife.

(2) Determination and promise: *Det skal aldri skje.* It shall never happen. *Du skal få juling.* You shall have a good hiding.

(3) A supposition = is supposed to be, is said to. Examples: *Han skal være rik.* He is supposed to be rich. Cf. German: **Er soll reich sein.**

(4) An agreed arrangement: *Vi skal møtes klokka 12 på stasjonen.* We are to meet at twelve at the station.

(5) Hopelessness as in sentences like: *Hva skal jeg gjøre?* What shall I do? *or* What am I to do?

skulle corresponds to English 'should' when expressing a moral obligation = ought to. *Du skulle venne deg til å tåle andre folks meninger.* You should (or ought to) accustom yourself to tolerate other people's opinions.

In case of an agreed arrangement Norwegian **skulle** corresponds to English: was, were to. Cf. (4) *Vi skulle møtes på stasjonen. Toget skulle gå klokka ti over tolv (12.10). Vi skulle dra på fisketur.* (Cf. (*d*) on the diagram in para. 162.)

174. **vil** generally suggests volition or a personal desire. English: will, be willing to, want to, like to, wish.

vil ha often corresponds to: want, (would) like. *Vil De ha te eller kaffe?* Would you like tea or coffee? *Jeg vil helst ha kaffe, takk.* I would rather have coffee, please. *Jeg vil ikke* (= *jeg har ikke lyst til å*) *gå hjem ennå.* I don't want to go home yet. *Gjør som du vil.* Do as you like (or please). *Ta hva du vil.* Take what you like.

Idiom: *Jeg vil(le) gjerne* = I should like to. Cf. German **Ich möchte gern.**

The shop expression corresponding to English **want** is **skulle ha.** *Jeg skulle ha et par sko, et par hansker* (gloves), *en pakke sigaretter,* etc.

175. The infinitive construction **I want you to come** does not exist in Norwegian. In such cases two clauses have to be used. *Jeg vil at du skal komme.* I expect you to say yes. *Jeg venter at du skal si ja.* Similarly with an infinitive after an interrogative pronoun or adverb. I don't know what to do = *Jeg vet ikke hva jeg skal gjøre.* He didn't know when to stop = *Han visste ikke når han skulle stoppe.*

Other Auxiliaries

176.

	Infinitive	Present	Past Tense	Past Participle
(1)	*kunne*	*kan*	*kunne*	*kunnet*
	be able to	can	could	been able to

The Norwegian **jeg kan** usually covers the English: I can, I am able to, and sometimes: I may.

Examples: *Du kan synge meget pent hvis du virkelig vil.* You can sing very beautifully, if you really want to. *Kan De snakke norsk?* Can you speak Norwegian? In the last sentence '*snakke*' can be omitted: *Kan De norsk?* **Kan** in this special case is equivalent to English 'know'.

Asking for permission, English: may, *Kan jeg (få) låne pennen din et øyeblikk?* May (or can, as in Norwegian) I borrow your pen for a moment?

	Infinitive	Present	Past Tense	Past Participle
(2)	*måtte*	*må*	*måtte*	*måttet*
	to have to	must	had to	have had to

Vi må hjelpe ham. We must help him. *Noe må gjøres.* Something has to be done. Past tense: *Jeg måtte gå før forestillingen* [ˇfɔːrəstilliŋən] *var slutt for å nå toget.* I had to go before the performance was finished to catch the train. *Jeg har måttet gjøre det* = *Jeg er blitt nødt til å gjøre det.* I have had to do it.

In polite questions = may, might: *Må jeg (få lov til å) komme inn?* May I come in?

	Infinitive	Present	Past Tense	Past Participle
(3)	*burde* [ˇburdə]	*bør* (ought to)	*burde*	*burdet*

This verb denotes what is the most proper and suitable thing to do. *Man bør gå tidlig til sengs.* One ought to go to bed early. *Jeg syns du burde be ham om unnskyldning.* I think you ought to ask his pardon.

	Infinitive	Present	Past Tense	Past Participle
(4)	*tore* (dare)	*tør* [tørr]	*torde* [ˇtɔːrə]	*tort* [tɔːʳʈ]

Hun tør ikke gå alene i mørket. She dare not walk alone in the darkness. *Han torde ikke påstå at det var sant.* He dared not maintain that it was true. Sometimes *tore* also indicates a vague possibility: *Det torde være vanskelig.* It might be difficult. *Tør jeg spørre hvem De er?* May I ask who you are?

(5) *få* get—*fikk*—*fått* is used in many connections and with various meanings:

(a) A vaguely expressed compulsion 'had better': *Du får nok gjøre som jeg sier.* You had better do as I say.

(b) Asking or granting permission=may, or might: *Får jeg komme inn?* May I come in?—also *Får jeg lov* [lɔːv] *å komme inn? Kan jeg få snakke med sjefen?* Can I see the manager? Lit.: speak with. *Du får gjøre som du vil.* You may do as you like.

(c) To manage, be able, get a chance to: *Jeg fikk ikke sove i natt.* I couldn't sleep last night. *Å få begge endene til å møtes* = to make both ends meet. *Å få en til å le, gråte,* etc., to make one laugh, weep, etc. It is frequently used in conjunction with past participle of the main verb. Example: *Jeg fikk kjøpt noen få epler i går.* I managed to buy a few apples yesterday. Useful idioms: *få til* = manage, succeed in doing; *jeg får det ikke til* I can't manage (because I am too clumsy perhaps). *få se* catch sight of; *få høre, vite* learn, get to know. *Fikk du se ham?* Did you catch sight of him? *Jeg fikk ikke vite noenting.* I didn't get to know anything. *Jeg fikk høre (vite) at han hadde reist.* I heard (or learned) that he had left.

(d) To express futurity in expressions like: *Vi får se.* We shall see. *Den som lever, får se.* Lit. He who lives, will see.

(6) *la* let—*lot*—*latt*: *La ham gå.* Let him go.

Note: Common to all the verbs of this type is the lack of '*å*' before the following infinitive.

Vocabulary

på restaurant [restu'raŋŋ] c. at a restaurant
servitør c. waiter
ordne [ˇɔrdnə] arrange, fix
hjørne [ˇjøːˈɳə] n. corner
passe (-et) suit
spisekart n. menu, bill of fare
meny [me'nyː] c. menu
biff c. beef
ørret c. trout
steke (-te) fry
vinkart n. wine list

rødvin ['røːviːn] c. red wine
hvitvin ['viːtviːn] c. white wine
likør [li'køːr] c. liqueur
velge, valgte, valgt choose, select
dessert [de'sæːr] c. dessert, sweet
is c. ice cream
varme c. warmth, heat
regning [ˇreiniŋ] c. bill, account
øyeblikk n. moment

Exercise 27a

På restaurant

Servitøren. God aften. Hva ønsker De?

Herr N. Vi skulle gjerne ha et hyggelig bord for tre personer.

S. Det skal vi straks ordne. De kan få det bordet i hjørnet der borte.

Herr N. Takk, det passer fint. Kan jeg få se spisekartet (menyen)?

S. Vær så god.

Herr N. Hva vil De anbefale i dag?

S. Biffen er meget god, og så har vi fin-fin ørret.

Fru N. Jeg vil gjerne ha en biff.

Herr N. Og du, min datter?

Fröken N. Jeg vil heller (*rather*) ha fisk, stekt ørret for eksempel.

Herr N. Jeg tror jeg vil prøve biffen, jeg også. Vel det blir to biff og en stekt ørret.

S. Det skal bli. Skal det være noe å drikke til?

Herr N. Ja, kunne jeg få se vinkartet? Jeg tror et glass rødvin vil passe bra til biffen, men du unge dame, som har valgt fisk, burde vel helst ha et glass hvitvin, ikke sant.

Frøken N. Nei, jeg vil ikke ha noe å drikke til maten. Jeg vil heller ha et glass likør til kaffen.

Herr N. Som du vil.

*   *   *

Herr N. Hva skal vi så velge til dessert? Hva sier dere om (*to*) is?

Begge damene: Det vil smake godt i denne varmen.

* * *

Herr N. Kunne jeg få regningen, takk.
S. Et øyeblikk. Vær så god.

Vocabulary

sint på angry with
'femtoget the five o'clock train
luft c. air

hefte (-et) detain
hilse (-et) noen give s.o. one's
  best regards

Exercise 27b

Translate:

Where are you going? I can't talk with you now. I am to
meet my wife at the station and I don't dare to come too
late. She will get very angry with me if I do (that). Is she
coming by the five o'clock train? Yes. You ought to take a
taxi. That would be much better. Oh no, you must not say
that. Then I would not get any (*noe*) fresh air. I understand.
I shan't detain you. Will you and your wife be at home
tonight? Yes, I think so. I will ring you later. Good-bye
and don't forget to give my best regards to your wife. I
shan't forget (it).

Vocabulary

i all hast in a hurry
dessuten [de ˇsuːtn̩] besides
overraskelse c. surprise

underrette (-et) inform
Jeg håper endelig [ˇendəli] I
  do hope

Exercise 27c

I wouldn't have gone away if I had known that you were in
(the) town. Why didn't you tell me that you were coming?
I had to leave in a hurry and didn't get time to write.
Besides, it was (supposed) to be a surprise. I do hope you
will inform us next time you are coming. I promise (transl.
det lover jeg).

Vocabulary

politi [poliˈtiː] n. police
ˇ**bonde** pl. ˈbønder farmer
tvile (-te) på doubt
alvorlig [allˈvoːˀli] serious
følge [ˇfølgə] c. consequence

permisjon [pærmiˈʃoːn] c. leave,
  furlough
sjåfør [ʃɔˈføːr] c. driver
reparere [repaˈreːrə] **(-te) to**
  repair

Exercise 27d

Connect the following sentence pairs, making the necessary changes.

1. Jeg spurte om ...	1. Han skal reise i morgen.
2. Politiet fortalte at ...	2. Det vil få alvorlige følger.
3. Bonden tvilte på at ...	3. Det vil lønne seg (*pay*).
4. Per mente (=trodde) at ...	4. Han vil få permisjon.
5. Sjåføren sa at ...	5. Bilen må repareres.

CHAPTER XV

PRONOUNS AND PRONOMINAL ADJECTIVES

Personal Pronouns

177. The personal pronouns may be arranged in the following way:

Singular

1st person	2nd person	3rd person[1]		
			c.	n.
Nominative:				
jeg I	*du* you	*han* he, *hun* she	*den*	*det* it
Object form:				
meg me	*deg* you	*ham* him, *henne* her	*den*	*det* it

Plural

1st person	2nd person	3rd person (all genders)
Nominative:		
vi we	*dere* you	*de* they
Object form:		
oss us	*dere* you	*dem* them

[1] Note: The third person singular also has a genitive form *hans* his, *hennes* her, *dens* and *dets* its, and similarly the second and third person plural: *deres* your, their. But all these are used as possessives, and are consequently mentioned under that paragraph.

178. As regards the forms *du* and *deg*, these are only used between members of the same family and between intimate friends or acquaintances; in other words, if you are what the Norwegians call '*dus*' with the person. If not, you had better use the more polite forms (with a capital D). Nominative: *De* (originally third person plural) and object form: *Dem*, with the corresponding possessive adjective: *Deres*.

For the use of *du* and *De* it may be good to compare with French *tu* and *vous*. But it takes less time to become '*dus*' in Norway than in France.

Furthermore young people far more rapidly drop the polite and formal forms among themselves than the older generation, who observe the rules of etiquette more strictly.

Examples: *Vil De ikke sette Dem? De har glemt hatten Deres.* In commercial correspondence: *Vi har mottatt Deres brev av 15. januar.*

179. A much-debated point in Norwegian, as in English, is whether one should say: *Det er* **meg** or *det er* **jeg**. *Han er eldre enn* **meg** or **jeg**. *Han er like så gammel som* **meg** or **jeg**. Common usage would in most cases prefer the object form **meg**, at least when the pronoun is stressed: **Meg** *var det ikke*. If the expression is followed by a relative clause the subject form **jeg** is often preferred. *Det var* **jeg** *som gjorde det*.

Vocabulary

i det siste lately
på flere uker for several weeks
reise (-te) bort leave, go away
nevne (-te) mention
gå på skole go to school
ja da oh, yes
rart n. of rar adj. strange
kan kanskje may

grunn c. ground, reason
ringe (-te) (til) en phone (up) somebody
God dag Hallo
så snart (som) as soon as
utmerket adj. splendid, grand
hils ham så mye fra oss give him our best regards

Exercise 28a

Practise reading and then translate:

Olav: Si meg, har du sett Per i det siste? Odd: Nei, jeg har ikke sett ham på flere uker. Olav: Tror du han er reist bort?

Odd: Han nevnte at han ville reise til Oslo for å gå på skole. Har du hørt noe om (*about*) det? Olav: Nei, ikke et ord. Odd: Kjente du ham godt? Olav: Ja da, vi var 'dus', og svært gode venner. Odd: Da er det (*it is*) rart han ikke har fortalt oss at han skulle reise. Han hadde kanskje ikke tid til å besøke oss før han dro.

Olav: Det kan kanskje være grunnen. Jeg vil ringe til hans søster og spørre henne om hun vet noe. Men der kommer jo hans bror. Broren: God dag, dere vet kanskje at Per er reist, eller har han ikke fortalt dere det? Olav og Odd: Nei, vi vet absolutt ingenting. Broren: Han sa han skulle skrive til dere så snart han kom til Oslo.

Olav og Odd: Det er utmerket. Hils ham så mye fra oss begge to (lit. from both of us).

Vocabulary

gå for'bi pass (by)
en fremmed a stranger
mann (here) husband
i ettermiddag this afternoon
etterpå afterwards

spille (-te) kort [kɔ'ţ] n. play cards
skitur ['ʃiːtuːr] ski-ing trip
ikke—på lenge
  not—for a long time
morsom funny (comical)

Exercise 28b

Translate:

1. Do you (polite form) know him? No, I have never seen him before. None of us know him. He must be a stranger in our town. He passed me yesterday in (*på*) the street. Mrs Olsen certainly knows (tr. knows certainly) what he is called (use the correct form of *hete*). I will ask her. She knows everything (*alt*). She and her husband are coming to us for (*til*) coffee this afternoon. Afterwards we are going to play cards. I didn't know that you (pl.) played cards. Oh yes, we do (it) occasionally (see adv. page 92). Do you (polite form) play cards? No, never.

Where are the boys? They are on (a) ski-ing trip. I haven't seen them for a long time. Have you sold your house? No, I

haven't sold it yet. My children are too fond of it. Will you
hear a good story? Yes, if it is good and funny.

'**heller—ikke** neither—nor

2. Who (*hvem*) did it? It was not I. Nor I either. Was it
you who did it? No, it was not he. He is bigger than you.
He is almost (*nesten*) as big as you.

The Reflexive Pronoun 'seg' [sei]—Reflexive Verbs

180. Special attention should be paid to the reflexive pronoun **seg** in Norwegian, as there is no equivalent in English
(cf. German **sich**, French **se**). This **seg** always refers back
to the subject in the clause where it occurs, but is only used
when the subject is in the third person singular or plural.
Thus it corresponds to English oneself, himself, herself,
itself, themselves. *Han hengte seg.* He hanged himself,
Slo hun seg? Did she hurt herself? In the first and second
persons the ordinary object forms of the personal pronouns
are used. *Slo du deg?* Did you hurt yourself?

The complete paradigm of a so-called reflexive verb will
then be:

Infinitive: *å more seg* to enjoy oneself, to have a good time.

jeg morer meg ..	..	..	I enjoy myself.
du morer deg ..	..	..	you enjoy yourself.
De morer Dem	..	..	„ „ „
vi morer oss ..	..	..	we enjoy ourselves.
dere morer dere	..	..	you enjoy yourselves.

Seg—3rd person, singular and plural:

han *morer* **seg**	..	..	he enjoys himself.
hun *morer* **seg**	..	..	she enjoys herself.
det (*barnet*) *morer* **seg**	..	it (the child) enjoys itself.
den (*katten*) *morer* **seg**	..	it (the cat) enjoys itself.
de *morer* **seg**	..	..	they enjoy themselves.

181. When the English forms **myself, yourself**, etc., are
used in an emphatic role, they correspond to Norwegian
selv [sell]. Examples: I did it myself = *Jeg gjorde det selv.*

You saw it yourself = *Du så det selv*. Thus *Jeg vil vaske meg selv* would mean: I will wash myself myself.

The Reflexive Verbs

182. The reflexive verbs have a much wider application in Norwegian than in English. Many verbs also have a reflexive form beside them, very often with idiomatic meaning, e.g. **å komme** = to come, but **å komme seg** means to recover, improve.

Here is a list of some very useful examples:

bar'bere seg shave
be'stemme seg make up one's mind
bry seg om care about
finne seg i put up with
for'andre seg change
for'sove seg oversleep
føle seg feel
gifte seg marry
glede seg be glad
glede seg til look forward to
hvile seg rest
'innbille seg imagine
kjede seg be bored
klippe seg have a haircut
kle på seg dress
kle av seg undress
legge seg lie down, go to bed
legge på seg put on weight
like seg like it, feel comfortable

liste seg steal, slink
lønne seg be of advantage, pay
more seg have a good time
nærme seg approach
'oppføre seg behave
reise seg rise, get up
røre seg move
se seg omkring have a look round
sette seg sit down, be seated
skaffe seg get oneself, procure
skamme seg be ashamed of oneself
skynde seg hurry up
slå seg hurt oneself, get hurt
ta på seg put on ⎱ about
ta av seg take off ⎰ clothes
tenke seg imagine
vise seg (1) appear, (2) prove to be, (3) show off

Vocabulary

såpe c. soap
prest c. minister, parson
preken c. sermon

foretrekke [ˈfoːrətrekkə] prefer, conjugated like **trekke** irr.

Exercise 29a

For translation

Examples of the use of the reflexive pronoun:

1. Han satte seg i en stol. 2. Jeg legger meg klokka elleve om (*in*) kvelden. 3. Hun føler seg vel. 4. Gutten brente seg. 5. Mannen falt og slo seg. 6. Jeg vasket meg med såpen. 7. Piken skar seg i fingeren (*cut her finger*). 8. Hun brydde

seg ikke[1] om det. **9.** Soldatene reiste seg (*rose to their feet*).
10. Jeg kunne tenke meg det (*so*). **11.** Vi tenkte oss at han
gjerne ville komme (*that he would like to come*). **12.** Døren
åpnet seg, og en katt listet seg inn. **13.** Da de hadde satt
seg, begynte presten prekenen.

The command *Sit down!* may be translated either reflexively
Sett deg!, politely *Sett Dem!*, or like English *sitt ned!* The
same applies to *Lie down!*, *Legg deg (Dem)!* or *Ligg ned!*

Exercise 29b

Translate into Norwegian: **peis** c. open fireplace   **kniv** c. knife

1. She married for money. **2.** They felt happy. **3.** I feel
better now. **4.** You must not sit down. **5.** The old people
preferred to go to bed. **6.** I do not care what he says. **7.** He
burnt himself. **8.** I have a wash every morning. **9.** I could not
imagine that he was there. **10.** He got up and went out of the
room. **11.** He sat down near (*ved*) the fireplace to (*for å*)
warm himself. **12.** I cut my finger with a knife. **13.** You have
not changed much.

183. *After a preposition* **seg** corresponds to the personal
pronouns in English.

Example: *Han tok henne med seg.* He took her with him.
Han hadde ikke noen penger på seg. He had no money on
him. *De delte eplet mellom seg.* They shared the apple between
them.

The Possessives
The Possessive Adjectives

184. We have already mentioned the possessive adjectives
in connection with the declension of the ordinary adjectives.
But a few further points remain to be explained. We discovered that these adjectives followed the strong declension,
and our paradigm will therefore be as follows:

	Common	Neuter	Plural
my	*min stol*	*mitt bord*	*mine stoler, mine bord*
your	*din stol*	*ditt bord*	*dine stoler, dine bord*
our	*vår stol*	*vårt bord*	*våre stoler, våre bord*

[1] The negative **ikke** is always placed after the reflexive pronoun in
principal clauses. Cf. page 55.

The spelling reform of 1938 has also permitted fem. forms such as *mi, di* which are placed after the fem. noun: *boka mi* (never *boka min*).

185. In addition to these we have the indeclinable possessives which are actually the genitive of the personal pronouns (see note, page 108): *hans* his, *hennes* her, *dens*, *dets* its, and finally: *deres* your, plural, also their, and the polite form *Deres* your, singular.

186. As regards the use of these adjectives, it should be noted that there is a growing tendency to place them after the noun, with the latter in its definite form. Thus nearly always in colloquial speech, e.g. *stolen min, bordet mitt,* plural *stolene mine, bordene mine, boken* (or *boka*) *hans, boken min* (or *boka mi*), plural: *bøkene hans, bøkene mine*. (Cf. page 65.)

In colloquial speech: *min nye hatt* sounds rather formal and literary, so we should generally put the definite article of the adjective in front: *den nye hatten min*, and in the plural: *de nye hattene mine*. To begin with, however, the English student is advised to put the possessive adjectives in front in conformity with his own language.

Exercise 30

Drill in the use of the possessive adjectives:

Mitt hus er nytt

Instead of *hus*, insert in turn the following nouns:

frakk c. coat   *bord* [boːr] n. table   *lampe* c. lamp

Change them into the plural afterwards.

Din nye hatt er pen.

Replace *hatt* by: *bilde* n. picture, *bil, hest*. Afterwards in the plural.

Unlike English, Norwegian uses the possessive adjectives in front of nouns for abusive purpose:

din tosk you fool!, *din idi'ot* you idiot!, *din slyngel, din kjeltring* you rascal!

Vocabulary

tilstand c. condition
snipp c. collar of a shirt
skitten dirty

tur c. here: turn
sjanse [ˈʃaŋsə] c. chance

Exercise 31a

1. Hans hår var grått. 2. Jeg tviler på hans ord. 3. Hennes tilstand er alvorlig. 4. Din far har kjøpt vårt hus. 5. Mitt land er større enn *ditt* (N.B.). 6. Hvorfor er din snipp så skitten? Kan du ikke låne en av mine? 7. Hvem har fortalt deg at boken er hans? 8. Når går ditt tog? 9. Nå er det din tur. 10. Mine sjanser er små.

From example No. 5 it will be seen that the pronoun has the same form whether used adjectivally or as a pronoun proper.

Example: *Dette er ditt eple.* English: your apple. *Eplet er ditt.* English: yours.

Vocabulary

dyr expensive
vente (-et) på wait for
interesse c. interest
stolthet c. pride

gris c. pig
sau c. sheep
ku f. cow

Exercise 31b

Translate into Norwegian:

1. It is not my turn. 2. My books are more expensive than yours. 3. Your brother is waiting for you. He has your hat and coat. 4. My mother's greatest interest is to work in our garden. 5. Her son is her greatest pride. 6. Have you seen their farm, their pigs, their sheep and cows? 7. Which (*hvem*) of his sons do you like best?

The Reflexive Possessive

187.

Common	Neuter	Plural
sin	*sitt*	*sine*

= his, her(s), its, one's, their(s)

(there is also a feminine form *si* —but rare. Cf. note, page 114.)

The reflexive pronoun '*seg*' [sei] and the so-called *reflexive possessive* '*sin*' (declined as *min* and *din*) should really be treated together, as what has been said about the former also applies to the latter.

The English has no equivalent to this pronoun; you should therefore devote special attention to it.

In English the possessive adjective 'his' is used in both these sentences: (1) *His* watch is expensive. (2) He took *his* watch. Actually the last statement implies an ambiguity, as 'his' may mean: his own watch, or somebody else's. The context will throw light upon the matter, so that possibilities of misunderstanding are usually rare.

Let us now translate the two sentences into Norwegian: (1) *Hans klokke* (or: *Klokka hans*) *er dyr*. (2) *Han tok* **hans** *klokke*, or: *Han tok* **sin** *klokke*. If we used the first version, of sentence No. 2: *hans klokke*, it would not be his own watch. If that were the case, we should have to use: *sin*. Thus the rule is:

If the possessive adjective refers back to a subject in the third person (N.B.), singular or plural, we use the reflexive possessive *sin* for English: one's, his, her, hers, its, their or theirs. (Cf. *seg* in para. 180.) It is never used in the nominative case.

Here is the complete paradigm:

Singular:

jeg tok *min hatt*	..	I took my hat
du tok *din hatt*	..	you took your hat

Polite:

De tok *Deres hatt*	..	you took your hat

Third person, singular:

han *tok* **sin** *hatt*	..	he took his hat, i.e. his own
hun *tok* **sin** *hatt*	..	she took her hat, i.e. her own
barnet *tok* **sin** *hatt*	..	the child took its hat, i.e. its own

Plural:

vi tok *våre hatter*	..	we took our hats
dere tok *deres hatter*	..	you took your hats

Third person, plural:

| de *tok* **sine** *hatter* .. | they took their hats, i.e. their own |
| **gjestene** *tok* **sine** *hatter* | the guests took their hats, i.e. their own |

188. Again: 'seg' and 'sin' always refer back to the subject when this is a noun or pronoun in the third person, either singular or plural.

Note: In the following example the reflexive possessive refers to the logical subject:

Jeg bad ham om å trekke sin søknad tilbake. I asked him to withdraw his application.

Exercise 32

Practice in using *sin* (*sitt, sine*)

1. After the war he will go back to his country.
2. Can't you see his face, or is it too dark?
3. The little boy had eaten all his (own) food.
4*a*. The men had forgotten to take their (own) money with them.
4*b*. Do you believe it was their money?
4*c*. Do you believe the money was theirs?
5. The English never lose their good spirits (*hu'mør* n.).
6. Ole and his brother had always been good friends.
7. The watch was not his. It was mine.
8. Wessel in one of his amusing poems tells the story about 'the Smith[1] and the Baker'.
9. The father saw two men speaking to his daughter.
10. 'Where is the money?' 'I took my part of it and they took theirs.'
11. The soldiers rode through his garden.

Demonstratives

189. There are two chief demonstratives, which are inflected in gender and in number as follows:

[1] a smith = *en smed* [smeː].

	Common	Neuter	Plural
Nom. Obj.:	*denne* this	*dette*	*disse* these
Poss.:	*dennes*	*dettes*	*disses*
Nom. Obj.:	*den* that	*det*	Nom.: *de* those
Poss.:	*dens* its	*dets*	*deres* yours
			Obj.: *dem* those

(*a*) **Denne,** n. **dette,** pl. **disse** indicate like English 'this, pl. these' that the thing or person in question is quite near, while **den,** n. **det,** pl. **de** give the idea of remoteness 'that one, those'.

Examples:

Denne blyanten er mye bedre enn **den.** This pencil is much better than that one. *Dette huset er større enn* **det.** This house is bigger than that one.

To make the situation still clearer **her** (here) is usually added to **denne, dette, disse** and **der** (there) to **den, det, de.** *Denne blyanten* **her** *er mye bedre enn* **den der** (or **den der borte** = over there). *Det brevet* **her** *er mitt, men* **det der** (*borte*) *er ditt.* You will notice that after all these demonstratives the noun generally appears in its definite form ('double definition').

(*b*) You will also see that the demonstrative **den, det, de, dem** is in form identical with the personal pronoun (English 'it') and the so-called 'definite article' of the adjective (English 'the') except that the article has no objective form **dem.** *The difference is indicated by stress.*

Illustrations

	Personal Pronoun	Demonstrative
hunden the dog	*den er* **stor** it is big	but **den** *er stor*
		that one is big
huset the house	*det er* **stort** it is big	but **det** *er stort*
		that one is big
In the plural:	*de er* **store** they are big	but **de** *er store*
		those are big

> *hunden er stor* the dog is big

but **den** *hunden er stor* that dog is big

> *hundene er store* the dogs are big

but **de** *hundene er store* those dogs are big

In the phrase: *den* (unstressed) *lange veien* the long road, we have the article, but if extra stress is put on *den* we get the demonstrative **DEN** *lange veien* **THAT** long road.

(c) The possessive form **dennes** is hardly ever used, except in business letters: *Jeg har mottatt Deres brev av 15.* **dennes** (abbreviated **ds.**). I have received your letter of 15th inst.

(d) Note specially: Where English uses **this**—**these, that**—**those** as subject of the verb 'to be' with a following noun (sg. or pl.) in the predicate Norwegian always uses the neuter singular form, **dette er/var, det er/var** ... Cf. para. 55.

Examples:

dette *er en bok* this is a book, **dette** *er bøker* these are books, **det** *er en blyant* ['bly:ant] that is a pencil, **det** *er blyanter* those are pencils.

(e) For expressions like **den som** = he who, **de som** = those who, see relative pronouns. Note: **den** *boken du kjøpte i går, har jeg lest.* **The** book you bought yesterday I have read.

(f) Another difference from English is the use of the genitive form of the noun instead of the demonstrative pronoun plus a preposition as in English in sentences like: *Norges 'handelsflåte er større enn Sveriges* ['sværjəs]. Norway's merchant-fleet is bigger than *that of* Sweden.

190. There are also some other words generally classed among the demonstratives. These are:

c.	n.	pl.
slik [ʃliːk] such	*slikt*	*slike*

the synonym:

sådan	*sådant*	*sådanne*

colloquially shortened to:

sånn	*sånt*	*sånne* (also permissible in writing)

191. Finally some indeclinable words:

begge both, *samme* the same, *selv*[1] self.

Note on **selv** [sell].

selv takes the ending **-e** when used adjectivally before a noun, **selve** [ˇselvə] **kongen.** The king himself. *I selve London.* In London proper. It even has a superlative, **selveste paven.** The Pope himself, in person. **selv** emphasizes a pronoun or a noun. (English myself, yourself, etc.) *Jeg skal gjøre det* **selv.** *Han så det* **selv.** Cf. reflexive verbs, para. 181.

selv can also have adverbial function meaning **even,** and is then always placed in front. *Selv et barn vet det.* Even a child knows that.

Exercise 33

Insert the correct form of

Den. 1. *Hva kaller du . . . gaten?* **2.** *Har du malt . . . bildet selv?* **3.** *. . . bøkene der er ikke mine, så du kan ikke ta . . .* (emphatic).

Denne. 1. *. . . huset er gult.* **2.** *. . . bildene er gode.* **3.** *. . . snøen er bløt.* **4.** *. . . er en vakker dal.* **5.** *. . . er ikke mine brev.*

Slik or **Sånn. 1.** *. . . folk er hyggelige* (pleasant). **2.** *Han likte ikke . . . arbeid.* **3.** *Har du sett en . . . tosk.*

---

[1] Another form permitted by the New Spelling Reform is 'sjøl', identical with the form used in the dialects and familiar speech.

Vocabulary

selskap n. party
'engelsk English
etter after
veldig great, terrible
slit n. toil, hard work
topp c. top, summit, peak
hvile (-te) ut rest
'anstrengende strenuous
klatre (-et) climb
klatring c. climbing
fører c. guide,
forskjellig [fɔ'ʃelli] different, various
vann n. 1, water; 2, lake
lengst farthest
'venstre left
'nettopp just, exactly
tind [tinn] c. peak
likeså—som quite as—as

jeg synes it seems to me
pigg c. spike, here: peak
rundt omkring round about
se ut look like
'synsbedrag n. optical illusion
tine bort (-te) melt away
for'retningsmann c. business man
deilig lovely, nice
slå seg ned settle down
hytte f. hut
fjellmann mountaineer
materiale [mat(ə)ri'a:lə] n. material
hit here, hither
rygg c. back
ˇsannelig really, indeed
'nedstigning c. descent
fjellkjede c. mountain range

Exercise 34a

På Galdhøppiggen

Et selskap med (of) engelske turister hadde etter et veldig slit nådd toppen av Galdhøpiggen, som er det høyeste fjellet i Norge. De hvilte først godt ut etter den anstrengende klatringen, men så begynte de å spørre føreren om navnene på de forskjellige toppene, dalene og vannene som de så rundt omkring seg.

En ung dame spurte: 'Hva heter det fjellet der?' Føreren: 'Mener De det lengst til venstre.' Damen: 'Ja, nettopp.' Føreren: 'Den fjelltoppen De ser der, er den berømte Glitretind, som er omtrent likeså høy som denne her.' En eldre dame sa: 'Jeg synes at alle disse toppene rundt omkring oss er høyere enn selve Galdhøpiggen.' Føreren: 'Det kan kanskje se slik ut, men det er bare synsbedrag.' Damen: 'Men den snøen vi ser på Glitretinden, tiner den aldri bort?' Føreren: 'Den ligger året rundt.' Tredje turist, en ung forretningsmann fra Manchester: 'Dette er et deilig sted. Her tror jeg vi slår oss ned for godt. Men, si meg, hvem har bygd denne vesle hytta her. Føreren: 'Det er den kjente fjellmannen Knut Vole. Han bar alle materialene opp hit på sin rygg.' Turisten: 'Det må sannelig ha vært et anstren-

gende arbeid. Jeg synes det er mer enn nok når en bærer seg
selv oppover. Men før vi begynner på nedstigningen, må De
enda en gang (*once more*) fortelle meg hva hele denne
fjellkjeden heter.' Føreren: 'Jotunheimen.' 'Ja visst (*Yes,
of course*). Jeg glemmer alltid det navnet.'

The Reciprocal Pronouns

192. There are only two: **Hverandre** [vær ˅andrə] and
Hinannen [hi ˅naɳ] (each other), the former being the one
more frequently heard. *Hinannen* is mainly a 'bookish'
word, and was originally used of two persons as is still the
practice with some people.

Example: *De hadde ikke sett hverandre på mange år.* They
had not seen each other for many years. *De elsket hverandre.*
They loved each other. These pronouns can also take a
genitive ending as in English: *De lånte hverandres bøker.*
They borrowed each other's books. *De leser hverandres brev.*
They read each other's letters.

Vocabulary

nevne (-et) mention
'sammen together
grunn c. reason
på samme tid = samtidig
  at the same time
i det hele (tatt) on the whole
skjønt conj. although
sint på angry with
ganske or **temmelig** quite
ge'mytt n. nature, temperament

syn n. **på** view(s) on
opti'mistisk optimistic
tro c. **på** belief in
'derimot or **på den annen**
  side on the other hand
tvile (-te) på to doubt
tvil c. doubt
evne c. faculty
skildre (-et) describe
verker pl. works (i.e. books)

Exercise 34b

Translate:

Ibsen and Bjørnson

Ibsen and Bjørnson are very often mentioned together. The
reason is that they lived at the same time, and knew each
other well. They wrote to each other for (*i*) many years,
and were on the whole good friends although they were
often angry with each other. They had quite different
natures, and quite different views (*use singular*) on many
things. Bjørnson was more optimistic than Ibsen, and had a

strong belief in himself. Ibsen, on the other hand, was always doubting his own faculties and this doubt he described in many of his works.

The Interrogative Pronouns

The interrogative pronouns are:

Hvem who, whom, **Hva** what, **Hvilken** which, n. **Hvilket,** plural **Hvilke.**

193. **Hvem** relates only to persons and is not used adjectivally. It has the same form whether used as subject or object.

Example: Subject—*Hvem er du?* Who are you? Object— *Hvem traff du i går?* Whom did you meet yesterday?

A preposition is usually put at the end of the sentence.

Example: *Hvem talte du med?* Whom did you speak to? *Hvem har du fått den gaven av?* From whom have you got that gift?

194. The genitive form of this pronoun is **Hvis** [viss] whose. *Hvis hatt er dette!* Whose hat is this? This **hvis,** however, is very often avoided in the spoken language. In the example quoted above, we should say: *Hvem eier denne hatten?*

Note: Whereas the English language would use *Which* (= *hvilken*) in a sentence like: Which of the two brothers did you meet? Norwegian more often uses: *hvem. Hvem av de to brødrene møtte du? Hvem av søstrene giftet han seg med?* Which of the sisters did he marry?

195. **Hva** on the other hand refers to inanimate objects. It also differs from *hvem* in that it is sometimes used adjectivally.

As subject: *Hva er det?* What is it? As object: *Hva sier du?* What do you say? With a preposition: *Hva tenker du på?* What are you thinking of?

The use of **Hva** as an adjective is very restricted.

Example: *Hva nytte kan du ha av det?* What benefit can you

draw from that; Of what advantage can that be to you? *Hva tid kom du?* What time did you come? *Hva nytt?* What's the news?

196. Hvilken, hvilket, plural **hvilke** (used both about persons and things) corresponds to English *what* and sometimes to *which* or *which one*.

Example: *Hvilken by kommer du fra?* What town do you come from? *Her er to billeder. Hvilket foretrekker du?* Here are two pictures. Which do you prefer?

This interrogative, however, has a somewhat literary flavour, and in the spoken language it is often replaced by *hva for en*, n. *hva for et*, plural *hva for (noen)*. *Hva for en by mener du? Hva for et bilde foretrekker du? Hva for en gate er dette?* or more frequently: *Hva er dette for en gate?* What street is this? *Hva er dette for (noen) bøker?* What books are these? (Note the use of *dette* in both questions, cf. para. 189(d)). *Hva for noen venner har du invitert?* What friends have you invited? *Hva for noen fjell er det vi ser der?* What mountains are those which we see there?

Note also the common expression: *Hva slags*, or *hva for slags* (what kind of). *Hva slags mennesker er det?*[1] What kind of people are *they*? *Hva slags tre er det?* What sort of tree is it?

197. Finally it must be added that **Hvilken** is frequently used in exclamations corresponding to English *what*.

Example: *Hvilken tosk jeg har vært!* What a fool I have been! *Hvilken skandale!* What a scandal! *Hvilken skam!* What a shame!

Instead of *hvilken* the spoken language would mostly use *for en* (n. *et*), plural *for noen*. *For en tosk.* What a fool! *For et syn!* What a sight! Plural: *For noen rare dyr.* What strange beasts. *For noe tøys!* What nonsense!

If you have not quite heard what a person has said to you, and you want him to repeat it, you could say either: *Hvilket? Hva behager?* I beg your pardon, or among intimate friends: *Hva sa du?* What did you say? or just the very informal: *Hva?* What?

---

[1] Here Norwegian uses the impersonal pronoun *det (it)*, whilst English employs the personal pronoun.

Vocabulary

renn n. race, competition
skje (-dde) happen, occur
mangel ['maŋŋel] c. lack
gidde (gadd-giddet) care, bother
virkelig indeed
idrett c. sport
stjerne [ˇstjæːˈɳə] c. star
prestere (-te) perform, achieve
premie ['preːmjə] c. prize
rekord [rəˈkɔrd] c. record
skøyte c. skate
uvesentlig unimportant
apropos (aproˈpoː] by the way

spansk Spanish
journalist [ʃoˈɳaˈlist] c. journalist
skildre give an account of, describe
inntrykk n. impression
gal here: mad
planke c. board
bratt steep
stup n. precipice
flakse flap
slå seg i hjel kill oneself
u'trolig incredible

Exercise 35a

Hvilken bok er det du har der?—Å, det er *Hvem er hvem.*
Hvem var det du skulle lese om?—Det var en stor skikonge.
Jeg har glemt hvilke renn han vant, og hvilket år det
skjedde.—Kan det være så viktig?—Hva er det du sier?
Hvilken (= *For en*) mangel på interesse du viser for vår
nasjonalsport.—Jeg gidder da virkelig ikke å huske hva alle
disse idrettsstjernene har prestert, hvem som har vunnet
første premie i Holmenkollen hvert år f. eks. og hvem som
har verdensrekorden på 500 meter på skøyter. Slike ting
er da ganske uvesentlige. Apropos, har du hørt historien
om den spanske journalisten som så hopprennet i Holmenkollen for første gang.—Nei, hva sa han?—Jo, han skildret
sine inntrykk på følgende måte:

'Nordmennene er helt gale. De binder noen treplanker om
bena, og så setter de utfor bratte stup, flakser i luften som
fugler og kommer ned igjen uten å slå seg i hjel. Helt utrolig.'

—Jeg synes ikke den historien var så veldig morsom.—
Hvilken mangel på humoristisk sans!'

Vocabulary

støy c. noise

rot n. mess (muddle)

Exercise 35b

1. Whom did you give the letter?
   Whose car is that?
   Who told you that?

2. What do you want (What will you have)?
What is the best hotel in Oslo?
What books have you read?
What friends did you meet?
What newspapers do you generally read? (use *pleie*).
What did you (pl.) talk about?
I did not know what to do.

3. Which glass do you prefer?
Which of the boys is the cleverest?
I did not know which way to go (tr. which way I should go).

4. What a noise. What a mess.
What a fool I have been not seeing that (tr. who did not see that).

198. Compare:

Interrogative   *Hva er hendt?* What has happened?
Indef. relative   *Jeg vet ikke* **hva som** *er hendt.* I don't know what has happened.

Interrogative   *Hvem gjorde det?* Who did it?
Indef. relative   *Jeg så ikke* **hvem som** *gjorde det.* I didn't see who did it.

Rule: When the interrogatives **hva** (what) and **hvem** (who) are subjects in the subordinate clause they are generally followed by the relative pronoun **som.**

The Relative Pronouns

199.   (1) **som** [sɔmm] is strictly speaking the only relative pronoun the foreigner need bother about. It is invariable and corresponds to English **who, whom, which,** and **that,** when these are used as relative pronouns.

som may stand:

(*a*) as subject, e.g. *Hun hadde en bror som snakket norsk.*

(*b*) as object, often omitted as in English. *Her gir jeg tilbake brødet* (*som*) *jeg lånte av deg.* Here I am giving back the loaf (which) I borrowed from you.

(*c*) with a preposition, which must always follow at the end of the sentence. It can also be omitted here as in English.

Den piken (som) du danset med, var min søster. The girl you danced with was my sister. *Porten (som) de kjørte gjennom, var meget smal.* The gate (which) they drove through was very narrow.

(*d*) **som** has no genitive form. **Hvis** (genitive of *hvem*) may sometimes be used instead, but it should be remembered that this word is not colloquial.

Example: *Jeg møtte en mann, hvis navn jeg har glemt.* Whose name I have forgotten. But it is better to say: . . . *en mann som jeg har glemt navnet på.*

(2) **hva** can be used as a relative pronoun after **alt** (all, everything), but it can also very well be left out. *Hun fikk alt (hva) hun bad om.* She got everything she asked for. *Jeg gjorde alt (hva) jeg kunne for henne.* I did everything I could for her.

Other Relative Pronouns

200. For the sake of the written language we should perhaps also note a few other relative pronouns, which, however, are constantly losing ground in everyday conversation.

(1) **der** is scarcely ever heard in modern speech. It can only be used as a subject, in order to avoid the clash of two 'som's'.

(2) **hvilken** as relative pronoun is still used by some people. This pronoun can take a preposition in front of it.

Example: *Porten, gjennom hvilken* (through which) *vi kjørte.* It may sometimes refer to the contents of a whole sentence. *Han sa han hadde gjort det, hvilket* (which) *ikke var sant.*

(3) **hva** can also have this last function: *Han trodde han husket det, hva* (which) *han slett ikke gjorde. Han kalte seg ingeniør* [inʃ(ə)n'jøːr] (engineer), *hva* (which) *han slett ikke var.* (*slett ikke* = not at all.) The colloquial language very often uses: *noe (som)* in this connection. *Han holdt en tale, noe (som) han aldri hadde gjort før.* Something (that) he had never done before.

(4) The indefinite relatives: *den som* = he who; plural: *de som* = those who. *Den som ler sist, ler best*; *det som*, or *hva som* (*som* is very often omitted) = that which, what. *Mente du det du sa* (or: *hva du sa)?* Did you mean what you said?

Vocabulary

kamerat [kamə'raːt] c. comrade, friend
en gang once
være ute å gå be (out) walking
få øye på catch sight of
smette irr. v. slip
bli stående igjen be left standing
bjørn c. bear
snuse (-te) ⎱sniff, smell
lukte (-et) ⎰
snute c. snout
pust c. breath
tegn [tein] n. **til** sign of

rusle (-et) jog, slouch
krabbe (-et) crawl
hviske (-et) whisper
nøye adj. and adv. here: exactly, quite
livløs lifeless
sige (irr. v. **ei -e**) **over ende** drop to the ground
som om as if
ransake (-et) ransack, examine
alt sammen all of it
fare c. danger, emergency
stund c. time, while
prøve (-de) test

Exercise 36

De to kameratene og bjørnen

To gode venner var en gang ute og gikk på en vei. Rett som det var (*all of a sudden*), fikk den ene øye på en bjørn, og han smatt opp i et tre uten å si et ord til kameraten sin. Som vel var (*fortunately*), hadde den gutten som ble stående igjen[1] på veien, hørt folk si at bjørnen aldri rører en livløs. Derfor seig han over ende og lå som om han var død.

Bjørnen ransaket ham både vel og lenge, snuste og luktet og stakk snuten inn i øret hans. Men gutten holdt pusten og lå ganske stille. Da bjørnen ikke så noe tegn til liv, ruslet han til skogs igjen.[1]

Da all fare var over, krabbet den andre gutten ned fra treet, og de to vennene gikk sammen som før.

'Si meg en ting,' sa gutten som hadde sittet i treet, 'hva var det bjørnen hvisket i øret på deg?' (*in your ear?*). 'Å, jeg husker ikke så nøye alt sammen,' sa den andre. 'Men én ting minnes[2] jeg godt han sa. Jeg skulle aldri stole på en venn jeg ikke hadde prøvd i farens stund.'

Ordspråk. I nøden skal en kjenne sine venner. Hva er det tilsvarende ordspråk på engelsk?

[1] *Note on* **igjen.** *Igjen* may correspond to English: (1) again; (2) back; (3) left.

Examples: (1) When shall we meet again? *Når skal vi møtes igjen?*
(2) He shall have it back. *Han skal få det igjen.*
(3) I have no money left. *Jeg har ingen penger igjen.*

Useful idiom: *legge* (or *glemme*) *igjen* leave, or leave behind.

[2] Cf. para. 105

The Indefinite Pronouns and Adjectives

201. The indefinite pronouns can be divided into two categories: (1) Those that are used as pronouns only, and (2) those used both adjectivally and as true pronouns.

As Pronouns only

202. **man** is only used as subject. There is no real equivalent to this pronoun in the English language. It may be rendered either by: one, you, they, or by passive forms. (See para. 102.)

Example: *Man sier.* They say, people say, or better: It is said. *Man vet hva man har, men ikke hva man får.* You know what you have, but not what you are going to get. *Man vet aldri hva som kan hende.* There's no knowing what may happen.

203. **en** may replace **man** as subject.

Example: *En vet aldri.* One never knows, or you never know. It should be observed that **en** also may be used in the object case and has, moreover, a genitive form **ens**.

Object case: *Man vet aldri hva som kan hende en.* One never knows what may happen to one(self). Genitive case: *I slike stunder går ens tanker tilbake til hjemlandet.* On such occasions one's thoughts go back to the home country.

Vocabulary

bad n. 1, bath, 2, bathroom
kjenne seg som feel like
dusj c. shower
herde [ˈhærdə] **seg** harden oneself

riktig here = **virkelig** really
sunt adv. healthily
gymnastikk [gymnaˈstikk] c. gymnastics, exercise
like etter at just after

Exercise 37 on **en** (*man*)

Read and translate:

Det er godt (*nice*) med et bad om morgenen. En kjenner seg som et nytt menneske, særlig hvis en tar en dusj etterpå. En bør alltid ta en kald vask etter det varme badet for å herde seg. Hvis en riktig vil leve sunt, skal en ta morgengymnastikk like etter at en har stått opp, og så gå inn i badet.

As Pronouns and Adjectives

But most of the indefinite pronouns can be used adjectivally as well, just as in English. Here are the most common ones:

Common	Neuter	Plural
noen some, any, some- body, anybody	*noe*	*noen*

204. (*a*) In affirmative sentences **noen** corresponds to some, somebody, neuter **noe** to some, something. *Noen sier hun er død.* Some (or somebody) say(s) she is dead. *Noen mennesker er lurere enn andre.* Some people are smarter than others. *Det må være noe i det.* There must be something in it.

(*b*) In negative and interrogative sentences **noen** corresponds to English: any or anybody, neuter **noe** to any or anything.

Example: *Kjenner De noen norske sanger?* Do you know any Norwegian songs? *Ja, men jeg kan ikke noen utenat.* Yes, but I do not know any by heart. *Han fikk ikke noe svar.* He did not get any (or an) answer. Instead of neuter *noe*, an enlarged form *noenting* may be used: *Har du hørt noenting hjemmefra?* Have you heard anything from home?

205. The neuter form **noe** can also be put in front of collective and material nouns whatever the gender, meaning: **something (anything) of,** which is originally a partitive genitive.

Example: *Har du fått noe mat?* (*mat* is c. gender). English: Have you got some (any) food? *Vi har ikke fått noe melk i dag.* We haven't had any milk today.

206. Finally **noe** serves to modify an adjective, corresponding to English: 'somewhat'.

Det kan synes noe vanskelig. It may seem somewhat difficult. *Jeg har en engelsk bok her, men den er noe tung å lese.* I have an English book here, but it is somewhat heavy reading. Lit.: somewhat heavy to read.

noe in these sentences means the same as: '*litt*' (a little, a bit).

Vocabulary

penger N.B. pl. money
bank c. bank
om conj. if
bryte irr. **seg inn** break into

poesi [poə'siː] c. poetry
smak c. taste
drama ['draːma] n.; pl. **dramaer**
slik som like

Exercise 38a

Fill in the correct forms of *noen*, *noe*, and translate afterwards:

Har du n.. penger? Nei, kan du låne meg n..? Jeg kan fortelle deg n.. nytt, n.. riktig (*really*) spennende. N.. tyver har brutt seg inn i banken og stjålet n.. hundre tusen kroner.

Har du lest n.. av Bjørnson? Jeg har lest n.. få skuespill og et par dikt. Han har skrevet n.. fine dikt som du må lese. Du vet kanskje at n.. av hans skuespill har vært spilt i England? Jeg liker n.. av Ibsens verker bedre. Ja, n.. liker Ibsen, andre liker Bjørnson. Det ville ikke være bra om alle hadde (*the*) samme smak.

Men jeg har ikke funnet n.. som kan bygge opp et drama slik som Ibsen. Å gå på teater er n.. av det morsomste jeg vet.

Vocabulary

få tak i get hold of
kjøtt n. meat

for—siden ago

Exercise 38b

Some believe there are people on the moon. I have bought some flowers for (*til*) you. I didn't think you could get hold of any today. They had some left. Have you got any meat? Yes, I got some, but it was very difficult. Did you see the car? No, I did not see any car. Some friends arrived an hour ago, some of our very (*aller*) best friends from Drammen.

| c. | n. | pl. |

207. *ingen* no, nobody, none; *intet, ingen.*

ingen is the direct opposite of **noen**, and therefore the expression: '**ikke noen**,' as we have already seen, often replaces **ingen**, especially in colloquial speech. The neuter

intet is now almost invariably a paper word, so when speaking we use either **ingenting,** which is always treated as a noun, or **ikke noe,** which, as we know, can be used adjectivally as well.

Example: Pronominally—*Ingen visste noe om det.* Nobody knew anything about it. *Jeg kjenner ingen her i byen.* I know nobody in this town. *Han visste ingenting* (or *ikke noe*). He knew nothing.

Proverb: *Det skjer intet nytt under solen.* There is nothing new under the sun. *Noe er bedre enn ingenting.* Something is better than nothing. *Det er ikke noe rart.* That is nothing strange.

Adjectivally: *Jeg har ingen anelse* [ˇaːn(ə)lsə] *om det.* I have no idea about it. *Det gir ingen mening.* It does not make sense. *Småguttene hadde ikke noe hjem.* The youngsters had no home. *Vi hadde ingen* (or *ikke noen*) *penger.* We had no money.

Note the following example, where the noun is omitted in the second sentence: *Du har noen penger, men jeg har ingen.* You have some money, but I have *none.*

	c.	n.	pl.
208.	*annen* [ˇaːn] other, else;	*annet* [ˇaːnt]	*andre.*

=another, some other. *Vent til en annen dag.* Wait till another day. *En annen gang.* Another time. *Det er en annen historie.* That is another story. *Den ene—den andre,* one—the other: *den ene dagen etter den andre gikk.* One day after the other passed.

209. Note: The Norwegian **annen** does not have the meaning of 'additional' which **another** can have, e.g. Could I have another cup of coffee, please? *Kunne jeg få en kopp kaffe* **til? En annen kopp** means **a different cup,** which would imply that you were not satisfied with the first one. I need another ten kroner. *Jeg trenger ti kroner til.*

Rule: When 'another' has the meaning of 'additional' it must be translated with **til.**

210. = other. *Jeg har annet* (or *andre ting*) *å gjøre.* I have other things to do. *Er det noen andre nyheter?* Is there any other news? *Vær så vennlig og bruk den andre inngangen!* Use the other entrance, please!

Some idioms translated: Somehow or other = *på en eller annen måte*, someone or other = *en eller annen*, the other day = *forleden* [fɔʳˈleːdn̩] *dag*, every other day = *hver'annen dag*.

211. = else. *Vil De ha noe annet i stedet?* Will you have something else instead? *Ingen annen* = no one else. *Ingen annen enn du vet om det.* No one but you knows about it.

= different. *Det er no ganske annet.* That is something quite different. Cf. para. 209.

      c.   n.   pl.

212. *all* all; *alt, alle*.

Before material words: *All maten ble spist. All makt i denne sal* (i.e. *Stortinget*). All power in this room. *Kjemp for alt hva du har kjært.* (First line of a well-known song.) Fight for all/everything that is dear to you. *Alt eller intet.* All or nothing, *alt = allting. Når enden er god, er allting godt.* All is well that ends well. *Alle de andre.* All the others. *Det er noe alle vet.* Everybody knows that. *Vi vet alle at . . .* We all know that . . . (note place of **alle**). Very often **sammen** is added to **alle**. *Vi vet alle sammen at . . . God natt alle sammen!* Good night everybody! Idioms: **allslags** all kinds of, **fremfor alt** above all, **Når alt kommer til alt.** After all, **En gang for alle.** Once and for all. **overalt** = everywhere.

      c.   n.

213. *(en)hver* (every, each), *(et)hvert*.

Han kom hver dag. Emphatic: *Hver eneste dag.* Every single day. *Hver dag har nok med sin egen plage.* Each day has enough with its own sorrow. *Alle og enhver* each and everybody.

Idiom: *hver for seg* = separately. *Tell dem hver for seg.* Count them separately. *Hver for seg er de ganske hyggelige, men sammen er de fæle.* Individually they are quite nice, but together they are horrible.

      c.   n.   pl.

214. *Mangen* many a; *mangt, mange*.

This word is composed of **mange** and the indefinite article

c. **en,** n. **et,** but the feeling for the article gradually disappeared, which is clearly shown by the fact that it can be
added anew.

mangen en, mangt et.

mangen gang many a time, more often *mange ganger. Man
hører så mangt* (= *så meget*) so much. The comparative of
mange is **flere,** which can also have a more independent
meaning = several. *Jeg har gjort det flere ganger* = several
times, but *flere folk enn . . .* = more people than *. . . mange
flere* = many more.

Interrogatives as Indefinite Pronouns

215. (1) The interrogative pronouns can also be used as
indefinite pronouns in conjunction with the two words **som
helst.**

Examples:

Du kan spørre (ask) **hvem som helst.** anybody, whoever
you like.

Han kan spille (play) **hva som helst.** anything, whatever
it is.

Du kan velge (choose) **hvilken som helst.** whichever you
like (with neuter *hvilket* and plural *hvilke*).

(2) Moreover, the same generalizing idea can be expressed
by using the word **enn** instead (very often preceded by the
adverb **nå** or **så**).

Examples:

Hva du   (*nå,* or *så*) **enn** *sier.* whatever you say.
Hvem du (,, ,, ,,) **enn** *er.* whoever you are.
Hvilken du (,, ,, ,,) **enn** *tar.* whichever you take.

(3) The same construction can be applied with regard to
the adverb **hvor** = (1) where, (2) how (before adj. and adv.),
e.g.: **hvor som helst** (anywhere); **hvor** *du* **enn** *går* wherever
you go; **hvor** *flink du* **enn** *er* however clever you are.

Learn the following words:

dikter c. poet
humo'ristisk humorous
være‑til stede, ved be present at
komme til å here: happen to
side c. side
ved siden av beside, by

foretaksom [ˈfɔːrətaːksɔm] enterprising
i løpet av in the course of, during
videre further
forlovet [fɔrˈloːvət] engaged to be married

Exercise 39a

Translate into English:

Fort gjort

Johan Herman Wessel er en kjent norsk dikter som skrev muntre humoristiske vers. Han var en gang til stede ved en stor middag, hvor han kom til å sitte ved siden av en meget foretaksom dame. Denne damen var svært interessert i Wessel, og i løpet av samtalen spurte hun plutselig dikteren: 'Hvorfor er De ikke gift, herr Wessel?' 'Jeg har ikke noen penger,' svarte Wessel. 'Men det har *jeg*,' sa damen. Historien forteller videre at før de reiste seg fra bordet, var de alt forlovet.

Vocabulary

linje c. line
trett av tired of
elvebredd c. river bank
et par ganger once or twice

kikke (-et) ned i peep into
samtale c. conversation
Hva nytte c. kan en ha av ... What is the use of ...

Exercise 39b

Translate into Norwegian:

The first lines of *Alice in Wonderland*.

Alice was beginning to get very tired of sitting (tr. to sit) by her sister on the bank, and having nothing to do; once or twice she had peeped into the book her sister was reading, but it had no pictures or conversations (in it),[1] 'and what is the use of a book,' thought Alice, 'which has not got[1] any pictures or conversations?'

[1] to be left untranslated.

CHAPTER XVI

THE PRESENT PARTICIPLE

216. The Norwegian Present Participle in **-ende** pron. [(ə)nə] can be used:

(1) As an adjective: *en dansende pike* a dancing girl.

(2) As an adverb: *Han snakket engelsk helt glimrende.* He spoke English quite excellently. *Han har en påfallende pen kone.* He has a strikingly pretty wife.

(3) After the verbs **bli** (= for'bli = remain, stay), **komme, finne:** *Bare bli sittende!* Just remain seated! *Han kom gående.* He came walking. *Jeg fant ham liggende i gresset.* I found him lying in the grass.

(4) After the verbs **se** (see) and **høre** (hear) the infinitive is used in Norwegian. *Jeg så ham komme* (or a complete clause: *at han kom* I saw him coming). *Jeg hørte ham spille Beethoven.* I heard him play(ing) Beethoven.

Note: I like to listen (*or* listening) to the radio. *Jeg liker å høre (på) radio.* He has stopped smoking. *Han har sluttet å røke.*

(5) After certain verbs English uses the present participle. Ex.: *She sat reading a novel.* In such cases Norwegian must use co-ordinated verbs. *Hun satt og leste.* Lit. She sat and read. *Hunden lå og sov.* The dog lay sleeping.

217. Very often an English participial construction must be rendered by a whole clause. It may be:

(1) A relative clause: A man going to Norway. *En mann som reiser til Norge.* He sent me a letter telling me about his life. *Han sendte meg et brev hvor han fortalte meg om sitt liv.*

(2) A clause of time: (On) opening the letter, he saw that ... *Da han åpnet brevet, så han at ...* Before leaving he gave me a book. *Før han gikk, ga han meg en bok.* (Before he left ...)

(3) A causal clause: Being too young I did not get in. *Da jeg var for ung, kom jeg ikke inn.* As I was too young ... Cf. page 161.

CHAPTER XVII

PREPOSITIONS

218. In the course of our study we have already learned some prepositions. These are rather tricky in any language, so we ought to devote a little more attention to them. Always look out for them and their uses in the text.

219. av (1) (part) of.

Jeg fikk bare en liten del av pengene.	I got only a small part of the money.
En venn av meg, oss, etc.	A friend of mine, ours, etc.
Hans far er medlem av Stortinget.	His father is a member of the Storting (i.e. the Norwegian Parliament).
Måltidet bestod av brød og melk.	The meal consisted of bread and milk.
Koppen er laget av tre -or just: *Koppen er av tre.*	The cup is made of wood.

Note expressions like: *en kopp te, et glass vin, en flaske melk, et par sko, ski; et par dager* a couple of days, etc., where English has the preposition 'of', whilst Norwegian places the words in apposition. The same with dates: *den 14. juli, den fjortende juli* the fourteenth of July.

(2) reason, cause.

Jeg dør av spenning.	I am dying of suspense.
Han er grønn av misunnelse.	He is green with envy.
Hun gråt av glede.	She wept for joy.

(3) Denoting the agent = **by**, see para. 106.

Jeg leser et dikt av Bjørnson.	I am reading a poem by Bjørnson.
Hun leser en roman av Lie.	She is reading a novel by Lie.

220. bak, bakom = behind.

Mannen bak disken.	The man behind the counter.
Bak teppet.	Behind the curtain.
På baksiden av huset.	At the back of the house.

221.   blant or **iblant** = among.

Han er lystig blant venner.	He is merry among friends.
Blant annet.	Among others.
adv. *iblant*	occasionally

222.   etter (1) = after.

Mannen fulgte etter meg.	The man followed (after) me.
Hunden løp etter bilen.	The dog ran after the car.
Vi skal gjøre det etter frokost.	We shall do it after breakfast.

(2) = in search of, for.

Din mor leter etter deg.	Your mother is looking for you.
Hva er det du ser etter?	What are you looking for?
Jeg lengter etter sommeren.	I am longing for the summer.

(3) = according to.

Etter loven er dette galt.	According to law this is wrong.
Alt gikk etter planen.	Everything went according to plan.
Etter hva jeg har hørt . . .	From (according to) what I have heard . . .

223.   for = for.

Jeg skal gjøre det for deg.	I will do it for you.
Ikke for Dem, mine damer.	Not for you, my ladies.
Gjør det for min skyld.	Do it for my sake.
For alt jeg vet.	For all I know.
Hvor mye ga du for bilen?	How much did you pay for the car?
Den er borte for alltid.	It is gone for ever.

Note: *i stedet for* (or *istedenfor*) instead of, *å være redd for* to be afraid of, *for to år siden* two years ago.

English 'for' occasionally corresponds to Norwegian **til** or **om**; see paras. 240(3), 237(2).

Her er et brev til deg.	Here is a letter for you.
Be ikke meg om hjelp!	Do not ask me for help!

224. foran ['forran] = in front of, before. The opposite of **bak**.

Hun satt foran meg på kino.	She sat in front of me in the cinema.
Foran og bak.	In front and at the back.
Dagbladet er alltid foran.	Dagbladet is always ahead.

225. forbi [for'bi:] past, by.

Han gikk forbi meg uten å hilse.	He passed without greeting me.
Kan jeg få komme (slippe) forbi Dem?	Can I get (slip) past (by) you?

226. fra and **i'fra** = from.

Fra morgen til aften.	From morning to night.
Har du hørt fra ham?	Have you heard from him?
Gå ikke ifra meg.	Do not leave me.
Gutten kom fra Norge.	The boy came from Norway.
Fra tid til annen.	From time to time.
Fra dag til dag.	From day to day.

227. før (1) = before.

Før Kristi fødsel ['føtsəl] c.	Before Christ.
Før siste krig.	Before the last war.

(2) = till, in negative statements.

Jeg så ham ikke før i går.	I did not see him till yesterday.
Jeg har aldri forstått deg før i aften.	I have never understood you till tonight.

228. gjennom ['jennɔm] or **igjennom** = through.

Gjennom tykt og tynt.	Through thick and thin.
De kjørte gjennom porten.	They drove through the gate.
Jeg lærte ham å kjenne gjennom herr O.	I got to know him through Mr O.

229. hos [hoss] (1) = with, in one's company; cf. French **chez**.

Jeg bor hos min onkel.	I live with my uncle, i.e. at my uncle's.
Vi gjør ikke det hos oss.	We don't do that in my country (*or* where I come from).
Vi skal ha noen kjente hos oss i dag.	We are having some acquaintances at home today.

(2) = at, in one's house, shop, etc.

Jeg har vært hos barbereren.	I have been at the barber's.
Du får kjøpt tøy hos skredderen.	You will be able to buy material at the tailor's.

230. i (1) = in.

Min bror arbeider i haven.	My brother is working in the garden.
Andersens bor i Oslo.	The Andersens live in Oslo.

(2) = at; in connection with smaller towns, streets, etc.

Min søster bor i Larvik.	My sister lives at Larvik.
I Kirkeveien 23.	At 23 Church Road.

= at; time.

I samme øyeblikk.	At the same moment.
I begynnelsen.	At the beginning.

(3) = into; often in conjunction with adverbs like: **inn, ut, ned,** etc.

Piken falt i vannet.	The girl fell into the water.
Svømmeren hoppet ut i elva.	The swimmer jumped into the river.
Ballen trillet ned i hullet.	The ball rolled into the hole.

(4) = for; denoting length of time, however, often omitted.

Krigen varte i fem lange år.	The war lasted for five long years.
Mine foreldre bodde der bare (i) noen få uker.	My parents only stayed there (for) a few weeks.

(5) = during, in the course of. See **under.**

I de siste årene av sitt liv bodde han i Sverige.	During the last (latter) years of his life he lived in Sweden.

(6) Useful prepositional phrases of time:

i dag today	**i år** this year
i morgen tomorrow	**i fjor** last year
i morges [i ˇmɔrrəs] this morning	**i vår** this spring
	i fjor vår last spring
i ettermiddag this afternoon	**i høst** this autumn
i kveld, i aften this evening, tonight	**i fjor høst** last autumn
	i sommer this summer
i natt last night	**i vinter** this winter

Example: What are you going to do tonight? *Hva skal du gjøre i kveld?*

231.   ifølge [iˇfølgə] = according to.

232.   innen = within, about place usually **innenfor.**

Du må betale regningen innen en uke.	You must pay the bill within a week.
Innenfor (or innen) rekkevidde.	Within reach.

233.   inntil/see **til** = to, close to.

Tett inntil veggen.	Close to the wall.

234.   med [meː] (1) = with, in company with.

Jeg reiste (sammen) med ham til London.	I went with him to London.
Jeg har arbeidet sammen med ham i mange år.	I have worked with him for many years.

(2) = with, by (the help of); suggesting instrument with which the action is performed.

Han slo meg med stokken.	He beat me with the stick.
Det er ikke pent å spise med kniven.	It is not nice to eat with the knife.
Reise med tog, fly, bus.	Travel by train, air, bus.
Turisten betalte med sjekk.	The tourist paid by cheque.
Snakke, tale med noen.	Speak with, to (= converse) somebody.
Snakke, tale til noen.	Address, accost somebody.
Med største fornøyelse.	With the greatest pleasure.
Med stor vanskelighet.	With great difficulty.

235. mellom ['mellɔm] = between.

Mellom oss sagt.	Between us.
Alt mellom himmel og jord.	Everything under·the sun.

236. mot or **imot** (1) = towards; direction.

Han kom imot meg.	He ´came towards me.
Mot slutten av uken.	Towards the end of the week.
'Mot kveld' av Agathe Backer Grøndahl.	'Towards evening' by A. B. G. (a famous Norwegian composer).

(2) = against.

Vi hadde vinden mot oss.	We had the wind against us.
De som ikke er med oss, er mot oss.	Those who are not with us are against us.
Hva har De imot meg?	What have you against me?
Å kjempe mot fienden.	To fight (against) the enemy.

(3) = to, *gjøre mot* = do to.

Gjør mot andre hva du vil at de skal gjøre mot deg.	Do to others what you want others to do to you.
Være snill, vennlig mot.	Be nice, kind to (towards).

The opposite is:

Være lei or slem mot.	Be unkind, nasty to.

237. om [ɔmm] (1) = about, of. In a great number of expressions where 'om' introduces a topic.

å skrive om to write about, *å lese om* to read about, *å høre om*, to hear about, *å snakke, tale* om to talk, speak about, *å tro, mene om* to think about, *å vite om* to know about, *å si om* to say about, *å fortelle om* to tell about, etc.

N.B.—What are we going to do about it? = *Hva skal vi gjøre ved det?*

Fortell meg om det.	Tell me about it.
Hva mener du om det (ham)?	What do you think about it (him)?
Han sa ikke noe om det.	He did not say anything about it.

I går så vi en film om Norge.	Yesterday we saw a film about Norway.
Den handlet om Norges fiske'rier.	It dealt with (was about) the fisheries of Norway.
Taleren snakket om Irland.	The speaker talked about (on) Ireland.

(2) = for, expressing a wish: *be* or *spørre om* ask for, *tigge om* beg for.

(3) = in, during, on; about a time or season when something usually takes place.

Om sommeren bader vi.	In summer we go swimming.
Om vinteren går vi på ski.	In winter we go skiing.

Similarly:

om våren in spring	*om høsten* in the autumn
om morgenen in the morning	*om natten* at night, by night
om formiddagen in the forenoon	*om dagen* in the daytime, by day
om ettermiddagen in the afternoon	*om aftenen, om kvelden* in the evening

Note the following phrases where English lacks preposition: *tre ganger om dagen* three times a day, *to timer om uken* two hours a week.

(4) = in, after a lapse of a certain time: *om fem minutter* in five minutes, *om ti år* in ten years.

Jeg skal være tilbake om ti minutter.	I shall be back in ten minutes.

(5) = about, around; denoting place.

Drei om hjørnet.	Turn around the corner.
Hun hadde et belte om livet.	She had a belt round her waist.

But in this meaning, *omkring* [ɔm'kriŋ] is more used, or combinations like: *rundt (om)* and *rundt omkring*.

Rundt om i verden. Round about the world. *Rundt haven gikk det et gjerde* [ˇjæːrə] (= a fence) or *Omkring haven*, etc.

(6) N.B. for 'about', meaning approximately, Norwegian uses: *om'kring, om'trent, 'cirka (ca), en* (= some).

Han er omkring førti år.	He is about 40.

238. over ['ɔːvər] (1) = over, across, above.

Hun gikk over gaten.	She went across the street.
Han svømte over elva.	He swam across the river.
Fuglen fløy over taket.	The bird flew over the roof.
Det går over min forstand.	It is beyond me.

(2) = of, comprising.

Et kart over Oslo. (= *et oslokart.*)	A map of Oslo.
En liste over passasjerene. (= *en passasjerliste.*)	A list of the passengers.

(3) = over, more than.

Det er over seks år siden nå.	It is more than six years ago now.

(4) With verbs and adjectives:

Klage over complain about (of), *forbauset over* surprised at, *skuffet over* disappointed in, *være klar over* be aware of.

239. på (1) = on, on top of, in.

på bordet on the table, *på scenen* [ˇseːn(ə)n] on the stage, *på fjellet* in the mountains, *på gaten* in the street.

(2) = in, at; in many place-names with *øy* island, *berg* or *fjell* mountain, and smaller inland towns: *på De britiske øyer* in the British Isles, *på Island* in Iceland, *på Lillehammer* at Lillehammer.

Note: *gå på skole(n)* go to school, *gå på kino* go to the cinema, *gå på apoteket* go to the chemist's.

(3) = of—instead of a genitive.

navnet på gaten the name of the street, *tittelen på boken* the title of the book, *nummeret* ['nomrə] *på billetten* the number of the ticket.

(4) = at, about time.

På den tid.	At that time.
På Harald Hårfagres tid.	At the time of Harold the Fairhaired.

(5) **På** is very much used in connection with verbs and adjectives: *tenke på* think of, *tvile på* doubt, *stole på* rely on, *skjenne på* scold, *høre på* listen to, *vente på* wait for, *svare på et brev* answer a letter, *minne en på* remind somebody of, *være sint på* be angry with.

Idiom: *På denne måte(n)* = In this way.

240. til (1) = to; denoting the direction.

Vi skal til byen i dag.	We are going to town today.
Min sønn kom til Oslo forrige mandag.	My son came to Oslo last Monday.

(2) = till, about time limits.

Jeg kan bli til klokka fem.	I can stay till 5 o'clock.
Vent til jeg kommer.	Wait till I come.
Kontortiden er fra ni til fire.	Office hours are from nine to four.

(3) = for, meant for (cf. **for**, para. 223).

Det er brev til deg.	There is a letter for you.
Skal De ha egg til frokost.	Do you want an egg for (your) breakfast.
Til minne om . . .	In memory of . . .
Oversette fra norsk til engelsk.	Translate from Norwegian into English.

241. under ['unnər] (1) = under, below, beneath.

Vi rodde under brua.	We rowed under the bridge.
Det er intet nytt under solen.	There is nothing new under the sun.
Han bor i etasjen under meg.	He lives on the floor just below me.

(2) = during, in the course of a special period.

Jeg besøkte henne under mitt opphold i Bergen.	I visited her during my stay in Bergen.
Under krigen tjenestegjorde jeg under oberst K.	During the war I served under Colonel K.
I (løpet av) de siste få år.	During the last few years.

unntagen [unn'taːgən] = **unntatt** ['unntatt] = except.

Alle vet det, unntagen mor.	Everybody knows it, except mother.

242.   uten = without.

Uten tvil.	Without doubt.
Jeg kan ikke leve uten deg.	I can't live without you.
Proverb: *Uten mat og drikke du(g)er helten ikke.*	Without food and drink, the hero is not much good.

243.   utenfor = outside.

Han bor et stykke utenfor byen.	He lives some way outside the town.

244.   ved (1) = by the side of, near, at.

De satt ved bordet og spiste.	They sat at the table eating.
Mine foreldre bor like ved stasjonen.	My parents live just near the station.
Min svigerfar bor ved sjøen.	My father-in-law lives by the sea.
Båten ligger ved brygga (kaien).	The boat is alongside the quay.
Slaget ved Waterloo	The Battle of Waterloo
Studere ved universitetet.	Study at the university.
Vi stanset ved porten.	We stopped at the gate.
Stolen står borte ved vinduet.	The chair is over by the window.

(2) = by, through, by the help of; indicating the means or methods by which the action is performed, often in connection with the infinitive.

Han reddet livet ved å svømme.	He saved his life by swimming.
Ved hjelp av	By the help of, by means of
Ved egen hjelp	By one's own effort
Ved egne midler	By one's own means
Due to: *Ved en misforståelse*	By a misunderstanding

(3) = at, approximate time.

Han ble skutt ved daggry.	He was shot at dawn.
Ved farens død reiste han hjemmefra.	On the death of his father he left home.

Vocabulary

knekke (-te) crack
nøtt f. nut
mark c. worm
markspist worm-eaten
med det samme at the same
  moment
fanden [ˇfaːŋ] the devil
tvinge (irr. a-u) force
knapp c. button
nål f. needle
hull n. hole
knappenålshull n. pin-hole
selvfølgelig [selˈfølgəli] of
  course
ikke før—før no sooner—than
pinne c. peg
stykke n. piece, here distance

smie f. smithy
smed [smeː] c. smith
sund }
iˈstykker} to pieces
hammer c. hammer
ambolt c. anvil
sint angry
storslegge [ˇstoːʳʃleggə] f.
  sledgehammer
bit c. bit, piece
tak n. roof
fly (irr. øy-øy) av fly off
som om as if
brake (-et) make noise
hytte f. hut
ramle (-et) ned tumble down,
  collapse

Exercise 40a

Read aloud. Then try to relate it.

Gutten og fanden
Et norsk folkeeventyr (folk-tale)

Det var en gang en gutt som gikk på en vei og knekte
nøtter. Så fant han en som var markspist, og med det
samme møtte han fanden. 'Er det sant,' sa gutten, 'det de
sier at fanden kan gjøre seg så liten han vil, og tvinge seg
gjennom et knappenålshull?' 'Ja, selvfølgelig,' svarte
fanden. 'Å, la meg se deg gjøre det; kryp inn i denne nøtta
hvis du kan,' sa gutten. Og fanden gjorde det. Men han var
ikke før kommet inn gjennom markhullet, før gutten satte
i en liten pinne. 'Nå har jeg deg der,' sa han, og stakk nøtta i
lomma.

Da han hadde gått et stykke, kom han til en smie. Der gikk
han inn, og bad smeden om han ville slå sund nøtta for
ham. 'Ja, det skal være lett gjort,' sa smeden, og tok den
minste hammeren han hadde, la nøtta på ambolten og slo
til, men den ville ikke i stykker. Så tok han en litt større
hammer, men den var ikke stor nok heller. Han tok da en
enda større en, men nei, - nøtta ville ikke i stykker. Men
så ble smeden sint og tok storslegga. 'Jeg skal vel snart få

deg i stykker,' sa han og slo så hardt til at nøtta gikk i tusen biter, og halve smietaket fløy av, og det braket som om hytta skulle ramle ned.

'Jeg mener fanden var i nøtta, jeg,' sa smeden.

'Ja, han var så,' sa gutten.

Note: Look carefully at the punctuation of this piece and see if there are any striking differences between English and Norwegian in the use of the various stops.

Vocabulary (gloser)

like ved just by
eie (-de) own
ve'randa c. veranda
neppe or nesten ikke hardly
på grunn av on account of
busk c. bush
alle slags all kinds of
blomst [blɔmst] c. flower
rose [ˇroːsə] c. rose
sti c. (foot)path
føre (-te) lead
plante (-et) plant
hekk c. hedge

hoved [ˇhoːvəd] main
inngang c. entrance
etasje [əˈtaːʃə] storey (floor)
pleide or brukte used to
i 'nærheten in the neighbourhood
vende (-te) mot v. face
buss c. bus
på vei til on its etc. way to
brygge f. kai c. quay
være interessert i be interested
  in
avstand c. distance

Exercise 40b

I have *for* many years lived just *by* the Oslofjord *in* a small town which is called Moss. My parents own a large beautiful house there. *In front of* it there is a veranda *with* large windows. One can hardly see our house *from* the street *on account of* the garden *with* all the trees and bushes. *In* summer it is full *of* all kinds of flowers and roses. A footpath leads *up to* the house, and *on* each side *of* this path a hedge is planted (tr. is there planted a hedge). If one goes *through* the garden, one comes *to* the main entrance. The house consists *of* three storeys *with* seven rooms *on* (tr. *in*) each floor. *Behind* the house there is a wood, and here we used to play *in* the afternoon when (*når*) we came home *from* school (tr. the school).

Ten years *ago* there were no houses *in* the neighbourhood, but *during* the last years *about* a dozen new houses have been built *on* both sides *of* the street.

My window faces the street and I can see all the buses and cars which drive *past* our house. They are *on* their way either *to* the quay or the station.

I lived *with* my parents until I was twenty years old. Later I went *to* Oslo *in order to* study languages which I have always been interested *in*. (Note place of adverb in a subordinate clause.)

I went home *in* my holidays as the distance *between* Oslo and Moss is not (note place of adverb here) more than sixty kilometres, or *about* thirty-seven English miles.

During my stay *in* Oslo I made (tr. got) many friends *from* all parts *of* the country, and I saw and learnt many things which I have never heard *of* before.

Vocabulary

være ferdig med have finished
høre (på) radio c. listen to radio
apparat [appaˊraːt] n. apparatus
ˊradioapparat wireless set
hjørne n. corner
skruˊ (-dde) på screw, switch on
stille (-te) inn på tune in on
kikke (-et) peep, glance
program [proˊgramm] n. programme
Norsk Rikskringkasting Norwegian State Broadcasting

ˊutgjøre constitute, make up
spennende thrilling, exciting
fotballkamp c. football match
idrettsstevne n. sports meeting
kringkaste (-et) broadcast
kåseri [kɔsəˊriː] n. short talk
foredrag [ˇfɔːrədraːg] n. lecture
aktuell current, topical
emne n. subject, topic
interˊvjue (-et) interview
værmelding c. weather forecast
ˊnyhet (pl. -er) c. news
post [pɔst] c. here: item

Exercise 40c

Radio

Når jeg er ferdig med dagens arbeid, liker jeg å sitte hjemme og høre radio, især i de lange vinterkveldene. Radioapparatet står i hjørnet av stua, og alt jeg behøver å gjøre, er å skru det på og stille inn på den stasjonen jeg ønsker.

Hver dag kikker jeg i radioprogrammet som Norsk Rikskringkasting sender ut. Her er det noe for enhver smak. Musikken utgjør den største delen av programmet—førti proˊsent eller kanskje mer. Det spilles både lett musikk og tyngre klassiske verker. Sanger synges av førsteklasses sangere og sangerinner. Det blir sendt skuespill og andre dramatiske arbeider. Spennende historier og fortellinger for barn blir lest i barnetimen hver lørdag ettermiddag. Viktige fotballkamper og idrettsstevner blir kringkastet.

Man får høre kåserier og foredrag om aktuelle emner, og kjente folk blir intervjuet. Den daglige værmeldingen og nyheter (dagsnytt) er populære poster på programmet, og tidssignalet sendes tre ganger om dagen.

Dagens sending avsluttes svært ofte med nasjonalsangen. Og da er det tid til å si God natt.

Revise Passive, page 56.

Første vers [væʃʃ] av *Den norske nasjonalsang*

> Ja, vi elsker dette landet
> som det stiger[1] frem[2]
> furet,[3] værbitt[4] over vannet,
> med de tusen hjem,
> elsker, elsker det og tenker
> på vår far og mor
> og den saganatt[5] som senker[6]
> drømme[7] på vår jord.[8]

[1] (e—e) irr. rise; [2] *frem* = *fram* forward, forth; [3] furrowed; [4] weather-beaten; [5] *saga—night* symbolizing Norway's ancient history; [6] (-*et*) bring down, lower; [7] obs. for *drømmer* dreams; [8] earth.

English version, see page 217.

Prepositions before the Infinitive
Rendering of the English Gerund

245. One of the first things that is bound to strike an Englishman learning Norwegian is the special use of the infinitive. It has already been mentioned that any kind of preposition can be placed in front of it without affecting the form of the infinitive at all. In other words there is no form corresponding to the English *-ing* form used after prepositions and certain types of verbs.

Examples:

He left **without saying** good-bye.	*Han gikk* **uten å si** *farvel.*
After having eaten.	**Etter å ha** *spist.*
I enjoy **ski-ing.**	*Jeg liker* **å gå** *på ski.*

246. A great many nouns, adjectives and verbs are followed by prepositions plus the infinitive. To find the right preposition here may sometimes be difficult. English may have a preposition plus *-ing* form, or just the infinitive with '*to*'. Of the vast number of expressions of this kind a few useful examples will be singled out by way of illustration.

Nouns:

håp n. **om å se**	hope **of seeing**
sjanse **for å få**	chance **of getting**
middel **til å finne**	means **of finding**
forsøk **på å gjøre**	attempt(s) **at making, to make**

Adjectives and Past Participles:

glad **i å lese**	fond **of reading**
lei *trett* } **av å vente**	tired **of waiting**
sikker **på å beholde**	sure **of keeping**
glad **over å se**	glad **to see**
forbauset **over å høre**	surprised **to hear** (at hearing)
redd **for å dø**	afraid **to die**
god, flink **til å tegne**	good, clever **at drawing**

PREPOSITIONS **153**

Verbs:

anklage (-et)⎫
be'skylde (-te)⎭ *en for å*

accuse someone of
+ *-ing* form

Examples:

Naboen vår er blitt **beskyldt for å ha** *stjålet en sekk po' teter.*

Our neighbour has been **accused of having** stolen a sack of potatoes.

247. One further point should be mentioned, where English *'to'* is used for Norwegian: (1) **å**; (2) **for å**; (3) **til·å.**

(1) The infinitive with *å* is very frequently used as an object of a verb and also, though far more rarely, as a subject. In many instances English could here employ the *-ing* form, which goes to show that the infinitive is really a noun here.

Examples—*As a subject:*

Å lære å gå på ski er ikke så lett.

To learn to ski is not so easy.

Å være eller ikke være, det er spørsmålet.

To be or not **to be,** that is the question.

As an object:

Jeg lærte **å kjøre** *i fjor.*
Hun glemte **å svare.**

I learnt **to drive** last year.
She forgot **to answer.**

(2) **for å** is used of purpose = in order to, with the object of.

So whenever *to* is equivalent to: *in order to*, use **for å** in Norwegian.

Examples:

Jeg må (gå) på stasjonen **for å** *møte ham.*

I must go to the station to meet him.

Jeg har spart penger **for å** *kjøpe en gave til min søster.*

I have saved money to buy a present for my sister.

(3) **til å**—*'til'* is here a preposition in a more concrete sense than 'for' in *'for å'*. It is used in certain prepositional expressions in connection with nouns, adjectives and verbs.

Examples—*Nouns:*

Jeg har ikke tid **til å** *gjøre det.*	I haven't time to do it.
Det var grunn **til å** *tro det var sant.*	There was reason to believe it was true.
Jeg har stor lyst **til å** *gjøre det.*	I have a great mind to do it.
Du har rett **til å** *gjøre det.*	You have a right to do it.

Adjectives:

Han var ferdig **til å** *reise.*	He was ready to leave.

Above all when the adjective is used in connection with the adverbs: **for** (too) and **nok** (enough):

Du er **for** *ung til å gå til sjøs.*	You are too young to go to sea.
Det er **for** *godt til å være sant.*	It is too good to be true.
Han er dum **nok til å** *gjøre det.*	He is stupid enough to do it.

Very often after superlatives where the infinitive does the work of a relative clause:

Han var den første **til å** *le (= som lo).*	He was the first to laugh (who laughed).

Verbs:

Han ble oppfordret **til å** *synge.*	He was called upon to sing.
De tvang meg **til å** *tie.*	They forced me to keep quiet.

Note: *til å begynne med* = to begin with.

Infinitive in English rendered by Subordinate Clause in Norwegian

(See also para. 175)

248. The infinitive in English can be used in a more free and elastic way than in Norwegian. After verbs expressing desire and volition English employs the infinitive which, when rendered into Norwegian, must be transformed into a subordinate clause introduced by '*at*' (that). This '*at*', however, is very often omitted, especially in everyday speech, e.g.:

I want you **to do it**.	*Jeg vil* (at) **du skal gjøre det.**
I want you **to come**.	*Jeg vil* (at) **du skal komme.**

Nelson's famous words: 'England expects every man to do his duty,' must in Norwegian be rendered thus: *England venter at hver man gjør sin plikt.*

249. In cases where the infinitive is preceded by the adverbs how = *hvordan, hvorledes,* where = *hvor,* the pronoun what = *hva,* or the conjunction when = *når,* we find examples of the same phenomenon:

Infinitive	Subord. Clause
He showed me **how to do it**.	*Han viste meg hvordan jeg skulle gjøre det.*
She did not know **where to go**.	*Hun visste ikke hvor hun skulle gå (hen).*
I did not know **what to do**.	*Jeg visste ikke hva jeg skulle gjøre.*
He did not know **when to say stop**.	*Han visste ikke når han skulle si stopp.*

å omitted

250. Like English 'to', *å* is omitted after the modal auxiliaries and verbs like: *høre* hear, *se* see, *føle* feel.

After: *be* ask and *gidde* care to, some people leave out the *å,* others do not. Examples: *Jeg bad ham (å) komme. Han gadd ikke (å) gjøre det.* In the former sentence the preposition *om* (about) may be added, and then *å* cannot be omitted, e.g. *Jeg bad ham* **om å** *komme.*

Idioms:

få en til å gjøre en ting	make someone do a thing
jeg kan ikke la være å	I cannot help + *ing* form
jeg har ikke råd til å	I cannot afford to
være i stand til å	to be able to
få lov til å	get permission to

forláte leave—**forlót**—**forlátt.**

Exercise 41a

Study carefully and translate these isolated sentences into English:

Piken (here: *the maid*) holder på å lage mat.
Jeg er ikke i stand til å høre hva du sier.
Datteren fikk ikke lov til å forlate hjemmet.
Min onkel er alltid den første til å le når noe går galt.
Sønnen hadde ikke (noe) lyst til å reise utenlands (= til utlandet).
Her er det sannelig små sjanser til (*also:* for) å vinne.
Er du ferdig (*ready*) til å gå? Det var morsomt å se hvor lett han lærte å spille. Jeg kunne ikke la være å le.
Få meg ikke til å le, er du snill! Kapteinen hadde lite håp om å redde skipet fra å synke. Et drama av Ibsen er vel verdt å se. Jeg har ikke råd til å kjøpe billett.

Idioms:

bli kvitt noe, noen	get rid of something, somebody
ha det travelt med å	be busy (with) + -*ing* form

Vocabulary

forkjølelse [fɔr'çøː|sə] c. cold
ennå yet
sannsynlig likely
det er sannsynlig at han vil ...
  he is likely to
slå irr. (slo-slått) beat
skru (-dde) på screw, switch on
sjømann sailor

svømme (-te) swim
prøve (-de), forsøke [fɔ'ʃøːkə] (-te) try
flytte (-et) move
'praktisk practical
ˇplutselig suddenly
kjempe (-et) videre fight on

Exercise 41b

Practice in infinitive

My sister likes to hear music and she herself is (tr. and is herself) clever at playing (the) piano. My brothers like rowing and fishing. To do it now would be both difficult and dangerous. Last year I learned to read and speak Norwegian. Have you time to come to dinner? Our friends had promised to come to the station to say good-bye to us. I am tired of hearing the same story so many times. Haven't you found any means of getting rid of your cold yet? I was just going to bed when the telephone rang. I am afraid of meeting him as he is likely to beat me. She switched on the wireless to hear the latest news (use plural). The sailors saved their lives (*the* life) by swimming in the cold water. They had tried to save the ship first. The daughter went to the station to meet her father. I am busy moving, but do not know how to do it in the most practical way. Without saying a word he left the room. After having lived there for ten years he suddenly moved. I have (*a*) great mind to talk to him. The King encouraged the people to fight on.

CHAPTER XVIII

USE OF ARTICLES

In most cases the use of articles in Norwegian corresponds with that of English. There are, however, some exceptions.

251. *The indefinite article* is omitted before nouns denoting professions, trade, nationality, etc.:

Hans bror er lege.	His brother is a doctor.
Hun er enke.	She is a widow.
Han er nordmann.	He is a Norwegian.
Som lege må jeg si . . .	As a doctor I must say . . .

252. The indefinite article is sometimes lacking before nouns denoting concrete things used as object of a verb:

Min far har bil.	My father has a car.
Min sønn røker pipe.	My son smokes a pipe.
Hun har fått brev fra sin venn.	She has had a letter from her friend.
Han venter nå på svar.	He is now waiting for an answer.

253. *The definite article* is not used with names of hotels, ships, titles of newspapers:

Vi holder 'Times'.	We take 'The Times'.
Jeg bor på 'Grand' [graŋŋ].	I am staying at the 'Grand'.

254. *Definite article in Norwegian, but not in English.*

(*a*) Before abstract nouns (life, death, time, etc.):

Livet er kort.	Life is short.
Kast ikke bort tiden.	Do not waste time.
Jeg stoler på lykken.	I trust luck.

(*b*) Before names of streets:

Jeg bor i Storgaten.	I live in High Street.

(*c*) In some prepositional phrases:

gå i kirken go to church, *gå i byen* go to town, *bo i byen* live in town, *være på skolen* be at school, but *gå på kino* go to the pictures.

CHAPTER XIX

CONJUNCTIONS

255. In order to link together sentences, clauses, phrases, or single words we use **conjunctions.** You have already come across a fair number of these words, so this chapter will be more of a review lesson with some additional notes here and there.

For practical purposes we generally divide the conjunctions into two classes: (1) Co-ordinating conjunctions, and (2) Subordinating conjunctions.

I—Co-ordinating Conjunctions

256. These words join together in various ways sentences or words of a similar type.

(1) *og* [ɔː] and	(5) *enten—eller* either—or
(2) *både—og* both—and	(6) *'verken—eller* neither—
(3) *så vel som* as well as	nor
(4) *'eller* or	(7) *men* [menn] but
	(8) *for* [fɔrr] for

Examples:

(1) *Jeg skrev brevet og la det i postkassen.* I wrote the letter and dropped it into the letter-box. *Kvinner og barn.* Women and children. *Unge og gamle.* Young and old.

(2) *Han elsket både sitt land og sitt folk.* He loved both his country and his people.

(3) *Du, så vel som han, bør vite at slikt noe ikke går an.* You, as well as he, ought to know that such things are not done.

(4) *Vil De ha te eller kaffe?* Would you like tea or coffee?

(5) *Du kan få enten en kake eller et stykke brød.* You can have either a cake or a piece of bread.

(6) *Han visste verken ut eller inn* (idiom). He was quite bewildered.

(7) *Jeg ropte til ham, men han hørte meg ikke.* I shouted to him, but he did not hear me.

(8) *Jeg kommer ikke til å kjøpe det, for jeg har ikke råd.* I shan't buy it, for I can't afford it.

II—Subordinating Conjunctions

257. These conjunctions introduce various kinds of subordinate clauses.

The words **at** [att] that, and **om** [ɔmm] if, whether, both introduce noun clauses.

Han fortalte meg at huset var ødelagt. He told me that the house was destroyed. *Jeg spurte ham om han ville komme.* I asked him if he would come.

258. In Norwegian a noun clause (*atsetning*) can be preceded by a preposition.

Example: *Han kom inn uten at jeg merket det.* He entered without my noticing it. *Jeg er redd for at vi ikke greier det.* I am afraid we shall not manage it.

Temporal Conjunctions

259. First of all we must learn to distinguish between **da** and **når** (cf. German **als** and **wenn**), as English does not observe any such distinction, but uses 'when' for both. Here are the rules:

da is used about a single happening in the past.

Examples: *Da vi reiste, kom alle våre norske venner på stasjonen for å si adjø.* When we left, all our Norwegian friends came to the station to say good-bye. *Da jeg kom hjem, fant jeg døren låst* (locked).

når is used:

(1) About happenings in the future. *Når jeg kommer hjem, skal jeg ta meg et bad.* When I get home, I shall have a bath.

(2) For customary or repeated actions (both in the present and in the past).

Examples: *Når det regner på presten, så drypper det på klokkeren.* A common saying: When it rains on the parson, it drips on the sexton (i.e. each time it rains).

260. Other conjunctions of time are: *etter at* after, *før* before, *til* till, *mens* while, *siden* since, *idet* [i'de:] as.

Practice in the correct use of **da** and **når.**

Vocabulary

låse (-te) lock   **kjenne (-te) en igjen** recognize somebody—by sight, by voice, etc.

Exercise 42

Translate the following sentences into Norwegian applying the above rules. Take good care of the word order!

1. When it is nice weather I play tennis.
2. When I came home there was no food in the house.
3. When the war is over we shall all go home.
4. When we spoke to him he always said: 'I don't know.'
5. I will (*skal*) come when I have eaten.
6. When he went out this morning he forgot to lock the door.
7. I did not recognize him when I saw him on the station.
8. When people become old they get grey hair.
9. When it was five o'clock (tr. when the clock was five) the music began to play.
10. When we reached the top we were all hungry and tired.

Causal Conjunctions

261. da is also extensively used as a causal conjunction, corresponding to English: *as*. *Da vannet var for kaldt, kunne vi ikke bade.* As the water was too cold, we could not bathe. We have already come across **fordi** [fɔrˈdiː] because.

Others are: *siden* since, and *ettersom* as.

Example: *Siden jeg var bare åtte år, fikk jeg ikke være med.* Being only eight, I was not allowed to join.

Conditional Conjunctions

262. The two commonest ones are: **hvis** [viss] and **dersom** [ˈdæʃɔm] if, which can be used indifferently. *Vi skal dra på langtur hvis (dersom) været holder.* We are going on a long trip, if the weather holds.

om may also be used in special instances to introduce conditional clauses. *Det ville være trist om det var tilfellet.* It would be sad if that were the case.

Two other conjunctions should be mentioned: **så´fremt** and **i´fall** in case. They have, however, a somewhat 'bookish' colour.

The English: **unless,** can be rendered with **hvis ikke, med´mindre** or very often **uten.**

Example: *Du kommer ikke inn uten du har billett.* You will not get in unless you have a ticket.

The adverb *bare* = only, can act as a conditional conjunction = if only, in instances like: *Bare han kommer, er alt vel.* If he only comes, all is well. *Bare vi hadde penger . . .* If we only had money . . .

263. A condition can also be expressed without any conjunction at all by using the same word order as in a question ('inverted word order'). This is also found in English, but far less frequently than in Norwegian. *Skulle du se ham, be ham komme hjem.* Should you see him, ask him to come home. *Har du lyst, har du lov.* If you feel like it, you may do it. *Hadde jeg vinger, så ville jeg fly.* If I had wings, I would fly. *Skjer det en ulykke, tilkall politiet.* If there should be an accident, call the police.

Concessive Conjunctions

264. Those in frequent use are: *skjønt* [ʃønt] and *enda* [ˇenda], both meaning: though, and *selv om*, meaning: even if.

Skjønt det bare var mars, var det ganske varmt i luften. Although it was only March, it was quite warm in the air. *Selv om jeg hadde visst det, ville jeg ikke ha fortalt deg det.* Even if I had known it, I would not have told you.

Final Conjunctions

265. Denote purpose: **for at** = so that, or **så** = that. *Jeg tok på meg en frakk for at jeg ikke skulle fryse.* I put an overcoat on so that I should not be cold. Here you might just as well say: **så** *jeg ikke skulle fryse.*

Consecutive Conjunctions

266. Denote consequence or result: **så at** = so that, or just **så** = so.

Toget går om fem minutter, så det er best du skynder deg. The train will be leaving in five minutes, so you had better make haste. *så at* may be split up just as English: *so that.* *Snøen var så dyp at det var nesten umulig å komme fram.* The snow was so deep that it was almost impossible to get through.

Conjunctions of Comparison

267. First of all:

som = as. *Som du vil.* As you wish. Then combinations with **som**:

like, likeså—som = just as—as. *Han er like stor som deg.* He is just as big as you. *Jeg kan like* (or *likeså*) *godt fortelle deg alt sammen.* I may just as well tell you all about it.

så—som = as—as. *Han er så stor som deg.* In the following sentence **som** may be omitted. *Han gjør det så godt han kan.* . . . as well as he can.

som om = as if. *Hun lot som om hun ikke visste det.* She made as if she did not know.

enn, used with comparatives: *større enn, rikere enn*, etc., the pronoun 'annen', *ingen annen enn* no other than, and

the derived adverb *annerledes* differently, in a different way.
Det gikk annerledes enn han hadde tenkt.

jo—jo, jo—dess (desto) = the—the. *Jo lenger du venter,
desto mindre blir sjansene.* The longer you wait, the less
the chances. *Jo før jo heller.* The sooner the better.

Supplementary Note on Subordinate Clauses

268. (1) The use of the present participle instead of a
complete subordinate clause has no equivalent in Norwegian.

Example: The sentence—Being late, I did not get a seat,
must be translated: *Da jeg kom for sent, fikk jeg ingen plass.*
As I was late . . . Cf. para. 217.

The same thing applies to shortened 'sentences' like: When
a boy I used to ski. *Da jeg var gutt, pleide jeg å gå på ski.*
Come, if possible. *Kom hvis det er mulig.*

(2) We already know that if a principal clause is preceded
by a subordinate clause subject and predicate change places
in the former ('inverted' word order).

Da jeg var gutt, pleide jeg å. I used to.

Vocabulary

modig brave
skipsgutt c. prentice naut.
overraske (-et) surprise
stå på (irr.) here: last
tau n. rope
komme i ugreie get into
    disorder, entangled
rette (-et) på put right
farlig dangerous
til værs up in the air, aloft
kap'tein c. captain
eneste only
enke c. widow
rå f. yard naut. pl. **rær**
dekk n. deck

bølge c. wave
'derpå then
forsvinne [fɔ'ʃvinnə] irr. (a-u)
    disappear
fri'modig cheerful, fearless
vant shroud naut.
mast c. mast
levende alive
klatre (-et) climb
ekorn [ˇekko'r̩n] n. squirrel
krenge (-et) heel over
tape (-te) lose
mot n. courage
uskadd unscathed, safe
for'nøyd contented

Exercise 43a

Read and translate:

Den modige skipsgutten

Et skip var på vei til Amerika. Midt i Atlanterhavet ble det
overrasket av en storm som stod på i fem dager. Da stormen
var på det verste (*at its worst*), kom et tau i ugreie på en

av rærne. Dette måtte rettes på. Men det var farlig å gå til
værs i slik en storm. Kapteinen sa til en skipsgutt at han
skulle gjøre det. Det var en liten gutt, ikke mer enn tretten
år gammel, eneste barn til en fattig enke.

Gutten så først opp til råa og så (*then*) ned i bølgene som hele
tiden brøt inn over dekket og likesom (*as it were*) strakte
armene ut etter ham. Derpå så han på kapteinen og sa:
'Jeg kommer straks.' Han forsvant, men kom straks tilbake
og skyndte seg frimodig oppover vantet. Den mann som har
fortalt dette, stod på dekket ved masten og fulgte gutten
med øynene. Han spurte kapteinen: 'Hvorfor sender du
denne vesle gutten opp? Han vil ikke komme levende ned
igjen.' Kapteinen svarte: 'Menn faller hvor gutter står, han
der klatrer som et ekorn.' Mannen så opp. Nå var gutten
høyt oppe. Skuta krengte så sterkt at rærne nesten nådde
bølgetoppene. Men gutten tapte ikke motet, og innen
(*within*) et kvarter kom han ned igjen, uskadd og fornøyd.

Idioms:

(1) *Det er ikke min skyld.*   It is not my fault.
(2) *ha skylden for*   be responsible for, bear the
                              blame for
(3) *Det er best du går.*   You had better go.

Vocabulary

lang tid or **lenge** a long time
avis [a'vi:s] c. (news)paper
veksle (-et) change (money)
pund [punn] n. pound
'blakk' broke sl.
dyr (use the comparative in -ere) expensive

presang [pre'saŋŋ] c. present (gift)
være i stand til = **kunne** to be able to
nevne (-te) mention
takket være thanks to
'Golfstrømmen The Gulf Stream

Exercise 43b

1. You must see all my books while you are here.
2. It is quite a long time since I saw you last.
3. We had better buy the papers before we go.
4. If you should see him tell him that I am here.
5. Can you change a pound? No, I cannot, as I am broke.
6. We eat that we may live, but we do not live that we may eat.
7. The longer you wait the more expensive it will be. (*bli* or *være?*)

8. Because you have been so kind to (*mot*) me I want to give you a present.
9. Both you and I are able to drive (a) car.
10. As already mentioned we are leaving for Oslo next week.
11. Since you are asking I may just as well tell you.
12. Even if Norway lies far north the summers are quite warm, thanks to the Gulf Stream.

CHAPTER XX

WORD ORDER (Ordstilling)

269. In simple assertive sentences the word order in Norwegian is the same as in English.

Examples:

Det regner i dag.	It is raining today.
Skipet seilte samme aften.	The ship sailed the same evening.
Han kom for en uke siden.	He arrived a week ago.

Inversion

270. If, however, any part of the predicate is placed before the subject, the subject and verb change places. (N.B.—A conjunction is not a part of the predicate.) This change in the normal word order is called **inversion,** a feature which is also found in English, though not to such an extent as in Norwegian.

By way of illustration let us make some alterations to the above sentences:

I dag regner det.	Today it is raining.
Samme aften seilte skipet.	The same evening the ship sailed.
For en uke siden kom han.	A week ago he arrived.

Further examples:

Store er de ikke.	They are not big.
Nå må vi gå.	Now we must go.
Så sa han: '. . .	Then he said: '. . .

Inversion caused by Subordinate Clauses

271. If a principal clause is preceded by a subordinate clause, we also get inversion, e.g.:

Når jeg kommer hjem, leser jeg avisen. When I get home, I read the newspaper. *Hvis jeg får tid, skal jeg komme.* If I get time, I shall come. Cf. page 42.

Note especially: Skal du bli flink, sa han, må du øve flittig. If you want to become expert, he said, you must practise intensely.

If the principal clause comes first, we get the normal order.

Example: *Jeg leser avisen når jeg kommer hjem.*

Exercise 44a

Begin the following sentences with:

1. *da* then	Alle begynte å synge.
2. *i går* yesterday	Sønnen kom hjem fra England.
3. *snart* soon	Det blir kaldt.
4. *engang* once	Jeg trodde på julenissen (Santa Claus).
5. *likevel* yet, still	Han gjorde det.
6. *plutselig* suddenly	Min søster så en mann gå inn i huset.
7. *nå* now	Det er nok.

Place of Adverbs

The problem of placing the adverbs correctly has already been dealt with on various occasions (cf. page 42 and the negative *ikke* on page 53), so this will only be a summing up.

Important rule:

272. In *principal clauses* the adverbs and adverbial phrases are usually placed *after* the verb in simple tenses:

Han kommer alltid sent hjem.	He always comes home late.
Det hender ofte.	It often happens.
Det hender ikke ofte.	It does not often happen.
Jeg møtte også min nabo.	I also met my neighbour.

In compound tenses, however, the adverb generally comes after the auxiliary, as in English.

Du har aldri/ikke forsøkt.   You have never/not tried.
Det vil alltid skje.   That will always happen.

273. In *subordinate clauses* the negative **ikke** and some other adverbs, especially such as denote time, are placed before the verb. Cf. paras. 75(2) and 95.

Jeg visste at han ikke ville komme.   I knew that he would not come.

Min venn sier at han aldri har forsøkt.   My friend says that he has never tried.

Siden De allerede (alt) vet det, behøver jeg ikke si det.   Since you already know it, I need not tell you.

274. Special note on **ikke**.
If in a simple sentence the object is a pronoun, the negative comes after. If on the other hand, the object is a noun the normal word order is preserved.

Jeg så ham ikke.[1]   I did not see him.
Jeg kjenner henne ikke.   I do not know her.
Jeg klarer det ikke.   I do not manage it.

But normal order in compound tenses:

Jeg har ikke sett ham.   I have not seen him.

Normal order with a noun:

Jeg kjente ikke fyren.   I did not know the fellow.

Vocabulary

kon'tor office
gå på kon'toret go to the office
bære irr. (a—å) carry
mappe c. case
'høyre, 'venstre right, left
matpakke c. food parcel
to'bakk c. tobacco
lunsj [lønʃ] c. lunch
pause c. break, pause

sette stor pris på appreciate very much
slappe (-et) av relax
nyte irr. (ø—y) enjoy
siga'rett c. cigarette
disku'tere (-te) discuss
pro'blem n. problem
for det meste, mest mostly
sport c. sport

[1] But stressed of course: *Jeg så ikke* **ham.**

Exercise 44b

When I go to the office in the morning I carry a black case in (my) right hand. If you ask me what I have in the case my answer is: two things only—my food parcel and my tobacco. We have our lunch between 11.30 and 12 o'clock (in letters please). Since this is our only break during the day we appreciate it very much. It is the only time of (*på*) the day when (*da*) we can relax, drink a cup of coffee, enjoy a cigarette and discuss the problems of the day (use the -*s* genitive). The men at (*på*) the office mostly talk about sport and cars.

Vocabulary

prest c. minister, parson
klokker c. sexton
svær big
kar c. fellow
hovedvei c. main road
notis [no'ti:s] c. notice
opp på siden av alongside
kappe c. gown
krage c. collar
hovmod ['hɔvmo:d] n. arrogance
vant til accustomed to
ha ord for å være supposed to be, considered to be
ha lyst c. til desire, have a great mind to
gap c. fool
klok ⎱wise
vis ⎰

ja here: well
i stedet instead
trapp f. staircase
krone c. crown
scepter ['septər] n. sceptre
glitre (-et) glitter
nå interj. oh
øst east
vest west
jo-ho well
ja, ja very well
verdt worth
Vår'herre Our Lord
verdsette, (verdsatte, verdsatt) value, estimate
sølvpenge c. silver piece
nå, nå so, so
Å (interj.) why
feil adj. and adv. wrong

Exercise 45

Presten og klokkeren

Det var en gang en prest som mente han var slik en svær kar. Når han så noen komme kjørende mot seg på hovedveien, ropte han så høyt han kunne: 'Av veien, av veien, her kommer selve presten.'

Så hendte det en gang han kom kjørende at han møtte kongen. 'Av veien, av veien,' skrek han langt borte.

Men kongen tok ingen notis av ham og kjørte som vanlig, så denne gangen måtte presten av veien.

Men da kongen kom opp på siden av ham, sa han: 'I morgen skal du møte meg på slottet, og hvis du ikke kan svare på tre spørsmål som jeg vil gi deg, skal du miste både kappe og krage for ditt hovmod.'

Det var noe annet enn det presten var vant til. Rope og skrike, det kunne han, men det var også omtrent alt. Så reiste han til klokkeren, som hadde ord for å være mye klokere enn presten. Til ham sa presten at han ikke hadde lyst til å reise, for en gap kan spørre mer enn ti vise kan svare, sa han, og så fikk han klokkeren til å reise i stedet. Ja, klokkeren reiste, og kom til slottet med prestens kappe og krage på. Kongen selv møtte ham på trappa med krone og scepter, og var så fin at det glitret lang vei. 'Nå, er du der?' sa kongen. Ja, han var da det, det var sikkert nok. 'Si meg nå først,' sa kongen, 'hvor langt er det fra øst til vest?' 'Det er en dagsreise, det,' sa klokkeren. 'Hvorledes det?' sa kongen. 'Joho, solen står opp i øst og går ned i vest, og den reisen gjør den lett på en dag,' sa klokkeren. 'Ja, ja,' sa kongen. 'Men si meg nå, hvor mye tror du jeg er verdt slik som jeg står foran deg her.' 'Å, Vårherre ble verdsatt til tretti sølvpenger, så jeg kan vel ikke sette deg høyere enn til tjue ni,' sa klokkeren.

'Nå, nå,' sa kongen. 'Siden du er så klok på alle ting, si meg hva det er jeg tenker nå?' 'Å, du tenker sikkert det er presten som står foran deg, men der tenker du feil, for det er klokkeren.'

'Nå, så reis du hjem og vær prest, og la ham bli klokker,' sa kongen, og slik ble det.

In this story, written in a natural narrative style, there are a great many instances of 'inversion'. Go through them all carefully and try to find the reason for their occurrence in each case.

Ordspråk

Hovmod står for fall. Hva er det tilsvarende ordspråk på engelsk?

Vocabulary

samling c. collection
glassmester c. glazier
hode n. head, here: brain
flittig industrious
lese med to coach
gjette (-et) 1, guess, 2, solve
gåte c. riddle
for en stor del for the most part
eksamen [ek'sa:mən] c. examination, degree
studénteksamen matriculation exam.
velstående well-to-do
nabo c. neighbour(ing)
bygd f. country district
'studium n.; pl. **studier** study
lesning c. reading, study
slutt c. finish; and predicatively finished

gjerne 1, willingly, 2, expressing habit—usually
peis c. fireplace, grating
korte ['ko'ʈə] **(-et)** shorten, pass away
helt fra right from
hedning ['he:dniŋ] c. heathen
fullt og fast fully and firmly
troll n. troll, gnome
nisse c. goblin
dverg c. dwarf
overtro c. superstition
skap n. cupboard
kiste c. chest, drawer
bli enig om agree to, about
minne n. memory, remembrance
forfedre ['fɔrfe:drə] pl. ancestors
trykke (-te) 1, press, 2, print
popu'lær popular

Exercise 46

Chr. Asbjørnsen og ' Jørgen Moe [mo:]

Første del

De to eventyrene vi har lest: Gutten og fanden og Presten og klokkeren, er tatt fra Asbjørnsen og Moes eventyrsamling.

Peter Christen Asbjørnsen ble født i Oslo 1812. Far hans var glassmester. Peter hadde et godt hode, men var ikke særlig flittig på skolen. Så sendte faren ham opp til Norderhov på Ringerike. Der var det en prest som leste med slike karer til studenteksamen.

Jørgen Moe var sønn av en velstående bonde fra nabobygda Hole på Ringerike. Han var ett år yngre enn Asbjørnsen. Jørgen Moe skulle også lese til studenteksamen hos presten i Norderhov. Slik kom Asbjørnsen og Moe sammen, og de ble venner for livet. Jørgen Moe var meget interessert i sine studier og var svært flittig. Men Asbjørnsen likte ikke å lese, og det gikk ikke bedre med lesningen her på landet enn i Oslo. Etter et par år tok faren ham hjem igjen. Han ble ikke student før tre år etter Moe.

Annen del

Det var få bøker og aviser den gang. Når arbeidet for dagen var slutt, samlet folk seg gjerne om peisen og kortet tiden med å fortelle historier og eventyr og gjette gåter. Det var for en stor del de samme eventyrene som var blitt fortalt i flere hundre år. Flere av dem var helt fra hedningetiden. Nå trodde de ikke lenger på Odin og Tor. Men de trodde fullt og fast på troll og nisser og dverger, som av og til kom fram og viste seg for menneskene. Vi kaller alt slikt for overtro. Men i gamle dager trodde mange at det var sant det som ble fortalt i disse gamle historiene.

De to unge studentene skjønte at det var med eventyrene som med et gammelt skap eller en gammel kiste. De er minner fra forfedrene. Men snart ville de bli glemt. Derfor ble de enige om å samle alle de eventyr som folk fortalte, og få dem skrevet ned og trykt.

Disse eventyrene kom første gang ut i 1842, og nå er de like populære i Norge som fortellingene om Alice in Wonderland er det i England.

CHAPTER XXI

INTERJECTIONS AND EXCLAMATIONS

275. These words and phrases generally express emotions and reactions on the part of the speaker. Numerous as they are, there will be room for only a relatively small selection of them. Typical of them is also that small tone variations often add different nuances to them.

ah, åh, both express amazement as well as delightful and pleasant surprise:

Ah—det var god tobakk!	Ah—that is good tobacco!
Åh, så stor hun er!	Oh, isn't she big!

Åh said in a wailing tone is a general utterance of pain, often reiterated—heard at the dentist's.

au is also an utterance of pain or regret, but more abrupt.

Au, jeg skar meg i fingeren!   Oh, I cut my finger!

akk is more or less a sigh of disappointment or resignation, corresponding to German **Ach,** Eng. 'alas' or 'oh!' In everyday speech mostly used in combination with **ja.** *Akk ja, nå er sommeren forbi for i år.*

276.   The answering words **ja, jo, nei** are frequently used as interjections, alone or with some additions, very often to fill in a pause.

Ja, hva skulle jeg gjøre?	Well, what should I do?
Ja, ja ⎫ *Ja—ha* ⎭ *så er det gjort!*	Well, now it is done!
Ja vel.	Very well, O.K., all right, acknowledging an order.

The opposite is: *Nei vel.*

Du må handle raskt.	You must act swiftly.
Ja vel!	Very well!
Ikke si det!	Don't say it!
Nei vel.	All right, I won't.
Ja så?	Really! Is that so? You don't say!
Knut har giftet seg.	Knut has got married.
Nei, ja så?	Has he really?
Ja visst!	Yes, of course!
Er det sant?	Is it true?
Ja visst.	Yes, of course.

After a negative: *Jo visst.*

Det er ikke sant.	It isn't true.
Jo visst.	Yes, it is.

nei (*nei*) expresses amazement.

Nei, så flink du er!	I say, how clever you are!
Ærlig talt!	Honestly, frankly!

fy! (fie), for shame—shows contempt and disapproval.

Fy, skam deg.	Shame on you.
Fy, det var stygt gjort.	For shame, that was not nice.

pytt—never mind.

Pytt det gjør da ikke noe.   That doesn't matter.

huff
huttetu } *det er kaldt i dag!*   Ugh, it is cold today!

isj or **æsj** shows irritation and disgust.

Æsj, så kjedelig det var!   How annoying!

uff, slight despair and grumble.

Uff, skal vi ha fiskepudding i   Oh, are we going to have fish
dag også?   pudding today too?

hm expresses doubt just as in English.

Order or request:

kom an!   Come on! Let's go to it!
hør her!   Look here! Listen! I say!
Hør her, gutter, dere må ikke   I say, boys, you mustn't
  holde sånt leven ['leːvn̩]!   make such a noise!
pass deg!   Take care!
Pass opp or *se opp!*   Look out!

hei, hallo! (for hailing someone).

Hei, gutter!   Hi, boys!
Hallo, er det noen der?   Hallo, is anybody there?

In the shop:

Hallo, De glemte noe!   I say, you left something!

Expressions of startling surprise:

Du store min!   Good gracious!
Bevare meg vel!   Good heavens!

Showing sympathy:

Det var synd.   That is a pity. That is too
              bad.

Det var synd at du kom for   It is too bad you arrived too
  sent.   late.
Stakkars gutt!   Poor boy!

Expressions of approval and enthusiasm:

hurra [hurˈraː]*! bravo* [ˈbraːvo]*!*

Lenge leve!	Long live!
Hurra for syttende mai.	Hurrah for the 17th of May!
La oss rope et tre ganger tre hurra for fedrelandet!	Let us give three cheers for our native land!
Bravo, det var fint levert!	Bravo, that was beautifully done!

CHAPTER XXII

CONVENTIONAL PHRASES

These are very important, but not at all easy as they are often tied up with customs and etiquette in the country concerned.

277. (1) When the Norwegians meet in the morning they say: *god morgen* [go'mɔᵣn̩], less formally just *mor'n* ['mɔᵣn̩] = good morning.

In the evening: *god aften* or *god kveld* = good evening.

The same expressions are also used when parting.

(2) Other leaving or parting expressions are:

god natt = good night.
adjø [a'djøː] or *farvel* [far'vel] = good-bye.
ha det bra (godt) = best of luck, cheerio.
Du får leve så vel or just *lev vel da* = take care of yourself.

Then we have: *På gjensyn* [ˇjensy(ː)n] corresponding to German **Auf Wiedersehen** and French **Au revoir.**

When taking leave of a friend just before dinner time one generally says: *god middag* (no equivalent in English).

(3) To some of these parting expressions the adverb **da** is added, thus: *god morgen da*, which in colloquial speech is reduced to just *morn'a* ['mɔᵣna], *farvel da* [far'vella], *på gjensyn da*, etc.

(4) When we meet during the day, we may say: *god 'dag.* where the English would say: 'good morning', 'good afternoon', 'good evening' depending on the time of the day.

Young people would just say *mor'n* at all hours. To make them more cordial the greetings are often repeated: *mor'n, mor'n; god dag, god dag; adjø, adjø*.

(5) To people going (out) to some form of amusement you may say:

God fornøyelse	Have a good time.
['goː fɔrˈnøy(ə)lsə].	

(6) When the Norwegians meet again after a party, etc., they say:

Takk for sist.	Lit. Thank you for the last time.

278. A much-used phrase is *vær så god*, lit. be so good/kind, which may be heard in a great variety of situations.

(1) First of all it is used when you are handing something to someone or offering something, corresponding to German: **Bitte** and French **S'il vous plaît**. There is no real equivalent in English. 'Here you are' has not the same degree of politeness.

Vær så god, her er hatten Deres.	Here is your hat.

A Norwegian speaking English is inclined to insert an incorrect 'please' here.

Asking a favour:

Unnskyld, kan jeg få låne telefonen et øyeblikk?	Excuse me, may I borrow the telephone for a moment?

The answer is:

Ja, vær så god,	Why, certainly. Yes, of course.

When you have finished you say:

Takk for lånet!	Lit. Thanks for the loan!

The reply to that is: *Ingen årsak!*

Asking a favour is also expressed by:

Vil De være så vennlig/snill å ...	Would you be so kind as to ...

also *Ville* or *Kunne De*, etc. ....

Ville De være så snill å lukke vinduet?	Would you be so kind as to shut the window?

(2) Quite often *vær så god* corresponds to English 'please'.

Vær så god og sitt ned.	Sit down, please.

In the big store:

Vær så god denne vei.	This way, please.

At the hairdresser's:

Vær så god neste.	Next, please.
Vær så god, det er servert [sær′ve:ʳ‍ʈ].	The table is ready.

The shop assistant says to the customer:
Vær så god, corresponding to something like: What can I do for you?

When you take the phone, you might say:
Vær så god (Your name first and then *vær så god*) besides 'hallo' as in English.

Used ironically in reply to a sentence like:

Jeg skal melde Dem til politiet.	I am going to report you to the police.
Ja, vær så god.	Please do. By all means. Go right ahead. Don't let anything stop you.

A command:

Du skal vær så god gjøre som jeg sier.	You will please do as I tell you.

279. The words of thanks are:

Takk, takk skal De ha, mange takk, tusen takk, hjertelig (cordial) *takk.*

Vil De ha en kopp te til ?	Would you like another cup of tea?
Ja, takk.	Yes, please. (The opposite is *nei, takk.*)

After a negation: *Vil De ikke, etc. ? Jo, takk.*

When you have finished a meal, do not forget to say: *Takk for maten* (Lit. Thanks for the food)! The host or hostess (*verten* [′væʳʈ(ə)n], *eller vertinnen* [væʳˇʈinn(ə)n] replies: *Velbekomme* [velbə′kɔmmə]. Lit. May it do you good.

280. Inquiring about health etc.:

Hvordan står det til?⎫
Hvordan har du det?⎭   How are you?

Hvordan lever du!   How is life?

The answer may be:

Jo takk, bare bra.   Very well, thank you.
Just fine, thank you.

281. Apologies:

To 'I am sorry the Norwegian equivalent is: *Om forlatelse*
[ɔmm fɔʳˈlaːtlsə] Lit. I ask for forgiveness. To 'excuse me'
the Norwegian equivalent is: *Unnskyld* [ˈunnʃyll].

Unnskyld, kan De si meg veien til Frognerparken? Excuse
me, can you tell me the way to the Frogner Park?

If you are so unfortunate as to tread on somebody's toe,
you should say: *Om forlatelse* (I am sorry, I beg your
pardon).

The sufferer is likely to reply: *Å, jeg ber* or less formally:
Å, det gjør ikke noe, or: *Det er ikke så farlig* (It doesn't
matter, it's quite all right).

Unnskyld at jeg forstyrrer   Excuse my interrupting you.
  Dem.
Unnskyld, De har vel ikke en   Excuse me, you haven't got
  fyrstikk, vel?   a match, have you?
Nei, dessverre [dəsˈværrə].   Unfortunately not. No, I'm
    sorry.

or slightly more formal: *Beklager* [bəˈklaːgər], I am sorry.
Jeg beklager at . . . I regret that . . .

If you have not heard what a person has said to you, the
formal expression is: *Hva behager* [bəˈhaːgər]? I beg your
pardon?

also: *Unnskyld, jeg hørte ikke hva De sa.* Very informal just
Hva? What?

CHAPTER XXIII

WORD FORMATION

282. By having some knowledge of Norwegian word formation you will be able to grasp the meaning of a lot of derivatives and compounds.

(1) The Norwegian language has a great facility for making compounds, usually written in one word.

stor by—storby big city, *storgård* great farm, *småpenger* small change, `ˇreisebyrå` n. travel bureau, *armbåndsur* n. wrist-watch.

(2) Genitive in English, compound in Norwegian:

dameveske lady's bag, *damehatt* lady's hat, *stolrygg* c. back of a chair.

(3) *Connecting links.*

Very often there is a connecting sound (vowel or consonant) between the different elements of the compound.

-e: *barnesko* children's shoes, *barnehave* c. Kindergarten, *gutteværelse* n. boys' room.

-s (originally the genitive *-s*): *landsmann* fellow-countryman, *årstid* season.

283. *Prefixes.*

(1) Negative prefixes are first of all **u,** which usually carries the stress `ˇuvenn` enemy, `ˇumoden` immature, `ˇuforsiktig` careless, but *umulig* [u'muːli] impossible. **mis-** `ˇmisforstå`, *mis'unne* envy.

(2) **be-, er-, for-,** are, as we know, un-accented prefixes (see page 12). **an-** on the other hand is stressed.

be'gynne begin, *er'klære* declare, *'angå* concern, *'ankomme* arrive.

284. *Noun suffixes.*

-inne, -ske indicate feminine gender: *venn* friend (male), *venninne* friend (girl), *lærer* teacher—*lærerinne* woman teacher, *sykepleier* male nurse—*sykepleierske* nurse.

Abstracts in **-dom** [dɔmm] 'dom', **-het** 'hood', **-skap** 'ship'.

-dom c. *ung* young—*ungdom* youth, *barn* n. child—*barndom* childhood, *vis* wise—*visdom* wisdom.

-het c. *falsk* false—*'falskhet* falsehood, *dum* stupid, foolish—*'dumhet* stupidity, foolishness, *kjærlig* amorous—*kjærlighet*, love.

-skap n. or c. *ekteskap* n. marriage, *vennskap* n. friendship, concrete: *landskap* n. landscape.

-else c. also denoting abstracts: *friste* tempt—*fristelse* temptation, *lede* lead—*ledelse* leadership, management, *stor* great—*størrelse* size.

-sel n., also c., *brenne* burn—*brensel* n. fuel, *lenges etter* long for—*lengsel* c. longing, *fange* capture—*fengsel* n. prison.

-e'ri ('-ry') n., denoting a place where some special activity is going on: *meieri* n. dairy, *vaske* wash—*vaskeri* n. laundry, *trykke* print—*trykkeri* printing press.

-tøy n., here in the sense of tool, gear or some other commodity: **verktøy** tool(s), **leketøy** children's toys, **kjøretøy** vehicle, means of transport, **fartøy** vessel, craft, even **syltetøy** jam.

285. *Adjectival suffixes.*

-aktig ('-ish'): *grå* grey—*gråaktig* greyish, *narr* fool—*narraktig* foolish, conceited, *fabelaktig*—fabulous.

-full: *tankefull* thoughtful, *praktfull* glorious, splendid (of *prakt* c. splendour).

-messig: ('-like') *regelmessig* regular, *bymessig* urban.

-(l)ig ('-ly'): *herlig* [ˇhæːrˌli] wonderful, *deilig* delicious, *farlig* dangerous, *kraftig* powerful.

-et(e), meaning full of: *støvete* dusty (see para. 129 (b)).

-løs (less): *fargeløs* colourless, *arbeidsløs* unemployed, *blodløs* bloodless.

-som is very common: *lang* long—*langsom* slow, *moro* c. fun—*morsom* funny.

-sk to denote nationalities: *fransk, engelsk, norsk, amerikansk*.

-bar ('able'): *holdbar* durable, often with a passive meaning, e.g. *brukbar* usable, i.e. that can be used.

286. *Adverbial suffixes.*

-vis: *heldig* lucky—*heldigvis* luckily, *par* pair—*parvis* in pairs, *del* part—*delvis* partly, *forhold* relations—*forholdsvis* comparatively.

287. *Verbal suffixes.*

-e formed from nouns: *land* n. land—*lande* to land; *mann* man—*bemanne* man (a ship), *mat* c. food—*mate* feed, *bil* c. car—*bile* to motor.

Quite a large number are formed by mutation of the vowel (umlaut)

sorg c. sorrow—*sørge* to mourn.
kam c. comb—*kjemme* to comb.
kamp c. battle—*kjempe* to battle.
krav n. claim—*kreve* to claim.
tall n. number—*telle* to count.
navn n. mention—*nevne* mention.

From adjectives:
tam tame—*temme* to tame.
lang long—*forlenge* to lengthen.
tom empty—*tømme* to empty.

-ne added to adjectives to describe a transition:

sort black—*sortne* darken. Cf. blacken.
blek pale—*blekne* become pale (to pale). Cf. Engl. strengthen, lengthen.

-ere ['eːrə] in loan-words *telefo'nere* telephone, *stu'dere* study, *le'vere* deliver, *konfer'ere* confer, etc.

CHAPTER XXIV

PUNCTUATION

The Norwegian rules of punctuation do not differ greatly from those in English.

288. Full stop is used after a complete sentence, but also after abbreviations, e.g. **dvs.** = *det vil si* (that is *or* i.e.), **jfr.** = *jevnfør* (cf.), **kr.** = *kroner*, but here the dot can be omitted, **kl.** = *klokka* (o'clock), **bl. a.** = *blant annet* (among others), **m.m.** = *med mere* and after ordinals **5.** (or **5te**) = *5th.*

Exceptions: In weights and measures the full stop is left out, **mm** = *'millimeter*, **cm** = *'centimeter*, **dm** = *'desimeter*, **m** = *meter*, **km** = *kilometer*, **1** = *liter*, **hl** = *hektoliter* (100 l), **g** = gram, **kg** = *kilogram* ['çiːlogram] or just *'kilo.*

289. Colon to introduce information.

Han sa: 'Det er kaldt i dag.'

Semicolon is not used so very much. It is more often than not replaced by a full stop. You may find it, though, before conjunctions like: **men** but, and **for** for, when these are introducing a complete sentence.

The rule is: *Always a stop mark in front of* **men.**

290. Hyphen is used to divide words and syllables at the end of a line and elsewhere where it is convenient for the sake of clarity.

Note specially: *barne- og ungdomsfilmer* = children and adult films.

291. Apostrophe is little used in Norwegian.—First of all it is used before the genitive **-s** if the noun also ends in **s**, e.g. *Under Paris's hustak.* Under the roofs of Paris. *Hans's kone.* Hans's wife.

292. Accents are mostly found in words of foreign (French) origin: words like: *kafé* café, *idé* idea, *renommé* reputation.

293. Comma is used:

(1) In enumeration: *sukker, salt og pepper.* N.B.—No comma before *og* here.

(2) Between two sentences connected by a co-ordinating conjunction:

Vi spiste først, og så badet vi. We ate first and then we went for a swim.

(3) With appositives (which are in fact 'non-restrictive clauses):

Oslo, Norges hovedstad, har ca. fire hundre tusen innbyggere. Oslo, Norway's capital, has about four hundred thousand inhabitants.

(4) By proper names in addresses:

Per, du lyver. Peter, you are lying.

(5) To set off mild interjections:

Ja, det er sant. Yes, that is true. With stronger interjections the exclamation mark is used.

(6) To set off a subordinate clause which precedes a principal clause:

Da jeg var gutt, bodde jeg i Arendal. When a boy I lived at Arendal.

(7) After a subordinate clause which is inserted in a principal clause:

De første mennesker vi traff, var to bønder. The first people we met, were two farmers. If the inserted clause is non-restrictive it is fully set off by commas. *Oslo, som er Norges hovedstad, har fire hundre tusen innbyggere.* Oslo, which is the capital of Norway, has four hundred thousand inhabitants.

(8) When the subordinate clause comes after the principal clause, a comma is used only if the former is non-restrictive and acts more or less as a parenthesis:

Jeg møtte min venn Per, som hadde vært på julebesøk. I met my friend Per, who had been on a Christmas visit.

ADVANCED READING AND TRANSLATING EXERCISES

Vocabulary

utlending c. foreigner
på besøk n. i on a visit to
oppdagelse c. discovery
i grunnen really
betydning c. importance
dagligtale c. everyday speech
forkorte (-et) [fɔr'kɔ'ʈə] shorten
oppkalle (-te) name
linje c. line
bane, short for jernbane c. railway
Slott [ʃlɔtt] n. Royal Castle
beliggenhet c. situation
høyde c. height, hill
lengde c. length
hovedinngang c. main entrance
statue ['sta:tuə] c. statue
plass c. here: square
spa'sertur c. stroll
forelesning c. lecture
'fortsette (-satte, -satt) continue
støte (-tte) på run into
vende (-dte) ut mot face
'omgi irr. surround
en rekke a number of

skogkledd forest-clad
ås c. hill
berømt famous
seilbåt c. sailing boat
ferge c. ferry
passasjer [passa'ʃe:r] c. passenger
'tilbringe (-brakte, -brakt) spend (the time)
klippe c. cliff
dyrke (-et) cultivate
badeliv n. lit. bathing life
glede c. joy, pleasure
foretrekke (-trakk, -trukket) ['fɔ:rətrekkə] prefer
på mindre enn in less than
sti c. path
sno (-dde) seg twist
gran f. Norway spruce
furu f. pine
terreng n. terrain
alder c. age
løype f. ski track
'opplevelse c. experience
fottur c. walking tour, walk

Exercise 47

Oslo by

En utlending på besøk i Oslo vil snart gjøre den oppdagelse at det i grunnen bare er én gate i byen som har noen større betydning for ham. Den heter Karl Johansgate, i dagligtalen forkortet til Karl Johan, og er oppkalt etter en svensk konge. Den går i'rett linje fra Oslo sentralstasjon til Slottet, som har en fin beliggenhet oppe på en høyde. Herfra kan man se gaten i hele dens lengde.

Hvis en går far Slottet nedover mot Oslo sentralstasjon, vil en på høyre hånd finne Nasjonalteatret. Foran hovedinngangen står statuer av Ibsen og Bjørnson, de to mest berømte norske dramatikere. På den andre siden av gaten ligger de gamle Universitetsbygningene med Universitets plassen foran, hvor studentene tar seg en spasertur mellom forelesningene for å trekke frisk luft. Fortsetter en nedover gaten, vil en støte på Stortinget, Norges Parlament. Det ble bygd i 1866, så det er ikke særlig gammelt. Oslo har en aldeles herlig beliggenhet. Den vender ut mot fjorden, og bakenfor er den omgitt av en rekke skogkledde åser. Denne fine beliggenheten har gjort Oslo til en ganske berømt turistby. I sommermånedene er fjorden full av seilbåter, og en ser stadig ferger, fullpakket med passasjerer som skal tilbringe dagen ved sjøen. Rundt omkring på klippene ligger folk som dyrker badelivets gleder.

Hvis man foretrekker en fottur i skog og mark, kan man bare ta Holmenkollbanen, og på mindre enn en time er man inne på skogstiene, som snor seg mellom gran- og furutrær. Om vinteren er hele dette terrenget snøkledd, og hver eneste søndag kan man da se tusenvis av Oslofolk i alle aldrer på ski i løypene. En norsk 'skisøndag' i Nordmarka, som terrenget rundt Oslo kalles, er en opplevelse man ikke så lett glemmer.

Vocabulary

inter'vju n. interview
tvil c. doubt
sjel c. soul
inter'vjue (-et) interview
det stemmer that's correct
stirre (-et) på stare at
briller spectacles
tydeligvis obviously
så vidt only just
fikk plas'sert seg managed to sit down
lund c. grove
alpelue f. beret
an'takelig probably
skjule (-te) hide, conceal
måne c. moon, pop. for bald head
rutet chequered

slips n. tie
nål c. pin
drive irr. here: run
reisebyrå n. travel bureau
vesentlig ['ve:sntli] mainly
skryte irr. av boast about
dårlig med scarce
Jeg liker meg godt idiom: I like it well (a lot)
være here: stay
omvendt reversed
rekkefølge c. order, succession
smigre (-et) flatter
Jeg for'drar ikke I can't stand
samtale c. conversation, talk
forbi past, here: over
ta fram take out, produce
hjemmefra adv. from home

Exercise 48

Et intervju

Han stod og leste *New York Times*, så det var ikke tvil i vår sjel at han var amerikaner.
— Vi ville gjerne intervjue Dem, sa vi.

— Det er helt i orden. Kom igjen—.

— De er fra Amerika?

— Det stemmer, sa vår venn og stirret på oss bak brilleglassene.

— Men skal vi ikke sette oss mens vi står?

Som sagt, så gjort. Vår venn gikk med stokk og hadde tydeligvis vond fot, for det var så vidt han fikk plassert seg på en av benkene i Studenterlunden. Han røkte på en stor sigar, og hadde på seg alpelue, antakelig for å skjule en måne, brune bukser uten press i, rutet jakke, gul skjorte, og grønt slips med sølvnål.

— Hvor kommer De fra?

— New York—. Jeg driver et reisebyrå, ikke stort, men lite, og kom hit med *Bergensfjord*, vesentlig for å se hva slags service skipet gir, slik at jeg kan fortelle mine kunder om de bør reise med det eller ei.

— Og hvilken konklusjon er De kommet til?

— Skipet er helt førsteklasses. Jeg skal skryte av det til alle kjente og ukjente, og for en tur vi hadde hitover! På Nordkapp var det aldeles fantastisk. Jeg har aldri vært der før, bare i Oslo, Bergen og Stavanger. Det var like etter krigen, og det var dårlig med mat i Norge den gangen, men nå er det helt annerledes.

Så det vanlige spørsmål:

— Hva synes De om Norge?

— Jeg liker meg meget godt her, og skulle gjerne komme tilbake enda en gang og være enda lenger.

— Hvorfor liker De landet vårt?

— For det første fordi alt er så rent her—

— For det andre fordi folk er så vennlige—

— For det tredje naturen, eller i omvendt rekkefølge om De vil.

— Vi føler oss smigret—

—Har De fått tid til å se Dem omkring?

— Å, ja da. Jeg har sett Kontiki, Fram, Vikingskipene, Rådhuset og Vigelandsanlegget.

Vår venn fordrar ikke å fly. Ikke fordi han er redd, men fordi det går for fort.

Så var samtalen forbi, og han tok fram sin avis og begynte å studere nytt hjemmefra.

Vocabulary

mål n. aim, goal
skape (-et) create, make
ankomst c. arrival
Pol c. pole
stikke irr. put
foregående preceding, previous
telt n. tent
tilstå irr. admit
handling c. action
foregå irr. occur
hastighet c. speed, haste
føre n. snow condition, surface
vekslende variable
gli irr. glide
smått stell idiom: in a poor way
mekanisk mechanical
tøye (-de) stretch
strekke (irr. **strakte, strakt**)
  stretch
glane (-te) stare
til gangs thoroughly
u'endelig endless
vidde c. mountain wilds
ljome [ˇjoːmə] **(-et)** echo
kjører c. driver
skrøne (-et) tell a yarn, lie

åpenlyst openly, obviously
jeg får heller være idiom: I had
  better be
opp'riktig frank, honest, sincere
ben straight, direct
stikk 'motsatt completely opposite to
an'ledning c. occasion (on =
  ved)
tiltale en attract one
bakvendt the wrong way about,
  topsy turvy
selvsagt of course
punkt n. point
uråd [ˇuːrɔː] impossible
instru'ment n. instrument
til rådighet c. at one's disposal
skille (-te) part, separate
lykkønske (-et) congratulate
gjensidig mutual
re'spekt c. respect
kraftig vigorous
neve c. fist
nevetak n. fist-shaking
veksle (-et) exchange

Exercise 49 (I)

Ved målet (av Roald Amundsen)

Om morgenen den 15. desember 1911 var været på sitt beste,
akkurat som skapt til ankomst til Polen. Jeg er ikke helt
sikker, men jeg tror vi stakk frokosten litt fortere i oss den
dagen enn de foregående, og kom oss noe raskere ut av
teltet, enda jeg må tilstå at denne handlingen alltid foregikk
med stor hastighet. Føret var denne dagen litt vekslende.
Av og til gled skiene godt, men av og til var det smått stell.
Det gikk framover denne dagen på samme mekaniske måte
som før. Det ble ikke snakket stort, men øynene ble brukt
så mye mer. Halsen til Hansen var dobbelt så lang den
dagen som den forrige, slik tøyde og strakte han den for
om mulig å se noen millimeter lenger. Jeg hadde bedt ham
før vi dro ut å glane ordentlig, og det gjorde han til gagns.
Men hvor mye han enn glante og så, fikk han likevel ikke
øye på annet enn den uendelige, flate vidda bortover.

Klokka 3 ettermiddag ljomet et samtidig 'holdt' fra kjørerne. Målet var nådd, reisen slutt. Jeg kan ikke si—enda jeg vet det ville ha gjort langt større effekt—at jeg stod ved mitt livs mål. Det ville være å skrøne vel mye og åpenlyst.

Jeg får heller være oppriktig og si bent fram at jeg tror aldri noe menneske har stått på et sted nettopp så stikk motsatt sine ønskers mål som jeg gjorde ved den anledning. Nordpolen hadde tiltalt meg fra jeg var barn, og nå stod jeg på Sydpolen. Kan det tenkes noe mer bakvendt.

Vi regnet nå at vi var på Polen. Selvsagt visste hver av oss at vi ikke stod på polpunktet—det ville være uråd å observere med den tid og de instrumenter vi hadde til rådighet. Men vi var så nær at de få kilometer som kanskje skilte, ikke kunne ha noe som helst å si.

Da vi hadde gjort holdt, samlet vi oss og lykkønsket hverandre. Vi hadde grunn til gjensidig respekt for det som var gjort, og jeg tror dette nettopp var hva vi følte og uttrykte med de kraftige nevetak som ble vekslet.

Vocabulary

flagg n. flag
høy'tidelig solemn
ferd c. trip, expedition
kjærlighet c. love
'stolthet c. pride
smell n. bang
folde (-et) seg ut unfurl
vaie (-et) fly, flutter
bestemme (or -te) decide
tilkomme irr. be one's privilege
takk'nemlighet c. gratitude
øde desolate
forlatt here: godforsaken
ta imot accept, take
ånd c. spirit
budt offered (from by irr. offer)
barkede (inflected form of barket) weatherbeaten
stang f. pole, staff
i været in the air
stund c. while, moment

langvarig lengthy, of long duration
seremoni [serəmo'niː] c. ceremony
venne (-te) seg av med break with the habit of
egn [ein] c. region
ikke så at not that
champagne [ʃam'panjə] champagne
kork c. cork
flømme (-te) flow
nøye (-de) seg med content oneself with
sel c. seal
kjøtt n. meat
tegn [tein] n. sign, token
passi'ar n. chat, talk
det tør hende idiom: it may be (happen)
bud n. message

Exercise 49 (II)

Flagget på Sydpolen

Etter denne første handlingen gikk vi til den neste, den største og mest høytidelige på hele ferden—å plante vårt flagg. Det var kjærlighet og stolthet som skinte ut av de 5 par øyne som så flagget, da det med et smell foldet seg ut i den friske brisen og vaiet på Polen.

Å plante flagget—denne historiske handlingen—hadde jeg bestemt at vi alle skulle være med på. Det tilkom ikke én mann å gjøre det, det tilkom alle dem som hadde satt livet inn i kampen og stått sammen i tykt og tynt. Det var den eneste måten jeg kunne vise mine kamerater takknemlighet på her på dette øde og forlatte sted. Jeg skjønte at de forstod det og tok imot det i den ånd det var budt dem. Fem barkede, frostbitte never var det som grep i stanga, løftet det vaiende flagget i været og plantet det som det første på den geografiske sydpol.

Den lille stunden vil sikkert minnes av oss alle som stod der den gang. Langvarige seremonier venner en seg av med i de egnene,—dess kortere dess bedre.

Selvsagt var det fest i teltet den kvelden—ikke så at champagnekorkene sprang og vinen flømmet, vi nøyde oss med et lite stykke selkjøtt til hver, og det smakte og gjorde godt. Noe annet tegn på fest innendørs hadde vi ikke. Ute hørte vi flagget slå og smelle. Passiaren gikk livlig i teltet, og mye ble det talt om. Det tør vel også hende at bud ble sendt hjem om hva vi hadde gjort.

Vocabulary

skandi'navisk Scandinavian
Ja here: in fact
forskjell c. difference
dia'lekt c. dialect
i al'minnelighet usually
'uttale (-te) pronounce
annerledes differently
tilfelle n. case, instance
uttrykk n. expression
vant til accustomed to
stort sett largely (speaking)
vo'kal c. vowel

konso'nant c. consonant
'gjenta irr. repeat
et lys går opp for ham a bell rings for him
'oppholde seg stay
hyggelig nice, pleasant
kompliment [kompli'maŋŋ] c. compliment
derimot on the other hand
neppe adv. hardly
ros c. praise
i hvert fall at any rate

lage (-et) make up, conceive
lystig gay, lively
moro c. fun
drosje [ˈdrɔʃʃə] c. taxi, cab
sted [steː] n. place, spot
etter hans mening in his
    opinion
kirkegård c. churchyard
være enig med agree with
'nettopp just, exactly

'ut på livet' have a gay time, on
    the spree
skape (-te) create
for'vikling c. confusion
misforståelse c. misunder-
    standing
lønne seg here: pay
krysse (-et) cross
grense c. border, limit

Exercise 50

De tre skandinaviske språk

De tre skandinaviske språk: svensk, dansk og norsk, er tem-melig like. Ja, det er så liten forskjell på dem at en kan nesten kalle dem dialekter.

Det er i alminnelighet ikke vanskelig for en nordmann å gjøre seg forstått f. eks. i Stockholm. Han finner naturligvis at svenskene uttaler de samme ordene litt annerledes i mange tilfelle og også bruker litt forskjellige ord og uttrykk, men han blir snart vant til det. Han har dessuten lest en del svensk i skolen.

Hvis han tar en tur til 'Kongens by' København, vil han kanskje til å begynne med ha noen vanskelighet med å forstå sine danske brødre. Ordene og uttrykkene er nok stort sett de samme, men danskene uttaler ofte vokaler og konsonanter på en ganske annen måte. Men etter at set-ningen er blitt gjentatt et par ganger, går det nok et lys opp for nordmannen. Har han oppholdt seg i byen noen dager, går det som regel meget fint.

Likevel er det en del ord som har helt forskjellig betydning i de tre skandinaviske språk. Vi kan nevne som eksempel *rar*. Når danskene og svenskene snakker om *en rar mann*, mener de en hyggelig mann. Det er med andre ord en kompliment. På norsk derimot betyr *en rar mann* en underlig eller merkelig (= *queer*) mann og kan neppe tas som noen ros.

Ett eksempel til: adjektivet *rolig* betyr i dansk og norsk fredelig, stille (=*quiet*), mens det i svensk har betydningen morsom (= *funny*). Det fins en morsom historie om dette ordet. Den skal være sann, men om den ikke er sann, er den i hvert fall godt laget.

En svenske kom en gang til en norsk by. Han var en lystig kar, og om kvelden ville han ha litt moro. Han tok en drosje, og da sjåføren spurte hvor han skulle hen, svarte svensken at han gjerne ville bli kjørt til et rolig sted. Sjåføren tenkte seg litt om og·kjørte ham så til kirkegården. Det var etter hans mening et rolig sted, og det kan man jo være enig med ham i. Men det var ikke nettopp et slikt sted svensken hadde ment. Han ville 'ut på livet', som vi sier.

Heldigvis er det ikke mange ord som er så forskjellige at det skaper slike forviklinger og misforståelser. Men det lønner seg å være litt forsiktig med hvilke ord man bruker når man krysser grensen.

PART III
KEY TO EXERCISES

1(a)

en sjø	sjøen	sjøer	sjøene
et dyr	dyret	dyr	dyrene
en gate	gaten	gater	gatene
en vei	veien	veier	veiene
en gutt	gutten	gutter	guttene
en by	byen	byer	byene
et belte	beltet	belter	beltene

1(b) to gutter, fire piker, sju epler, to brød, fem fisker.

2(a) Is he an Englishman or a Norwegian? He is a Norwegian, but the mother is English and the father an American. He has a sister. She is six years (old). Have you a sister? No, but I have two brothers, Arne and Olaf. Arne has five children—two boys and three girls. Olaf has two girls. They are from Drammen. It is five (Norwegian) miles from Oslo to Drammen. Have you been in Norway? Yes, but only in Oslo. I have many friends in Oslo.

2(b) Min far har to brødre og fire søstre. Olaf er min bror og Marit min søster. Vi er fra Norge, men vi har mange venner i England. Har du vært i England? Ja, men bare i London. Har din søster mange barn. Hun har fire barn. Hvor er barna nå? De er i London.

Vi har to armer, to hender, to ben og to føtter, men vi har ti fingrer og ti tær. Skogen har mange trær. Min by har tre bakere, men bare én lærer.

3(a) mannens hatt, bondens åker, krigens redsler, herr Hansens hund, Kongens klær.

3(b) Navnet på byen, sønnen til læreren, Konene til mennene, moren til barna.

4(a) I awoke early today, had my breakfast out in the open, and then jumped into the sea. It was glorious. I did not bathe yesterday. The water was too cold, only fifteen degrees Centigrade, but my wife bathed.

My brother has got me a book by Ibsen. I remember my teacher speaking much about him at school. My brother is expecting a letter from me, but I have lost the pen I had.

4(b) De reddet ham. Han hadde badet i sjøen og kunne ikke svømme. Guttene kastet steiner (ut) i vannet og jaget endene bort (=vekk). Han våkner tidlig og hopper ut av senga. Jeg hadde ikke børstet mitt hår (håret mitt). Hun ventet på meg i bilen.

5(a) We shared the cake between us. I felt the cold. I heard what you said. He drove the car into the garage. She read a book about Norway. I borrowed the book from her. I have studied Norwegian for over two years. They smiled at me. The student saved money and went abroad. He showed us the way. You have eaten up the cake.

5(b) Jeg lånte/har lånt en bok av ham.
Hun leste/har lest avisen hver dag.
Far kjørte bilen inn i garasjen.
Barna hørte/har hørt/barnetimen i radio.
Hun svarte/har svart nei.
Du viste/har vist meg huset til din bror.

6(a) Have you met my father? No. That was strange. I was to meet him here in front of the Town Hall at 2 o'clock, and now it is ten past. But there I see him. He has bought flowers for mother. She has her birthday today. Congratulations! Thank you. I have bought a present for her which I hope she will like. She liked the one I bought last year.

Who called out? Oh, it was only the newspaper boy. Norway has lost the football match against Denmark.

6(b) Jeg liker å lese bøker. Jeg leste om Nansen i går. Min søster liker å høre musikk, og har kjøpt mange plater. Hun likte ikke (den) hatten hun kjøpte i går. Jeg har kjøpt (meg) en pipe. Vis meg butikken hvor du kjøpte den.

7(a) I dreamt last night that I bathed in the Thames. The thief had hidden himself behind a tree. Where have you hidden the money? To hide is not to forget (lit. hidden is not forgotten). What do you call a man who lives in Norway? I call him a Norwegian. She called me a fool. The man and the wife were always working and did not distinguish between night and day. The boy played the piano all day. I understood well what he talked (was talking) about. My brother understood nothing.

7(b) Moren skjønte at gutten drømte. Hun glemte å svare. De kalte ham Gudmund. Hun hadde gjemt bort blomstene hun hadde kjøpt. Gutten skjønte hva de mente. Han hadde kjent henne i mange år. Jeg lærte å kjøre bil i fjor. Jeg vet hva du mener. Jeg trodde det.

8. Only the translation:

1. The smoke chokes (or: is choking) him. 2. She lays the cloth on the table. 3. The hen lays eggs. 4. He places the chair in the corner. 5. You count to a hundred. 6. Mother tells fairy tales. 7. Father hands me an apple. 8. I stretch myself in the morning. 9. That arouses great interest. 10. Mother wakes me early in the morning. 11. They elect a king. 12. Are you following my advice? 13. What are you asking about? 14. I am greasing my shoes. 15. The farmer sells butter. 16. You do not speak the truth. 17. She brings good news. 18. The wolf does great harm.

8(a) Late one evening I came to the town where my friend lived. I had his address, but did not know the town (was a stranger in the town) and did not know where his house was (lit. lay). The best thing would have been to take a taxi— that is done by most people—but I was a poor student and did not have (possess) a penny. The few crowns I had in my pocket when I started were used up. I practised the sentence: Can you (please) tell me the way to . . . Can you tell me the way to . . .

Most people understood what I said and tried to help me. 'Do you think I am able to find the house,' I asked. 'Oh yes,' they answered. 'It is so easy (I assure you). You can't miss it.' It was just what I did. It started to get dark, too. (It was getting dark, too.) I turned to the left and I turned to the right—then continued straight on, as they had told me, but the house, where was the house? Had it burnt down? At last I managed to find it. Two big fir trees had almost completely hidden it. I was saved. I had got a roof over my head, but I had indeed tried hard.

8(b)
1. Sangeren øvde daglig.
   Sangeren har øvd daglig.
2. Jeg strevde hardt, men lærte lite.
   Jeg har strevd hardt, men har lært lite.
3. Ørnen svevde høyt oppe i luften.
   Ørnen har svevd høyt oppe i luften.
4. Eleven prøvde å lære diktet utenat.
   Eleven har prøvd å lære diktet utenat.
5. Du behøvde ikke å betale.
   Du har ikke behøvd å betale.

In English:
1. The singer practises daily.
2. I try hard, but learn little.
3. The eagle hovers up in the sky.
4. The pupil tries to learn the poem by heart.
5. You do not need to pay.

8(c) Hun spiller meget godt. Hun øver både dag og natt. Jeg pleide å spille fiolin en gang, men nå har jeg glemt det helt, og jeg tør ikke prøve igjen (*or*: jeg våger ikke å prøve igjen). Jeg er ikke meget musikalsk, men jeg liker å høre musikk. Jeg er meget glad i Grieg.

9.
1. Tror du han vil komme (*or* kommer)? *Slightly more certain:* Mener du han kommer?
2. Jeg synes (*your personal taste*) hun er en av de søteste piker jeg har sett.
3. Har (er) han gått? Nei, jeg tror ikke det.
4. Forstyrr ham ikke. Han tenker.
5. Jeg tror det er best vi går.
6. Vi synes at du burde komme, eller hva synes du selv?
7. Jeg syntes jeg så en mann i rommet. (*I had a feeling . . .* Jeg trodde *etc. would mean, I believed . . .*)
8. Hun trodde jeg var femti. Jeg er bare førti.
9. Dette er veldig rart, synes jeg.

10. Dette er vanskelig å tro.
11. Det betyr krig.
12. Jeg tror ikke på mirakler.

10(a) My family are very fond of the sea and spent every summer holiday on 'Sørlandet'. We lived in a little cosy cottage which my parents rented. We often rowed out to an island to bathe, to fish and collect shells which lay strewn along the shore. If the wind started to blow (lit. If it started to blow), we turned and rowed homewards again. We always reached land and no accident happened (lit. there happened no accident), although mother prophesied that something would happen one fine day. She was almost right. We rowed out one morning in fine, quiet weather . . . not a cloud in the sky, no wind, no wave. We were going to fish for cod. In the afternoon a wind started to blow, and my brother who was rowing got so frightened that he lost an oar. There was only one thing to do—cry for help. We waved our arms shouting: Help! help! Father fortunately heard us. He sprang into a boat and rowed with all his might to reach us. He managed fine. We were saved, but an accident might easily have occurred if no one on the beach (shore) had heard us shouting (= when we shouted).

Proverb: All is well that ends well.

10(b) Er du glad i sjøen? Nei, jeg liker å feriere på fjellet. Jeg har en koselig liten hytte ikke langt fra Lillehammer. Er Lillehammer en stor by. Nei, heldigvis ikke. Jeg liker ikke store byer. Jeg kan ikke bo der. Jeg har hørt at luften på Lillehammer er så fin. Ja, det er riktig (*or* Ja, det stemmer) —og naturen! Jeg kaller det turistpropaganda (*or* Det kaller jeg turistpropaganda). Kall det hva du vil. Det er sant. Kom og se hvis du tror jeg lyver. Du vil ikke bli skuffet.

11(a) I awake every morning at seven o'clock, stretch myself and jump out of the bed and into the bathroom, brush my teeth and wash myself. Afterwards I dry myself with a towel, dress in a hurry—first underwear, shirt and trousers, stockings and shoes, then tie and finally a coat.

I am now fully dressed and eat my breakfast with a ravenous appetite. I always read the newspaper while I eat.

Rewritten in the past tense:

Jeg våknet hver morgen klokka syv, strakte meg og hoppet ut av senga og inn i badet, pusset tennene og vasket meg. Etterpå tørket jeg meg med et håndkle, kledde på meg i en fart—først undertøy, skjorte og bukse, strømper og sko, så slips og til slutt en jakke.

Jeg var nå fullt påkledd og spiste min frokost med glupende appetitt. Jeg leste alltid avisen mens jeg spiste.

11(b) Du sa du hadde en norsk venn. Ja, det er sant. Han bodde i Oslo, men pleide å reise til England om sommeren. Han sa han kunne ikke bo der, men likte å reise i England.

Jeg skal reise til Norge neste vår. Jeg har kjøpt en norsk bok som kostet ti shilling. Jeg lærer å lese og tale språket. Jeg har lært flere ord allerede. Det er veldig morsomt. Jeg kan si: God morgen. Det betyr 'good morning' på engelsk, og God aften som svarer til: 'Good evening.'

Min venn liker å ro og fiske. Jeg har besøkt ham flere ganger. Vi rodde over elva.

12(a) I seized the boy by the arm. The son wrote a letter home every week. My brother has written a book about Ibsen. The dog bit the boy in the leg and the boy howled.

12(b) The thief crept along the fence. You have broken your promise. The sportsman (hunter) has shot an elk and a fox. The water has frozen to ice.

12(c) He drank only two glasses. Have you found the ring? I found it when I put my hand in my pocket. The boy helped the girl on with her coat.

12(d) He carried her over the brook. I have cut my finger. He stole from the rich and gave to the poor.

12(e) Eve gave Adam an apple. Adam had not asked for it. No one has seen him. The girl looked at me with big eyes. My sister has lain ill for three days.

12(f) I took my hat and said good-bye. They let me go. The clock in the tower struck exactly twelve. We went to England by plane. We laughed and sang the whole way. She said she got up at eight every day. He who laughs last, laughs best (longest) (*et alminnelig ordtak*).

12(g) The plane arrived at Fornebu airport yesterday. I could not sleep last night. The storm kept me awake. I got up and took a long walk. My friend 'walked' to London yesterday. No, he did not. He 'went' to London.

13(a) A very learned professor, let us call him N. N., never found his clothes when he was going to dress in the morning. Therefore, he always arrived too late at the university. To avoid this, he wrote down where he had laid every piece of clothing in the evening.

He sat in bed writing:

The stockings on (top of) the shoes, the shoes under the bed, shirt, tie and coat over the back of the chair, underwear on the chair. At last (finally) he wrote: The professor in bed. Then he put out the light, and not long after he slept like a top (lit. stone).

When he awoke next morning he grasped the list and found all his clothes where they should be. But—the professor in bed he did not find. He arrived late that time too.

13(b) Han drakk et glass øl før han gikk til sengs om kvelden (aftenen). Mannen red alltid alene. Han tilbød meg bare ti pund for bilen. Piken tilga ham aldri. Arsenal har vunnet igjen. Han grep alltid sjansen når han så den. Jeg har ikke funnet henne. Hva sa Cæsar? Han sa: 'Jeg kom, jeg så, jeg vant.'

14(a)

1. Did you meet Per yesterday? Yes, I saw him in the theatre.

Did you know that he was there? No, I had no idea.

Did you recognize him? Yes, at once.

How did he look? He looked very well.

Did you speak a lot with him. Yes, in every interval.

Are you often in the theatre? I see almost everything that is on.

You never go to concerts? (Do you ever go to c.?) Yes, occasionally.

What do you like best, modern music or classical? I prefer the latter.

Do you play any intrument yourself? No, unfortunately, but you play the piano, don't you?
Do you remember that too? You have indeed a good memory.

2. Bor du i Oslo? Hører han ofte på radio? Skrev hun brev til kjæresten sin hver dag? Er han soldat? Ligger byen Narvik i Nord-Norge? Døde Bjørnson i Paris? Vil Deres kone ha en kopp te til?

3. Hun skriver et brev. Du studerer (Du holder på å studere) norsk, ikke sant? Han reiser (skal reise) i morgen, ikke sant? Hva gjør de? Spiller de bridge?

14(b) Fikk du (tak i) billetter til konserten? Ja, jeg var heldig. Når begynner konserten? Den begynner klokka åtte. Liker du å spille kort? Nei, jeg synes det er kjedelig. Spiller din bror tennis? Nei, han er mer interessert i fotball.

15(a) To learn to ski is not so easy as one thinks. Have you tried? No, I daren't. You must not be stiff. Don't forget to tie your skis on properly. Don't be afraid. 'Keep smiling' (lit. Take it with good humour) . . . Don't think that you can learn it in one day. Practice makes master ('practice makes perfect'). Don't you (very) often break your legs? (The pronoun *en* often corresponds to 'you' in English.) No, that doesn't often happen. It doesn't pay to be careless, of course. That is silly.

15(b) Visste du ikke at jeg kom? Nei, du har ikke skrevet. Jeg fikk ikke tid. Liker du ikke å se meg? Naturligvis, men jeg vet ikke hvor jeg kan finne en seng til deg. Jeg kan sove i en stol. Jeg behøver ikke en seng å sove i. Vær ikke tåpelig. Du kan sove på en divan. Ja, mange takk, det er ypperlig. Jeg har gjort det mange ganger.

16(a) Jeg leste i dag en roman. Helten blir narret ut i skogen og blir drept av en forræder. Ingen ser det. Men om noen få dager blir ugjerningen oppdaget. Forræderen blir fanget og straffet med døden.

16(b) Historien leses av mange barn. Prinsessen reddes av helten, som er bare en fattig mann. Han føres til slottet for å belønnes. Han gjøres til konge, og de lever lykkelig resten av livet.

With the auxiliary 'å bli':

Historien blir lest av mange barn. Prinsessen blir reddet av helten, som er bare en fattig mann. Han blir ført til slottet for å bli belønnet. Han blir gjort til konge, og de lever lykkelig resten av livet.

17. The correct forms of 'være' and 'bli':

1. ble, 2. ble, 3. var, 4. ble, 5. ble, 6. bli, 7. bli, 8. var, 9. var, 10. var blitt.

18. *At the Barber's*

A man went into a barber's shop to have a shave. As there were four or five customers before him, he had to wait for his turn. After a while the barber calls out: 'Next please!' Our man gets up in the chair, and the barber asks him as usual: 'Haircut or a shave?' 'A shave,' the man answers.

After a while the barber, who is very short-sighted, says: 'Have you eaten tomato soup for dinner today?' 'No,' the customer answers, astonished, 'I have eaten fish soup.' 'And afterwards?' 'Beef.' 'With jam to (on) it?' 'No, with onion.' 'Have you eaten pudding with red sauce as dessert?' 'No, fruit salad.' 'That is strange. Then I must have cut you after all.'

19.

En stor bok.	Et stort barn.	En stor båt.
Noen store skip.	Store epler.	Store menn.
En lang vei	Lang film.	Et langt ord.
Lange båter.		
Veien er lang.	Ordet var langt.	Skoene var lange.
Et høyt tre.	Høye trær.	Ingen høye fjell.
Mannen er høy	Huset er høyt.	Prisene er for
Trærne var blitt høye.		høye.

20(a) Den lange veien. De lange veiene.
Det lange bordet. Det lange stykket.
Den vakre haven. De vakre pikene. Det vakre huset.

20(b) Answer (*svar*):

denne is in the neuter *dette*, in the plural *disse*.

denne lange veien, disse lange veiene
dette lange bordet, dette lange stykket

denne vakre haven, disse vakre pikene
dette vakre huset.

21(a) *Norway's Independence Day*

The seventeenth of May is Norway's Independence Day and there is great rejoicing over the whole country on that day. It is a delight to see the long procession with all the happy children marching through the streets. All carry small beautiful Norwegian flags in their hands and they are dressed in their best clothes for the occasion.

In Oslo the children's procession is especially long. You may stand for a good two hours looking at it.

Each school has its own band, which all the time plays national marches and songs. You can hear the fresh tunes at a long distance. The boys are dressed in fine red, white, and blue uniforms, and the small girls in beautiful national costumes. The picturesque procession then marches in a big curve up to the beautiful castle.

The beloved King of the Norwegians, Olav V, is standing on the balcony greeting the young ones, and they cheer at the top of their voices.

The procession then goes on down towards the gay town. You see Norwegian flags and Norwegian colours everywhere and you meet smiling faces and you hear friendly words. Everybody is in high spirits, what we in Norwegian call 'perlehumør'.

In all the towns of Norway from north to south we find the same joy and gaiety.

21(b) Har du sett hans nye hus? 2. Han likte ikke å bo i store byer. 3. Vi hadde ingen penger. 4. Liker du Den glade enke? 5. Kjenner du den hvite dame? 6. Lillehammer er bare en liten by. 7. Den lille pike(n) hadde intet (=ikke noe) hjem å gå til. 8. Det var en pen liten pike. 9. Disse norske epler (eplene) er for små. 10. Vi kjøpte noen meget fine jordbær. 11. Været var fint. 12. Det var et fint ord for det. 13. Denne brune hatt(en) var meget dyr. 14. Hun skrev et langt brev til sin far. 15. Prisene er blitt for høye. 16. Jeg så noen store skip på havnen. 17. Han ga et dumt svar. 18. Det store egg(et) var råttent. 19. Jeg kan ikke se noe rødt hus. 20. Er det klart?

22(a) A man from Africa had been on a visit to Norway, and when he came back to his homeland his relatives and friends wanted to know how it was (how things were) up there in the high north. 'Well,' he said, 'there were two (kinds of) winters, one green winter and one white winter. But the green one was worst, because (lit. for) then they did not put the heat on (lit. they did not burn in the stoves).

22(b) Svar på spørsmålene (*Answers to the questions*).

1. Mannen var fra Afrika.
2. Han hadde vært på besøk i Norge.
3. De ville gjerne vite hvordan det var deroppe i det høye nord.
4. Med grønn vinter mente han den norske sommer(en), og med hvit vinter den norske vinter(en).
5. For da fyrte de ikke (i ovnene).

A doubtful compliment

She: Am I not just as beautiful as the day when we got married?

He: Oh yes, dear, but now it takes just a little more time.

22(c) Du er kanskje rik, men din far var rikere. Sissel er den kjekkeste pike i hele byen og den lykkeligste også. Oslo er mye (meget) større enn Bergen, men mye (meget) mindre enn London. England har større byer enn Norge. Det er dyrere å bo i en by enn på landet. Jeg er to år eldre enn min bror. Jeg var mye (meget) sterkere i mine yngre dager. Jo mer han drakk, desto tørstere ble han. Vær mer forsiktig (or forsiktigere) neste gang. Det er den aller beste tobakk jeg har prøvd. Svein er den høyeste gutt i klassen, men ikke den flinkeste.

23(a) *The Geography of Norway*

In Norway we find (lit. one finds) high mountains, deep valleys and swift-flowing rivers. The longest river is called the Glomma. It comes from the Aursund Lake and runs southward and flows into the sea near the town of Fredrikstad, one of the best known factory towns in Norway.

The Norwegian rivers have great speed and one waterfall follows after the other. They are also rich in fish, and English tourists go salmon-fishing in many of our rivers.

Norway has a long coast and the Norwegians started early to sail on the sea. They did not have such big ships as we have now. Surely you have heard about the beautiful Viking ships.

In these small ships they sailed to England and France. In modern times the Norwegians are well known as a seafaring nation. The country has a very big merchant fleet, one of the biggest in the world, and you (lit. one) can meet Norwegian ships on all oceans. The Norwegian flag flies in every big harbour.

Norway has many deep and long fjords. The longest is the famous Sognefjord, which cuts (lit. goes) a long distance into the country with high mountains on both sides. It is very beautiful and the foreign tourists admire it very much.

As we get further north the country becomes narrower and narrower. At the narrowest place, near the town of Narvik, it is just about 8 kilometres to the Swedish frontier. At the widest place the distance from the West Coast to Sweden is about 450 kilometres.

In the centre of this wide area lie Norway's highest mountain ranges: the Jotunheimen and the Rondane. The very highest mountain peak is called the Galdhøpiggen. It is 2,468 metres above sea-level and lies in the wild mountain area of Jotunheimen.

Norway's capital is called Oslo, and is the biggest town in the country. It is almost as big as the English coal town (of) Newcastle. Other great towns are for instance Bergen and Trondheim. Bergen is well known as a lively (busy) shipping town with an interesting history.

The same applies to Trondheim. They are both amongst the very oldest towns of Norway.

23(b) *Livet i en sjøby*

Jeg har to brødre og tre søstre. Min eldste bror heter Per Han er tre år eldre enn meg. Min yngste bror er fire år yngre enn meg, men mye høyere. Alle mine søstre er meget unge. Den eldste er bare sju år gammel. Alle har lyst hår og er meget vakre.

De er veldig glad i å leke.

Mine to brødre er meget sterke og liker å slåss. De er begge hissige, men de blir fort gode venner igjen hver gang de har trettet. Vårt hus ligger på toppen av en bakke, og vi har derfor en fin utsikt over sjøen nedenfor. Vi kan se alle de store skipene som kommer inn på havnen. Noen er hvite, andre er røde eller svarte. Det er meget travelt på kaien når en stor passasjerbåt kommer inn. Den lille byen er straks full av nye, ukjente folk: svensker, dansker, tyskere og engelskmenn. Hvis du kan snakke fremmede språk, kan du ha mange interessante samtaler med disse menneskene. Svenskene og danskene forstår vårt eget språk. Den neste morgen er (har) den fine båten forsvunnet, og byen er likeså stille som den var før.

24(a) *Names of months and seasons*

The year has twelve months. The first month is called January, the second February, the third March, the fourth April, the fifth May, the sixth June, the seventh July, the eighth August, the ninth September, the tenth October, the eleventh November and the twelfth December, which is the last month of the year.

In Norway Spring comes in the months of April and May, and in June, July and August it is Summer. Autumn comes in September and generally lasts till the end of November, when the Winter sets in with cold and snow. Some months have 31 days, such as January, March, May, July, August, October and December, while April, June, September and November have 30 days, and February has only 28, except every fourth year, when it has 29. That year is called Leap Year. A year usually has 365 days, but when it is Leap Year, 366. There are 52 weeks in a year. A week has 7 days.

The names of the days are Sunday, Monday, Tuesday, Wednesday, Thursday, Friday and Saturday.

24(b) Kan du fortelle (*or* si) meg hvor mange klokka er? Den er seksten minutter over elleve. Da må jeg (*Inversion*) si farvel. Mitt tog går kvart på tolv, og det tar minst tjue (tyve) minutter til stasjonen. Hvilken dato er det i dag? Det er den nittende juli. Hvor langt er det til Lillehammer?

Med tog er det ett hundre og åttifem kilometer, det vil si (*abbr.* dvs.) omtrent ett hundre og seksten engelske mil. Med bil er det to hundre kilometer eller 125 engelske mil. En engelsk mil er omtrent en komma seks kilometer, som du vet. Hvor mange timer vil det ta? Tre time og atten minutter, for å være nøyaktig. Hva er din adresse i Oslo? Storgaten 14, men vi skal flytte om fjorten dager. Hvor mange barn har du?—Tre sønner. De heter Per, Hans og Ole. Hvor gamle er de? Ole er født den niende juli nittenhundreogfemti. Hans er født den åtteogtyvende september nittenhundreogfemtitre. Per er født femte mai nittenhundreogfemtisju og da kan du selv regne ut hvor gambe de.

25. *En anekdote*

The Norwegian general, Helset, was known for his apt and amusing remarks. During a military exercise he discovered a motor-cyclist driving (lit. who drove) much faster than was allowed.

He stopped him, asking (lit. and asked) him how old he was. 'I am 21, sir,' answered the young man. 'How fast did you drive just now?' 'Oh, some 95 km per hour, I suppose.' The general shook his head saying (lit. and said): 'The question now, young man, is whether you want to drive at 95 and stay 21 or to drive at 21 and become 95.'

26(a)   Holmenkollen, 28th July, 1966.

Dear parents,
    Thanks for your letter. I got it exactly an hour ago and am sending you a few lines in a great hurry. I am very comfortable, especially as regards food and fresh air. Yesterday the whole family were out at Bygdøy bathing. The sun was shining as usual. Apparently it never rains here.

There were crowds of people everywhere, young and old, who were bathing and afterwards lying in the sun. The water was quite warm. Otherwise I would certainly not have dared to go in.

Afterwards we had coffee on the beach and smoked a cigarette or two.

I have not had a letter from Ola yet, but he will be writing soon, I expect.

Best regards,
Rolf.

26(b) Oslo, 25. august 1966.

Kjære venn!

Takk for ditt siste brev som jeg fikk akkurat for en uke siden. Jeg må fortelle deg at dette vil bli bare et kort brev. Du spør meg hva jeg har sett i Oslo. Jeg har sett mange interessante ting nylig, flere filmer og skuespill og har også hørt noen gode konserter. Jeg kan nå fortelle deg at neste måned skal jeg reise tilbake til England igjen. Derfor prøver jeg å se så mye av Norge som jeg kan.

Jeg har også nylig vært på en lang fottur i Nordmarka. Den var litt for lang for meg, så jeg var nokså trett da jeg nådde byen, men likevel likte jeg det. Du får nok av frisk luft. Du kan neppe finne noe som er bedre for deg, kan du? Vel, jeg må slutte nå.

Håper å se deg igjen snart.
Hjertelig hilsen
Gunnar.

27(a) *The waiter:* Good evening. What do you wish?

Mr N. We want (would like) a cosy table for three persons.

W. We will soon arrange that. You may have the table there, over in the corner.

Mr N. Thank you, that will suit us well. May I see the menu, please?

W. Here you are, sir.

Mr N. What would you recommend today?

W. The beef is very good, and we also have excellent trout.

Mrs N. I should like to have beef.

Mr N. And you, my daughter?

Miss N. I would rather have fish, fried trout for instance.

Mr N. I think I will try the beef myself. That will make two beef and one trout.

W. Very well (lit. that shall be). Do you want anything to drink?

Mr N. Yes, could I see the wine list, please? I think a glass of red wine will go well with the beef, but you, young lady, who have chosen fish, ought rather to have a glass of white wine, isn't that right?

Miss N. No, I won't have anything to drink with the food. I would rather have a (glass of) liqueur with the coffee.

Mr N. As you like.

*   *   *

Mr N. What shall we choose for dessert? What do you say to ice cream?

Both the ladies. That will certainly be good in this heat.

*   *   *

Mr N. Could I have the bill, please?

W. Just a moment. Here you are, sir.

27(b)   Hvor skal du (hen)? Jeg kan ikke snakke med deg nå. Jeg skal møte min kone på stasjonen, og jeg tør ikke komme for sent. Hun vil (*or* kommer til å) bli sint på meg hvis jeg gjør det. Kommer hun med fem-toget? Ja. Du burde ta en drosje. Det ville være meget (*or* mye) bedre. Å nei, du må ikke si det. Da ville jeg ikke få noe frisk luft. Jeg forstår. Jeg skal ikke hefte deg. Vil du og din kone bli hjemme i kveld? (*Or* Kommer du og din kone til å bli hjemme i kveld? *or just* Blir . . . hjemme i kveld?) Ja, jeg tror det. Jeg skal ringe deg senere. Farvel og glem ikke å hilse din kone så meget fra meg. Jeg skal ikke glemme det. Det skal jeg ikke glemme. ('skal' *here denotes promise more than future.*)

27(c)   Jeg ville ikke ha reist bort hvis jeg hadde visst at du var i byen. Hvorfor fortalte du meg ikke at du skulle komme? Jeg måtte reise (*or* dra) i all hast og fikk ikke tid til å skrive. Dessuten skulle det være en overraskelse. Jeg håper endelig at du vil underrette (*or present:* underretter) oss neste gang du kommer. Det lover jeg.

27(d)
1. Jeg spurte om han skulle reise (*or* dra) i morgen.
2. Politiet fortalte at det ville få alvorlige følger.

3. Bonden tvilte på at det ville lønne seg.
4. Per mente (= trodde) at han ville få permisjon.
5. Sjåføren sa at bilen måtte repareres.

28(a) Olav: Tell me, have you seen Per lately? Odd: No, I haven't seen him for several weeks. Olav: Do you think he has gone away? Odd: He mentioned that he would travel to Oslo to go to school. Have you heard anything about it? Olav: No, not a word. Odd: Did you know him well? Olav: Oh, yes, we were 'dus', and very good friends. Odd: Then it is strange that he hasn't told us that he was leaving. Perhaps he hadn't time to visit us before he left.

Olav: That may be the reason. I will 'phone his sister and ask her if she knows anything. But here (lit. there) comes his brother. The brother: Hallo, you know perhaps that Per has left, or hasn't he told you? Olav and Odd: No, we know absolutely nothing. The brother: He said he would write to you as soon as he arrived in Oslo.

Olav and Odd: That is grand. Give him our best regards.

28(b) 1. Kjenner De ham? Nei, Jeg har ikke sett ham før. Ingen av oss kjenner ham. Han må være (en) fremmed i byen vår (i vår by). Han gikk forbi meg i går på gaten. Fru Olsen vet sikkert hva han heter. Jeg vil spørre henne. Hun vet alt. Hun og hennes mann skal komme (or kommer) til oss til kaffe i ettermiddag. Etterpå skal vi spille kort. Jeg visste ikke at dere spilte kort. Å, jo da, vi gjør det av og til. Spiller De kort? Nei aldri.

Hvor er guttene? De er på skitur. Jeg har ikke sett dem på lenge. Har De solgt huset Deres (or Deres hus)? Nei, jeg har ikke solgt det ennå. Mine barn (barna mine) er for glad i det. Vil De høre en god historie? Ja, hvis den er god og morsom.

2. Hvem gjorde det? Det var ikke meg (jeg). Ikke meg (jeg) heller. Nei, det var ikke ham (han). Han er større enn deg (du). Han er nesten så stor som deg (du).

29(a) 1. He sat down in a chair. 2. I go to bed at 11 in the evening. 3. She feels well. 4. The boy burnt himself. 5. The man fell and hurt himself. 6. I washed myself with the soap. 7. The girl cut her finger. 8. She didn't care about it. 9. The soldiers rose to their feet. 10. I could imagine so. 11. We thought that he would like to come. 12. The door opened and a cat slunk in. 13. When they had sat down the minister started the sermon.

29(b) 1. Hun giftet seg for penger. 2. De følte seg lykkelige. 3. Jeg føler meg bedre nå. 4. Du må ikke sette deg. 5. De gamle (folk) foretrakk å legge seg. 6. Jeg bryr meg ikke om hva han sier. 7. Han brente seg. 8. Jeg vasker meg hver morgen. 9. Jeg kunne ikke tenke meg at han var der. 10. Han reiste seg og gikk ut av rommet (værelset). 11. Han satte seg ved peisen for å varme seg. 12. Jeg skar meg i fingeren med en kniv. 13. Du har ikke forandret deg meget.

30. *Singular:*
Min frakk er ny. Mitt bord er nytt. Min lampe er ny.

Plural:
Mine hus er nye. Mine frakker er nye. Mine bord er nye. Mine lamper er nye.

Singular:
Ditt nye bilde er pent. Din nye bil er pen. Din nye hest er pen.

Plural: Dine nye hatter er pene.
Dine nye bilder er pene. Dine nye biler er pene. Dine nye hester er pene.

31(a) 1. His hair was grey. 2. I doubt his words. 3. Her condition is serious. 4. Your father has bought our house. 5. My country is bigger than yours. 6. Why is your collar so dirty? Can't you borrow one of mine? 7. Who (has) told you that the book is his? 8. When does your train leave? 9. Now it is your turn. 10. My chances are small.

31(b) 1. Det er ikke min tur. 2. Mine bøker er dyrere enn dine. 3. Din bror venter på deg. Han har din hatt og frakk (*colloquially:* hatten og frakken din). 4. Min mors største interesse er å arbeide i vår have. 5. Hennes sønn er hennes største stolthet. 6. Har du sett deres gård, deres griser, deres sauer og kuer? 7. Hvem av hans sønner liker du best?

32. sin (sitt, sine). The reflexive possessive.

Remember: **sin** can never be used as part of the subject.

1. Etter krigen vil han reise tilbake til sitt land.
2. Kan du ikke se hans ansikt, eller er det for mørkt?
3. Den lille gutten hadde spist all sin mat (*or* all maten sin).
4a. Mennene hadde glemt å ta sine penger (*N.B.—plural in Norwegian*) med seg.
4b. Tror du at det var deres penger? (Sine *could not be used here as it would have no person to refer back to in the sentence.*)
4c. Tror du pengene var deres?
5. Engelskmennene taper aldri sitt gode humør.
6. Ole og hans bror hadde alltid vært gode venner. (Hans *here constitutes part of the subject.*)
7. Klokka var ikke hans. Den var min.
8. Wessel i et av sine morsomme dikt forteller historien om 'Smeden og Bakeren'. (*You would understand it better if the sentence were changed into:* Wessel forteller i et av sine morsomme dikt, etc.)
9. Faren så to menn snakke (*or* som snakket) med hans datter.
10. 'Hvor er pengene?' 'Jeg tok min del av dem (*N.B.—plural in Norwegian*), og de tok sin.'
11. Soldatene red gjennom hans have.

33. den. 1. Hva kaller du den gaten? 2. Har du malt det bildet selv? 3. De bøkene der er ikke mine, så du kan ikke ta dem. **denne.** 1. Dette huset er gult. 2. Disse bildene er gode. 3. Denne snøen er bløt. 4. Dette er en vakker dal. 5. Dette er ikke mine brev. **slik** or **sånn.** 1. Slike (sånne) folk er hyggelige. 2. Han likte ikke slikt (sånt) arbeid. 3. Har du sett en slik (sånn) tosk?

34(a) A party of English tourists had after great toil reached the top of the Galdhøpiggen, which is the highest mountain in Norway. First they had a good rest after the strenuous climb(ing), but then they began to ask the guide about the names of the different peaks, valleys and lakes which they saw around them.

A young lady asked: 'What is the name of that mountain there?' The guide: 'Do you mean that farthest to the left?' The lady: 'Yes, exactly.'

The guide: 'The peak you see there is the famous Glitretind, which is almost as high as this one.' An elderly lady said: 'It seems to me that all these peaks round about us are higher than the Galdhøpiggen itself.' The guide: 'It may look like it perhaps, but it is only an optical illusion.' The lady: 'But the snow we see on the Glitretind, does it never melt away?' The guide: 'It stays (lies) the whole year round.' Third tourist, a young business man from Manchester: 'This is a lovely spot. I think we will settle down here for good. But tell me, who has built this small hut here?' The guide: 'The well-known mountaineer Knut Vole. He carried all the materials up here on his back.' The tourist: 'That must indeed have been a strenuous job. I think it is more than enough to carry yourself uphill. Before we start on the descent you must once more tell me what the whole of this mountain range is called.' The guide: 'The Jotunheimen.' 'Yes, of course, I always forget that name.'

34(b) Ibsen og Bjørnson nevnes ofte (*or* blir ofte nevnt) sammen. Grunnen er at de levde på samme tid (*or* samtidig) og kjente hverandre godt. De skrev til hverandre i mange år, og var i det hele gode venner, skjønt de ofte var sinte på hverandre. De hadde (et) temmelig forskjellig gemytt og ganske forskjellig syn på mange ting. Bjørnson var mer optimistisk enn Ibsen og hadde en sterk tro på seg selv. Ibsen derimot tvilte alltid på sine evner, og denne tvilen har han skildret i mange av sine verker.

35(a) Which book have you got there? Oh, it is *Who's Who*. Who was it you were going to read about? It was a great King of Skis. I forget (lit. have forgotten) which races he won and which year it occurred. Is that so important? What are you saying! What lack of interest you are showing for our national sport! Indeed I do not bother to remember what all these sports stars have achieved, who has won the first prize in Homenkollen, and who has the world record in 500-metre skating. Such things are after all (= *da*) quite unimportant. By the way, have you heard the story about the Spanish journalist who saw the jumping in Holmenkollen for the first time? No, what did he say? Well, he described his impressions in the following way:

'The Norwegians are quite mad. They tie (strap) some wooden boards round their feet, and then they set out from steep precipices --flap in the air like birds and come down again without killing themselves. Quite incredible.'

I don't think that story was so terribly funny. No sense of humour!

35(b)
1. Hvem ga du brevet?
   Hvis bil er det? (*Coll.* Hvem er det som eier den bilen?)
   Hvem fortalte deg det?
2. Hva vil du ha? (Hva ønsker du?)
   Hvilket or Hva er det beste hotellet i Oslo?
   Hvilke bøker har du lest?
   Hvilke venner traff (møtte) du?
   Hvilke aviser pleier du å lese?
   Jeg visste ikke hva jeg skulle gjøre.
3. Hvilket glass foretrekker du (vil du helst ha)? (*Or coll.* hva for et glass, *etc.*)
   Hvilken or Hvem av guttene er flinkest?
4. For en støy (=et bråk)! For et rot! (hvilket rot *is rather stiff*). For en tosk (Hvilken tosk) jeg har vært som ikke så det!

36. *The Two Friends and the Bear*

Two good friends were once walking along a road. All of a sudden (the), one caught sight of a bear and he climbed up a tree without saying a word to his friend. Fortunately the boy who was left standing in (tr. on) the road had heard people say that a bear never touches a lifeless person. Therefore, he dropped to the ground and lay as if dead.

The bear examined him both well and long, sniffed and smelt and put his snout into his ear. But the boy held his breath and lay quite still. As the bear did not see any sign of life he jogged off to the wood again. When all danger was over the other boy climbed down from the tree, and the two friends walked together as before.

'Tell me one thing,' said the boy, who had been sitting in the tree, 'what was it the bear whispered in your ear?' 'Well, I don't exactly remember all of it,' said the other, 'but one thing I do remember his telling me. I should never rely upon a friend I hadn't tested in time of danger.'

Proverb: A friend in need is a friend indeed.

37. A bath in the morning is very nice. You feel absolutely refreshed (lit. like a new person), especially if you take' a shower afterwards. You always ought to take a cold shower after a hot bath in order to harden yourself. If you really want to live healthily you should take morning exercise just after getting up and then go into the bath.

38(a) Har du noen penger? Nei, kan du låne meg noen? Jeg kan fortelle deg noe nytt, noe riktig spennende. Noen tyver har brutt seg inn i banken og stjålet noen hundre tusen kroner.

Har du lest noe av Bjørnson? Jeg har lest noen få skuespill og et par dikt. Han har skrevet noen fine dikt som du må lese. Du vet kanskje at noen av hans skuespill har vært spilt i England? Jeg liker noen av Ibsens verker bedre. Ja, noen liker Ibsen, andre liker Bjørnson. Det ville ikke være bra om alle hadde samme smak. Men jeg har ikke funnet noen som kan bygge opp et drama slik som Ibsen. Å gå på teater er noe av det morsomste jeg vet.

Translation:

Have you any money? No, can you lend me some? I can tell you something new, something really exciting. Some thieves have broken into the bank and stolen some hundred thousand kroner.

Have you read anything of Bjørnson? I have read a few plays and a couple of poems. He has written some fine poems which you must read. You know perhaps that some of his plays have been acted in England? I like some of Ibsen's works better. Well, some like Ibsen, others like Bjørnson. It would be a pity (lit. It wouldn't be good) if everybody had the same taste. But I have not found anybody who can build up a drama like Ibsen. One of the most amusing things I know is to go to the theatre.

38(b) Noen tror at det er folk på månen. Jeg har kjøpt noen blomster til deg. Jeg trodde ikke at du kunne få tak i noen i dag. De hadde noen igjen. Har du fått noe kjøtt? Ja, jeg

fikk noe, men det var svært vanskelig. Så du bilen? Nei,
jeg så ikke noen bil. Noen venner kom for en time siden,
noen av våre aller beste venner fra Drammen.

39(a) *Quickly done*

Johan Herman Wessel is a well-known Norwegian poet
who wrote gay humorous verses. He was once present at a
big dinner, where he happened to be sitting beside a very
enterprising lady. This lady was very interested in Wessel,
and in the course of the conversation she suddenly asked the
poet:'Why aren't you married, Mr. Wessel?' 'I haven't got any
money,' answered Wessel. 'But I have,' said the lady. The
story goes on to tell that before rising from the table they
were already engaged.

39(b) De første linjene av *Alice in Wonderland*

Alice begynte å bli svært trett av å sitte ved siden av
søsteren på elvebredden og ikke å ha noe å gjøre. Et par
ganger hadde hun kikket ned i boken som søsteren leste
(holdt på å lese), men den hadde ikke noen bilder eller
samtaler, 'og hva nytte kan en ha av en bok,' tenkte Alice,
'som ikke har noen bilder eller samtaler.'

40(a) *The Lad and the Devil* (a Norwegian folk-tale)

Once upon a time there was a lad who went along a road
cracking nuts. He happened to find one which was worm-
eaten, and at the same moment he met the devil. 'Is it
true,' said the lad, 'what they say, that the devil can make
himself as small as he likes, and go through a pinhole?'
'Yes, of course,' answered the devil. 'Well, let me see you do
it; creep into this nut if you can,' said the lad. And the devil
did it. But he had no sooner got through the worm-hole,
than the lad put a small peg in the hole. 'I have got you safe,
now,' he said, and put the nut in his pocket.

When he had walked some distance he came to a smithy.
He went in there and asked the smith if he would crack that
nut for him. 'Yes, that's easily done,' said the smith, and
took the smallest hammer he had, laid the nut on the anvil,
and gave it a blow, but it didn't break. So he took a somewhat bigger hammer, but that wasn't big enough either.
Then he took a still bigger one, but no—the nut would not

break. This made the smith angry, and he seized the big sledgehammer. 'I shall soon make bits of you,' he said, and gave the nut such a blow that it flew into a thousand pieces, and sent half the roof of the smithy flying in the air. Such a crash! just as if the hut were tumbling down.

'I think the devil was in the nut,' said the smith.

'So he was,' said the lad.

40(b)   Jeg har *i* mange år bodd like *ved* Oslofjorden *i* en liten by som heter Moss. Mine foreldre eier et stort vakkert hus der. *Foran* det er det en veranda *med* store vinduer. En kan nesten ikke se vårt hus *fra* gata *på grunn av* haven med alle trærne og buskene. *Om* sommeren er den full *av* alle slags blomster og roser. En fotsti fører *opp til* huset, og *på* begge sider *av* denne stien er det plantet en hekk. Hvis en går (*or* Går en) *gjennom* haven, kommer en til hovedinngangen. Huset består *av* tre etasjer *med* sju rom *i* hver etasje. *Bak* huset er det en skog, og her pleide vi å leke *om* ettermiddagen når vi kom hjem *fra* skolen.

For ti år *siden* var (*or* fantes) det ingen hus *i* nærheten, men *i* (løpet *av*) de siste år er *omkring* et dusin nye hus blitt bygd *på* begge sider *av* gaten.

Mitt vindu vender *mot* gaten, og jeg kan se alle bussene som kjører *forbi* vårt hus. De er enten *på* vei *til* brygga eller stasjonen.

Jeg bodde *sammen med* (*or* hos) mine foreldre til jeg var tjue år gammel. Senere reiste jeg *til* Oslo *for* å studere språk som jeg alltid[1] har vært interessert *i*.

Jeg reiste hjem *i* mine ferier, da (*or* siden) avstanden *mellom* Oslo og Moss ikke er mer enn seksti kilometer, eller *omkring* (*or* ca.; omtrent) trettisyv engelske mil.

Under mitt opphold *i* Oslo fikk jeg mange venner *fra* alle deler (*or* kanter) *av* landet, og jeg så og lærte mange ting som jeg aldri[1] hadde hørt *om* før.

40(c)   *Radio*

When I have finished the day's work I like to sit at home listening (lit. and listen) to the wireless, especially in the

---

[1] Remember the place of adverbs in subordinate clauses is *before the verbs, even the auxiliaries.*

long winter evenings. The wireless set stands in the corner of the drawing-room, and all I have to do is to switch it on and tune in on the station I wish.

Each day I look (lit. peep) in the radio programme which the Norwegian State Broadcasting sends out.

Here is something to everybody's taste (lit. for every taste). The music constitutes (makes up) the greater part of the programme—forty per cent or perhaps more. Both light music and heavier classical works (stuff) are (is) played. Songs are sung by first-class male and female singers. Plays and other dramatic works are produced. Thrilling stories and tales for children are told in the Children's Hour each Saturday afternoon. Important football matches and sports meetings are broadcast.

One may hear short talks and lectures on current topics and well-known people are interviewed. The daily weather forecast and the news are popular items and the time signal is sent three times a day. The day's transmission very often ends with the National Anthem, and then it is time to say: Good night.

The Norwegian National Anthem: 'Ja, vi elsker'
(English version by G. M. Gathorne-Hardy)

> Yes, we love with fond devotion
> This, the land that looms
> Rugged, storm-scarred, o'er the ocean,
> With her thousand homes.
> Love her, in our love recalling
> Those who gave us birth,
> And old tales which night, in falling,
> Brings as dreams to earth.

41(a) The maid is preparing food. I am not able to hear what you are saying. The daughter was not allowed to leave the home. My uncle is always the first to laugh when something goes wrong. The son did not like to go abroad. Here there are indeed few chances of winning. Are you ready to go? It was great fun to see how easily he learned to play. I couldn't help laughing. Don't make me laugh, please. The captain had little hope of saving the ship from sinking. A drama of Ibsen is well worth seeing. I cannot afford to buy a ticket.

41(b)   Min søster liker å høre musikk og er selv flink til å spille piano. Mine brødre liker å ro og fiske. Å gjøre det nå ville være både vanskelig og farlig. I fjor lærte jeg å lese og snakke norsk. Har du tid til å komme til middag? Våre venner hadde lovt å komme på stasjonen for å si adjø til oss. Jeg er trett (*or* lei) av å høre den samme historien så mange ganger. Har du ikke funnet noe middel til å bli kvitt din forkjølelse ennå? Jeg skulle nettopp (*or* akkurat) gå til sengs da telefonen ringte. Jeg er redd for å møte ham, da det er sannsynlig at han vil slå meg. Hun skrudde på radioen for å høre de siste nyheter. Sjømennene reddet livet ved å svømme i det kalde vannet. De hadde forsøkt (*or* prøvd) å redde skipet først. Datteren gikk på stasjonen for å møte sin far. Jeg har det travelt med å flytte, men vet ikke hvordan jeg skal gjøre det på den mest praktiske måten. Uten å si et ord forlot han rommet. Etter å ha bodd der i ti år flyttet han plutselig. Jeg har stor lyst til å snakke til ham. Kongen oppfordret folket til å kjempe videre.

42. da og når

1. Når det er pent (*or* fint) vær, spiller jeg tennis.
2. Da jeg kom hjem, var det ingen mat i huset.
3. Når krigen er over, skal vi alle reise hjem (igjen).
4. Når vi talte til ham, sa han alltid: 'jeg vet ikke'.
5. Jeg skal komme når jeg har spist.
6. Da han gikk ut i morges, glemte han å låse døren.
7. Jeg kjente ham ikke igjen da jeg så ham på stasjonen.
8. Når folk blir gamle, får de grått hår.
9. Da klokka var fem, begynte musikken å spille.
10. Da vi nådde toppen, var vi alle sultne og trette.

43(a)   *The Brave Prentice*

A ship was on its way to America. In the middle of the Atlantic they were overtaken by (surprised by) a storm which lasted for five days. When the storm was at its worst, a rope got entangled on one of the yards. This had to be put right. But it was very dangerous to go aloft in such a storm. The captain told the prentice to do it. He was a little boy, not more than thirteen years old, only child of a poor widow.

The boy first looked up towards the yard and then down at the waves which all the time were breaking over the deck and, as it were, stretching their arms out for him. Then he looked at the captain and said: 'I will come soon.' He disappeared, but came back presently and hastened cheerfully up the shroud. The man who told this was standing on the deck near the mast and followed the boy with his eyes. He asked the captain: 'Why do you send this little boy up? He won't come down alive.' The captain answered: 'Men fall where boys stand; that one climbs like a squirrel.' The man looked up. Now the boy was high up. The ship heeled over so heavily that the yards almost reached the wave tops, but the boy didn't lose courage, and within a quarter of an hour he came down again, safe and contented.

43(b)

1. Du må se alle mine bøker (alle bøkene mine) *mens* du er her.
2. Det er ganske lenge *siden* jeg så deg sist.
3. Det er best vi kjøper avisene *før* vi går.
4. *Hvis* du skulle se ham, fortell (si) ham *at* jeg er her.
5. Kan du veksle et pund? Nei, jeg kàn ikke, *da* jeg er blakk.
6. Vi spiser *for at* vi skal leve, men vi lever ikke *for at* vi skal spise.
7. *Jo* lenger du venter, *desto* dyrere vil det bli (*or* blir det).
8. *Fordi* du har vært så snill mot meg, vil jeg gjerne gi deg en presang (*or* gave).
9. *Både* du *og* jeg kan kjøre bil.
10. *Som* allerede (*or* alt) nevnt, skal vi reise (*or* dra) til Oslo neste uke.
11. *Siden* du spør, kan jeg likeså godt fortelle (*or* si) deg det.
12. *Selv om* (*or* skjønt, enda) Norge ligger langt nord, er somrene ganske varme, takket være Golfstrømmen.

44(a)

1. Da begynte alle å synge.
2. I går kom sønnen hjem fra England.

3. Snart blir det kaldt.
4. Engang trodde jeg på julenissen.
5. Likevel gjorde han det.
6. Plutselig så min søster en mann gå inn i huset.
7. Nå er det nok.

44(b)   Når jeg går på kontoret om morgenen, bærer jeg en svart (sort) mappe i høyre hånd. Hvis du spør meg hva jeg har i mappen, er mitt svar: bare to ting —min matpakke og min tobakk. Vi har vår lunsj mellom halv tolv og tolv. Siden dette er vår eneste pause i løpet av dagen, setter vi stor pris på den. Det er den eneste tid på dagen da vi kan slappe av, drikke en kopp kaffe, nyte en sigarett og diskutere dagens problemer. Mennene på kontoret snakker for det meste om sport og biler.

45.   *The Parson and the Sexton* (Not literally translated.)

Once upon a time there was a parson, who was such a bully, that he screamed out a long way off, when anybody came driving towards him in the main road: 'Out of the way, out of the way! Here comes the parson himself!'

One day, when he was driving along and carrying on in this way, he met the king. 'Out of my way, out of my way!' he shouted, while still far off. But the king drove straight on and took no notice of him, so that time the parson had to pull his horse on one side. When the king came alongside him, he said: 'Tomorrow, you must appear at the palace, and if you cannot answer the three questions which I will ask you, you shall lose both your gown and your collar, because of your pride.'

That was something different from what the parson was accustomed to. He could bawl and shout and carry on terribly, but that was about all. So he went to the sexton, who was said to have a much smarter tongue than the parson. He told the sexton he had no mind to go, 'for a fool can ask more than ten wise men can answer,' said the parson, and so he got the sexton to go instead.

Well, the sexton set out and came to the palace dressed in the parson's gown and collar. The king received him at the door with crown and sceptre, and was so fine that he glittered a long way off.

'Oh, you are there, are you?' asked the king.

Yes, he was there, sure enough.

'Now, tell me first,' said the king, 'how far is it from east to west?'

'Why, a day's journey,' said the sexton.

'How do you make that out?' asked the king.

'Well, don't you see, the sun rises in the east and sets in the west, and he does it easily enough in a day,' said the sexton.

'Very well,' said the king; 'but tell me now, what you think I am worth, as I stand here before you.'

'Well, our Lord was valued at thirty pieces, and I suppose I cannot put you higher than twenty-nine,' said the sexton.

'So, so!' said the king, 'since you are so clever at everything, tell me what it is I am thinking about just now?'

'Why, you are surely thinking it is the parson who stands before you; but so help me, if you don't think wrong — for I am the sexton.'

'Be off with you—go home, and you be the parson and let him be sexton,' said the king, and so it was.

Proverb: Pride goes before a fall.

46. *P. Chr. Asbjørnsen and Jørgen Moe: Part I*

The two folk-tales we have read: The Lad and the Devil, and The Parson and the Sexton, are taken from Asbjørnsen and Moe's collection of folk-tales.

Peter Christen Asbjørnsen was born in Oslo in 1812. His father was a glazier. Peter had a good brain, but was not particularly industrious at school. His father then sent him up to Norderhov in Ringerike. Up there there was a minister who coached fellows like him for the matriculation examination.

Jørgen Moe was the son of a well-to-do farmer from the neighbouring district Hole in Ringerike. He was a year younger than Asbjørnsen. Jørgen Moe was also studying for the matriculation examination under the minister at Norderhov. This is how Asbjørnsen and Moe met and they became friends for life. Jørgen Moe was very interested in his studies and was very industrious. But Asbjørnsen didn't like books, and he didn't do any better in the country than in Oslo. After a couple of years his father took him home again. He didn't become a student until three years after Moe.

Part II

There were few books and newspapers then. When work was finished for the day, they used to gather round the fire and pass the time away in telling stories and folk-tales and in solving riddles. For the most part it was the same folk-tales that had been told for several hundred years. Several of them dated right back to heathen times. They didn't believe in Odin and Thor any longer. But they believed firmly in trolls and goblins and dwarfs who came out and showed themselves to people on occasion. We call all such things superstition. But in olden days they believed to be true all that was told them in these old stories.

The two young students realized that it was the same with the folk-tales as with an old cupboard or chest: they are a reminder of ancestors, but would soon be forgotten. They agreed therefore to collect all the folk-tales people told, write them down and have them printed.

These stories were first published in 1842, and are now as popular in Norway as the story of *Alice in Wonderland* is in England.

Advanced Reading and Translating Exercises

47. *The town of Oslo or Oslo City*

On a visit to Oslo a foreigner will soon discover (make the discovery) that there really is only one street of any particular[1] importance. It is called Karl Johansgate, in everyday speech shortened to Karl Johan, and is named after a Swedish King. It runs (lit. goes) in a straight line

[1] *større* (lit. greater, major) here = *særlig* (special, particular). Cf. para. 131.

from Oslo sentralstasjon to the Castle, which is beautifully situated up on a hill. From here one may see the
street in all its length.

If one walks from the Castle down towards Oslo sentralstasjon one will find the National Theatre on the right
hand. In front of the main entrance are (lit. stand) statues
of Ibsen and Bjørnson, the two most famous Norwegian
dramatists. On the other side of the street are (lit. lie) the
old University buildings with the University Square in
front, where the students take a stroll between the
lectures to get (lit. draw) fresh air.

Continuing down the street one will soon see (lit. run or
bump into) Stortinget, Norway's Parliament. It was built
in 1866, so it is not very (lit. especially, particularly) old.

Oslo has an absolutely glorious location. It faces the fjord
and behind is surrounded by a number of forest-clad hills.
This fine location has made Oslo into quite a famous tourist
town. In the summer months the fjord is full of sailing
boats, and one constantly sees ferries packed (full) with
passengers who are spending the day by the sea.

Round about, on the rocks, lie people enjoying (lit. cultivat-
ing) the pleasures of the seaside (lit. the bathing life). If one
prefers a walk in the country (lit. wood and field) one only
has to take the Holmenkollen railway, and in less than an
hour one is on the paths which twist between spruce and
pine trees. In winter the whole country is snow-clad
(covered with snow), and every single Sunday one can see
Oslo people by the thousand of all ages on skis on the
'tracks'. A Norwegian ski-ing Sunday in Nordmarka—
which the terrain round Oslo is called—is an experience
which is not easily forgotten.

48. *An Interview*

He stood reading the *New York Times*, so there was no
doubt in our minds that he was American. — We would like
to interview you, we said. — That's O.K. Fire away. —
You are from America? — That's correct, said our friend
gazing at us from behind his spectacles. — But how about
sitting down while we are standing (Norwegian facetious
way of putting it)? — No sooner said than done. Our friend

carried a walking-stick (Norw. went with a w.-stick), and obviously had a bad foot, for he only just managed to seat himself on one of the benches in Studenterlunden. He smoked a big cigar and was wearing (lit. had on him) a beret, presumably to hide a bald. head, a pair of brown baggy trousers, check coat (lit. jacket), yellow shirt, and a green tie with a silver tie pin.

— Where do you come from? — New York, I run a travel bureau, not big but small, and came here in the *Bergensfjord*, mainly to see what kind of service the ship gives so that I can tell my customers whether they should travel in it or not. — And what conclusion have you come to? — The ship is absolutely first class. I shall boast about it to all and sundry, and what a trip we had coming over! At North Cape it was absolutely fantastic. I have never been there before, only in Oslo, Bergen and Stavanger. That was just after the war, and food was scarce in Norway then, but now it is quite different. — Then the usual question. What do you think of Norway? — I like it very much here and I should like to come back another time (lit. once still) and stay (be here) even longer. — Why do you like our country? — Firstly, because it is so clean. Secondly, because the people are so kind. Thirdly, the scenery. Or in reverse order if you like. — We feel flattered. Have you had time to look round? — Oh, yes. I have seen *Kontiki*, *Fram*, the Viking ships, the city hall and the Vigeland Park.

Our friend can't stand flying, not because he is afraid, but because flying is too fast.

Then the conversation was finished and he took out his paper and started to study the news from home.

49 (I). *At the Goal*

On the morning of the 15th of December 1911 the weather was at its best, just as if made for the arrival at the Pole. I am not quite certain, but I believe we ate our breakfast a little faster that day than the previous ones, and got somewhat more quickly out of the tent, although I must admit that this event was always performed in a great hurry. On this day the surface was somewhat variable. Occasionally the going was good, but now and again it was quite bad. We continued this day in the same mechanical way as before.

Not much was said, but eyes were used so much the more. Hansen's neck was twice as long that day as the day before, from the way he stretched it to see some millimetre further. I had asked him, before we set out, to keep a good look-out and he did so thoroughly. But however much he stared and looked, he still saw nothing but the flat plateau stretching away unendingly.

At three o'clock in the afternoon a simultaneous 'halt' echoed from the sledge-drivers. The goal was reached, the journey finished. I cannot say—although it would have made a far greater effect—that I stood at the goal of my life. That would be to lie too much and too obviously.

I had better be frank and say straight out that I believe that no man has ever stood on a spot so completely opposite to his heart's desire as I did on that occasion. The North Pole had attracted me since I was a child, and now I stood at the South Pole. Can one imagine anything more topsy-turvy? We reckoned now that we were at the Pole. Of course, every one of us knew that we were not standing exactly at the Pole—that would be impossible to establish with the time and the instruments at our disposal. But we were so close that the few kilometres which perhaps separated could be of no importance whatsoever.

When we had halted we gathered together and congratulated ourselves. We had reason for mutual respect for what was achieved, and I believe that was exactly what we felt and expressed by the vigorous handshakes which we exchanged.

49 (II). *The Flag on the South Pole*

After this first act we went on to the next, the most important (lit. greatest) and the most solemn one of the whole expedition—to plant our flag. It was affection and pride which shone out of the five pairs of eyes which watched the flag, as with a crack it unfurled itself in the fresh breeze and fluttered over the Pole.

In planting the flag—this historic act—I had determined that we all should take part. It was no one man's job to do it; it was due to all those who had staked their lives in the struggle and stood together through thick and thin. This was the only way I could show my gratitude to my friends in this desolate and forsaken place. I realized that they understood this and accepted it in the spirit it was offered to them. It was five rough and frostbitten fists which seized the flagstaff, lifted the fluttering flag into the air and planted it as the first at the Geographical South Pole.

That brief moment will certainly be remembered by all of us who stood there then. Lengthy ceremonies are dispensed with in those regions—the shorter the better.

Naturally there was a celebration in the tent that evening. —Not that champagne corks flew and wine flowed. We made do with a small piece of seal meat each and it tasted good and had a pleasant effect.

Of other signs of celebration indoors we had none. Outside we heard the flag crack and bang. Chat in the tent was lively, and much was talked about. It may well be that messages were also sent home about what we had done.

50. *The three Scandinavian languages*

The three Scandinavian languages, Swedish, Danish and Norwegian, are fairly similar. In fact, there is so little difference between them that one can almost call them dialects.

Usually it is not so difficult for a Norwegian to make himself understood, say, in Stockholm. He finds, naturally, that the Swedes pronounce the same words a little differently, in many instances, and also use slightly different words and phrases, but he soon gets used to it. Besides, he has read some Swedish in school.

If he takes a trip to the 'King's Town', København, he will perhaps to begin with have some difficulty in understanding his Danish brethren. The words and expressions are true enough largely the same, but the Danes often pronounce vowels and consonants in quite a different way. But after the sentence has been repeated a couple of times, a bell rings for the Norwegian. When he has stayed in the town for several days, everything as a rule goes fine.

Still, there are a number of words which have a completely different meaning in the three Scandinavian languages. We can give as example 'rar'—When the Danes and the Swedes talk about 'en rar mann', they mean a pleasant man.

It is in other words a compliment. In Norwegian, on the other hand, 'en rar mann' means a strange or peculiar man, and can scarcely be taken as praise.

Another example: The adjective 'rolig' means in Danish and Norwegian peaceful or quiet, whereas in Swedish it has the meaning amusing or enjoyable. There is an amusing story about this word. It is said to be true, but if it isn't, it is at any rate well conceived.

A Swede once came to a Norwegian town. He was a lively chap and in the evening he wanted to have some fun. He took a taxi, and when the driver asked where he wanted to go, the Swede replied that he would very much like to be driven to a quiet place (= Swedish: to a lively spot). The driver thought for a while and then drove him to the churchyard. In his opinion that was a quiet place, and one must agree with him here. But it was not exactly the kind of place the Swede had had in mind. He wanted to have some fun, as we say.

Fortunately there are not many words which are so different that they create such complications and misunderstandings. But it pays to be a little careful over which words one uses when one crosses the border.

IRREGULAR VERBS

An Alphabetical List of the most important Irregular, or Strong Verbs

Those verbs with an asterisk (*) attached to them alternate between the strong and weak conjugation.

Those verbs marked with ¹ have weak conjugation when used transitively: *brente, hengte, knekte, rente, skvettet, slengte, smelte.*

Infinitive	Present	Past	Past Participle
adlyde obey	*adlyder*	*adlød*	*adlydt*
be(de) pray, ask	*ber (beder)*	*ba(d)*	*bedt*
bedra(ge) betray	*bedrar (bedrager)*	*bedro(g)*	*bedradd (bedratt)*
binde bind	*binder*	*bandt*	*bundet*
bite bite	*biter*	*bet*	*bitt*
bli(ve) become, remain	*blir (bliver)*	*ble(v)*	*blitt*

Infinitive		Present	Past	Past Participle
brekke break	..	*brekker*	*brakk*	*brukket*
[1]*brenne* burn	..	*brenner*	*brant*	*brent*
briste burst	..	*brister*	*brast*	*bristet (brustet)*
bryte break	..	*bryter*	*brøt*	*brutt*
by(de) order, offer	..	*byr(byder)*	*bød*	*budt*
bære carry, wear	..	*bærer*	*bar*	*båret*
dra(ge) draw, pull	..	*drar (drager)*	*dro(g)*	*dradd (dratt)*
drikke drink	..	*drikker*	*drakk*	*drukket*
drive drive, force	..	*driver*	*drev*	*drevet*
ete eat	..	*eter*	*åt*	*ett*
falle fall	..	*faller*	*falt*	*falt*
fare go, travel	..	*farer*	*for*	*faret*
finne find	..	*finner*	*fant*	*funnet*
flyte flow	..	*flyter*	*fløt*	*flytt*
fly(ve) fly	..	*flyr (flyver)*	*fløy*	*fløyet*
forlate leave	..	*forlater*	*forlot*	*forlatt*
forstå understand	..	*forstår*	*forstod*	*forstått*
forsvinne disappear	..	*forsvinner*	*forsvant*	*forsvunnet*
fryse freeze	..	*fryser*	*frøs*	*frosset*
fyke drift	..	*fyker*	*føk*	*føket*
få receive, get	..	*får*	*fikk*	*fått*
gale crow	..	*galer*	*gol*	*galt*
gidde care to	..	*gidder*	*gadd*	*giddet*
gi(ve) give	..	*gir (giver)*	*ga (gav)*	*gitt*
gjelde concern	..	*gjelder*	*gjaldt*	*gjeldt*
gli(de) glide, slip	..	*glir (glider)*	*gled*	*glidd*
glippe slip, fail	..	*glipper*	*glapp*	*glippet*
gnage gnaw	..	*gnager*	*gnog*	*gnaget*
gni rub	..	*gnir*	*gned*	*gnidd*
grave dig	..	*graver*	*grov*	*gravd*
grine fret, be cross	..	*griner*	*gren*	*grint*
gripe grasp	..	*griper*	*grep*	*grepet*
gråte weep	..	*gråter*	*gråt*	*grått*
gyse shudder	..	*gyser*	*gjøs*	*gyst*
gyte spawn, pour	..	*gyter*	*gjøt*	*gytt*
gyve fly (of dust)	..	*gyver*	*gjøv*	*gjøvet*
gå go	..	*går*	*gikk*	*gått*
[1]*henge* hang	..	*henger*	*hang*	*hengt*
hete be called	..	*heter*	*het or hette*	*hett*
hive throw	..	*hiver*	*hev*	*hevet*
hjelpe help	..	*hjelper*	*hjalp*	*hjulpet*
holde hold, keep	..	*holder*	*holdt*	*holdt*
hugge hew, cut	..	*hugger*	*hugg*	*hugget*
hvine shriek	..	*hviner*	*hven*	*hvint*
klinge sound	..	*klinger*	*klang*	*klinget*
klyve climb	..	*klyver*	*kløv*	*kløvet*
[1]*knekke* crack, break	..	*knekker*	*knakk*	*knekt*
knipe pinch	..	*kniper*	*knep*	*knepet*
komme come	..	*kommer*	*kom*	*kommet*

Infinitive	Present	Past	Past Participle
krype creep ..	*kryper*	*krøp*	*krøpet*
kvede poet. sing,			
chant	*kveder*	*kvad*	*kvedet*
la (te) let	*lar (later)*	*lot*	*latt*
le laugh	*ler*	*lo*	*ledd*
*li (de) suffer ..	*lir (lider)*	*led*	*lidt*
ligge lie	*ligger*	*lå*	*ligget*
lyde sound	*lyder*	*lød*	*lydt*
lyve lie	*lyver*	*løy*	*løyet*
løpe run	*løper*	*løp*	*løpt*
nyse sneeze	*nyser*	*nøs*	*nyst*
nyte enjoy	*nyter*	*nøt*	*nytt*
pipe pipe, whistle ..	*piper*	*pep*	*pepet*
ri(de) ride	*rir (rider)*	*red*	*ridd*
[1]*renne* flow	*renner*	*rant*	*rent*
rive tear	*river*	*rev*	*revet*
ryke break, smoke, intr.	*ryker*	*røk*	*røket*
se see, look	*ser*	*så*	*sett*
sige sink, move slowly			
forward	*siger*	*seig*	*seget*
sitte sit	*sitter*	*satt*	*sittet*
skjelve tremble	*skjelver*	*skalv*	*skjelvet*
skjære cut	*skjærer*	*skar*	*skåret*
skride proceed ..	*skrider*	*skred*	*skredet*
skrive write ..	*skriver*	*skrev*	*skrevet*
skrike cry, shriek ..	*skriker*	*skrek*	*skreket*
skryte boast	*skryter*	*skrøt*	*skrytt*
[1]*skvette* give a sudden			
start, splash ..	*skvetter*	*skvatt*	*skvettet*
skyte shoot ..	*skyter*	*skjøt*	*skutt*
skyve push	*skyver*	*skjøv*	*skjøvet*
[1]*slenge* dangle, idle	*slenger*	*slang*	*slengt*
slippe let go, drop ..	*slipper*	*slapp*	*sloppet*
slite wear out, toil ..	*sliter*	*slet*	*slitt*
slå strike	*slår*	*slo*	*slått*
[1]*smelle* crack ..	*smeller*	*smalt*	*smelt*
smette slip, get away			
quickly	*smetter*	*smatt*	*smettet*
smyge creep, sneak ..	*smyger*	*smøg*	*smøget*
snike (seg) sneak, slink	*sniker*	*snek*	*sneket*
snyte cheat	*snyter*	*snøt*	*snytt*
sove sleep	*sover*	*sov*	*sovet*
spinne spin	*spinner*	*spant*	*spunnet*
sprette leap, bounce	*spretter*	*spratt*	*sprettet*
springe jump, run ..	*springer*	*sprang*	*sprunget*
stige rise, increase ..	*stiger*	*steg*	*steget*
stikke stab, prick, put	*stikker*	*stakk*	*stukket*
stjele steal	*stjeler*	*stjal*	*stjålet*
strekke draw out, stretch	*strekker*	*strakk*	*strukket*

Infinitive	Present	Past	Past Participle
*stri (de) strive, struggle	strir (strider)	stred	stridt
stryke stroke, iron, fail in exams.	stryke,	strøk	strøket
stå stand	står	sto(d)	stått
*sverge swear ..	sverger	svor	svoret
*svi singe, smart ..	svir	sved	svidd
svike betray ..	sviker	svek	sveket
*svinge swing, turn ..	svinger	svang	svunget
svinne vanish, decrease	svinner	svant	svunnet
synge sing	synger	sang	sunget
synke sink	synker	sank	sunket
ta take	tar	tok	tatt
treffe meet with, hit ..	treffer	traff	truffet
trekke pull	trekker	trakk	trukket
tvinge force	tvinger	tvang	tvunget
vike yield, step aside	viker	vek	veket
vinde wind	vinder	vandt	vundet
vinne win	vinner	vant	vunnet
*vri twist, wring ..	vrir	vred	vridd
være be	er	var	vært

Forms in parentheses such as *bede* and *blive* indicate that they may still be seen in formal style and frequently in 19th and early 20th century literature. But in colloquial speech and modern prose only the short forms like *be* and *bli* are used.

VOCABULARY

Norwegian – English

Numbers refer to paragraphs unless otherwise indicated.

A

adjø .	good-bye 277
adresse c.	address 70
aften c.	evening, page 45, 230
aker c. see åker	
akkurat	just, exactly 84, 157
aktuell	current, topical 244
aldeles	completely, absolutely 157
aldri	never, pages 42 and 92
alene	alone 87
all .	all 212
aller .	emphatic, very 124, 128
allerede	already 75
allikevel, see likevel	
alt .	already 215; much too 147
altan c.	balcony 121
altså	consequently 139
alvorlig	serious(ly) 176
amerikaner c.	American 50(d)
amerikansk	American 285
and f.	duck 50
anelse c.	idea, inkling 91, 207
angripe (irr. v.) .	attack 106
anklage (-et) for	accuse of 246
ankomme (irr. v.)	arrive 86
anledning c.	occasion 121
anmode (-et)	request 98(a)
annen	other, second 135, 208
annerledes	different(ly) 151
ansikt n.	face 121
anstrengende	strenuous, page 121
anta (irr. v.)	suppose 139, 158
antakelig .	probably 171, 293
apotek n. .	chemist's shop 58
apparat n.	apparatus 244
appetitt c.	appetite 75
apropos	by the way 197
arbeid n. .	work 118(a)
arbeide (-et)	work 65
arm c. .	arm 53, 78(a)
at (conj.) .	that 257

av . . . . . by (passive) 106, of 219
av og til . . . . occasionally 91
avbryte . . . . break off, interrupt 159
avfyre (-te) . . . fire 159
avholdt . . . . beloved 121
avis c. . . . . newspaper 65
avlyse (-te) . . . cancel 95
avskjære (irr. v.) . . cut off 159
avslutte (-et) . . . end 244
avstand . . . . distance 244

B

bad n. . . . . bath(e), bathroom 75, 203
bade (-et) . . . . bath, bathe 64(b)
bak . . . . . behind 125(5)
baker c. . . . . baker 50(d)
bakke c. . . . , hill 131
bakket . . . . hilly 129(1a)
bakre . . . . rear 125(5)
bange . . . . frightened 120
bank c. . . . . bank 206
barbarisk . . . . barbaric 129(1a)
barber c. . . . . barber 107
barbere . . . . shave 107
barbersalong c. . . barber's shop 107
bare . . . . only 53, 64, 80(c), 262; just 157
barn n. . . . . child 52(1)
barndom c. . . . childhood 105
barnetog n. . . . children's procession 121
be (irr. v.) . . . ask (om = for) 82(5)
bedre . . . . better, quite good 125(4), 131
befolkning c. . . . population 140
begge . . . . both 191
begynne (-te) . . . begin 34
behandle (-et) . . . treat, deal with
behøve (-de) . . . need, require 69
behøves . . . . be necessary 103
bekk c. . . . . brook 81(d)
belte n. . . . . belt 48
belønne (-te) . . . reward 106
bemerke (-et) . . . remark
bemerkning c. . . . remark 139
ben n. . . . . leg, bone, page 25
bero (-dde) . . . . depend (på = on) 71
berømt . . . . famous, page 183
beskrive (irr. v.) . . describe 99
bestandig . . . . always, constantly 148
bestemme (-te) . . . decide, page 187
besøk n. . . . . visit 128
besøke (-te) . . . . visit 75
betale (-te) . . . . pay 70, 99

bety (-dde) . . . mean, signify 71
beundre (-et) . . . admire 131
biff c. . . . . beef 107
bil c. . . . . car 57, 64
bilde n. . . . picture 73
billett c. . . . . ticket, page 52
billig . . . . cheap 125(1)
binde (irri. v.) . . . bind, tie 95
bit c. . . . . bit. piece 244
bite (irri. v.) . . . bite 78(1)
bitter . . . . bitter 116(2)
bjørn c. . . . . bear, page 128
blad n. . . . . leaf 112, 115
blakk (sl.) . . . broke 268
blant . . . . among 221
blekk n. . . . ink 108(b)
blekkhus n. . . . inkstand 108(b)
bli (irri. v.) . . . get, become 78, 96
blomst c. . . . . flower 65
blyant c. . . . pencil 189
bløt . . . . soft 119(b)
blå . . . . . blue 119(a)
blåse (-te) . . . blow 75
bo (-dde) . . . . live (reside) 60
bok c. . . . . book 60
bombe ["bombə]c. . . bomb
bonde c. . . . farmer 50, 68
bord n. . . . . table 68
borger c. . . . . citizen 118(e)
bort, borte . . . away 125(5), 155
bortre . . . . farther 125(5)
bot f. . . . . patch 50
bra . . . . . fine excellent 120
brake (-et) . . . make a big noise 244
bratt . . . . steep 197
bred . . . . broad, wide, page 78
bredd c. . . . . (river) bank 215
brekke (irr. v.) . . break 95
brenne (-te) . . . burn 101
brev n. . . . letter 64, 112
briller . . . . spectacles, page 184
bringe (brakte, brakt) . bring 68
bror c., pl. brødre . . brother 50(c)
bruke (-te) . . . . use 65, 70
brun . . . . brown 121
bry seg om . . . care about 182
brygge f. . . . . quay 244
bryggeri n. . . . brewery
bryllup n. . . . wedding
bryte (irr. v.) . . . break 79(2), 206
brød n. . . . . bread, loaf 48

brått . . . suddenly 148
bue c.; (-et) . . . bow, curve 121
bukke (-et) . . . bow
bukse f. . . . . pair of trousers
busk c. . . . . bush, page 148
buss c. . . . . bus 244
butikk c. . . . shop 65
by c.. . . . town 48
by (irr. v.) . . . offer, bid, page 187
bygge (-de) . . . build 98(d)
bære (irr. v.) . . . carry 274
bølge c.; (-et) . . . wave 75
bør, burde . . . ought, should 176(3)
børste c.; (-et) . . . brush 64
både . . . both 191
   både—og . . . both—and 70, 256
båt c. . . . . boat, 54, 113

C

ca. (abbr. cirka) . . approximately 237(6)

D

da (cong. adv.) . . . when page 42, 259; then 148;
              after all 156; as 261
dag c. . . . . day 70
   i dag . . . . today 230(6)
   daglig . . . . daily 70
   dagligdags . . . daily, everyday 118(e)
dal c. . . . . valley 131
dam c. . . . . pond 48
dame c. . . . lady 57(2), 121
Danmark . . . Denmark 65
danne (-et); dannet (adj.) . shape; educated
dans c. . . . . dance 104
danse (-et) . . . dance 199(c)
danske c. . . . Dane 131
dato c. . . . . date 139
datter c.; pl. døtre . . daughter 50(c)
deilig . . . . pleasant, delicious, page 121
del c. . . . . part 140
dele (-te) . . . divide, share 65, 176
dengang . . . that time, then 108(b)
der . . . . there 5, 65
dérfor . . . . therefore 87
dérfra . . . . from there 153
dérimot . . . on the other hand 192
derpå . . . . then, page 92
dersom . . . . if 262
desémber . . . December 138
dessuten . . . besides 176

dessvérre	unfortunately; I am afraid 91, 1
detálj c. . . .	detail 131
dikt n. . . .	poem 70, 188
dikter c. . . .	poet 215(3)
diskutére (-te) . .	discuss 274
diván c. . . .	divan 95
dog (dɔ:g) . .	though, yet
doven [ˇdo:vən] .	lazy 116(2)
dra (irr. v.) . .	draw, drag; depart, go 83(6)
drakt c. . . .	dress, costume 121
dreie (-de) . . .	turn 70
drepe (-te) . .	kill 106, 107
drikke (irr. v.) . .	drink 80(3)
drosje [ˇdrɔʃʃə] c. .	taxi 70
dryppe (-et) . .	drip 259(2)
drøm n. . . .	dream
drømme (-te) . .	dream 65(e)
duk c. . . .	(table)cloth 68
dum	stupid 121
dusin n. . . .	dozen 141
dusj n. . . .	shower 203
dverg c. . . .	dwarf 274
dyp	deep 131
dyr	expensive, dear, pages 72 and 76
dyr n. . . .	animal 48
dýrisk . .	beastly
død c. (dø:d) . .	death 106
dø (-de, -dd) . .	die 246
død [dø:] (adj.) . .	dead 119(b)
dømme . . .	judge 65(c)
dør c. . . .	door 9
dårlig . . .	bad, -ly 144
dårlig med . . .	scarce, page 185

E

edru	sober 120
egen	own 117
egg n. . . .	egg 68
eie (de) . . .	own 244
ekorn n., c. . .	squirrel 268
eksamen c. . . .	exam. 98(a)
eksémpel n.; for eksempel	
abbr. f. eks. . .	example; for example (e.g.) 49, 131
eldre; eldst . .	older, elderly; oldest 128, 131
eléndig	miserable
elév c. . . .	pupil, page 38
eller	or 53
éllers	otherwise 154
elske (-et); elsket (adj.)	love 107; beloved 118
elv f. . . .	river, pages 44 and 78
emne n. . . .	subject, topic 244

fjell n.	mountain 113
fjellkjede c.	mountain range, page 121
fjellmann c.	mountaineer, page 121
fjellparti n.	mountain range, area, page 121
fjord ['fjo:r] c.	fjord 131
flagg n.	flag 121
flaske f.	bottle 140
flere; flest	more, several 75; most 244
flink	clever, expert 128, 271
flittig	industrious 271
fly, flyge (irr. v.)	fly, page 147
fly n.	plane 84(f)
flyger c.	pilot
flýplass c.	aerodrome 85(g)
flytte	move, page 156
folk n.	people 100
for (adv.) c.f. áltfor	too 147
for (prep.)	for 223
for á	in order to 87
for (conj.)	for 256
foran ['forran]	in front of, before 65, 224
forbi	past, by 225
fordí	because, as 261
fordømt	damned
forestilling c.	performance
foretaksom	enterprising
foretrekke (irr. v.)	prefer 121, 182
forfátter c.	author 159
forférdelig	terrible 147
forlóvet	engaged to be married 215
fornøyd	contented 268
fórrest	foremost 127
forrésten	however; by the way
forrétning c.	business, page 121
forræder c.	traitor 106
forrige uke, måned	last week, month
forsiktig	careful 128
forskjéllig	different, pages 121 and 189
forstá (irr. v.)	understand
forsvínne (irr. v.)	disappear 268
forsøke (-te); forsøk n.	try, attempt 268; attempt, trial 246
fort	quickly 145
fortau n.	pavement
fortélle (-talte, -talt)	relate, tell about 68, 237
fórtsette (-satte, -satt)	continue 70
foss c.	waterfall 131
fot c., pl. føtter	foot 50(a), 51
fra	from 226
frakk c.	coat 186
fram (frem)	forward 125(5), 155
fram og tilbáke	to and fro

glitre (-et)	glitter 274	
glo f.; pl. glør . . .	ember 50(b)	
god [go:]	good 119(b), 125(4)	
godt [gɔtt] (adv.) . .	well 144	
gran f.	spruce, page 183	
grave (-de) or (irr. v.) . .	dig	
greie (-de)	manage 69	
gren c.	branch 159	
grense c. . . .	border, frontier 131	
gripe (irr. v.) . . .	seize, grasp 87	
gris c.	pig 124(b), 186	
gro (-dde)	grow 71	
grunn c.	ground; reason 179	
grønn	green 112, 116(1)	
grå	grey 119(a)	
gråte (irr. v.) . . .	weep	
gul	yellow, page 185	
gutt c.	boy 45, 78(a)	
gyllen	golden 129(1)(c)	
gymnastikk [gymna′stikk] c.	gymnastics; exercise 203	
gå (irr. v.) . . .	go, walk 85(7)	
gård [gɔ:r] c. . . .	farm 29	

H

ha (hadde, hatt) . .	have 53	
hals c.	neck, throat 121	
halv [hall] . . .	half 33, 40	
halvdel c. . . .	half 140	
halvmåne c. . . .	half-moon 140	
halvpart c. . . .	half 140	
halvveis . . .	half-way 140	
hammer c. . . .	hammer 244	
hándelsflåte c. . . .	merchant navy 131	
handling c. . . .	action, page 186	
hard [ha:r] . . .	hard 29, 70	
hatt c.	hat, page 33	
hav n.	sea 131	
havn c.	harbour 121, 131	
hel	whole 115(g)	
heldig	lucky 91	
héller; helst . . .	rather, sooner; preferably 145	
heller ikke . . .	nor, neither	
helt (adv.) . . .	completely 70	
helt riktig . . .	quite right	
helt til . . .	as far as, right to 131	
helt c.	hero 106	
helteroman c. . .	heroic novel	
hende (-te) . . .	happen 40	
henge (-te); (irr. v.) (intr.) .	hang	
hente (-et) . . .	fetch	
her [hæ:r] . . .	here 5	
herr	Mr 59	

herre c.	gentleman 5, 6
hest c.	horse 186
hete (het(te), hett) . .	be called 90
hilse (-te)	greet 121
himmel c. . . .	sky, heaven 119(a)
hissig	hot-tempered 131
história c. . . .	story; history 106, 131
hit	here, hither 155
hjelp c.; (-e, irr. v.) . .	help 244(2) 80(3)
hjem n.	home 121
hjemland n. . . .	homeland 128
hjemme	at home 155
hjémover . . .	homeward, page 42
hjerte n.	heart
hjertelig	hearty 157
hjørne n.	corner 68
hode n.	head, page 170
holde (irr. v.) . . .	hold, keep 85(7)
hoppe (-et) . . .	jump 64(a)
hos	with 229
hotéll n.	hotel 35
hovedvei c. . . .	main road 274
hovedstad c., pl.—steder .	capital 90
hovmod [ˇhɔvmo(:)d] n. .	arrogance, pride 274
hugge (hugde or hugg) .	hew, cut
hull n.	hole 244
humør n.	humour 121, 188
humorístisk . . .	humorous 125
hund c.	dog 59, 78(a), 115(c)
hundre n.	hundred 68
hus n.	house 43
huske (-et) . . .	remember 64(a), page 128
hva (int. pron.) . .	what 65, 88, 195
hvem	who 65, 193
hver	every 65, 111, 131, 213
hver gang . . .	every time, page 79
hvil c.; hvile (-te) .	rest, page 121
hvilken (interrog. pron.) .	which 88, 196
hvis (conj.) . . .	if 75, 95, 203, 261
hviske (-et) . . .	whisper, page 128
hvit	white 119(b)
hvor	(¹) where 53; (²) how (before adj. and adv.) 88
hvórdan	how, in what manner 88, 128
hvórfor	why 88
hvórfra	from where, whence
hvorhen	where to
hvorledes	how 88
hyggelig	nice, cosy, page 106
hystérisk	hysterical 129(1)(a)
hær c.	army

høflig	. . . .	polite, -ly
høne f.	. . . .	hen 43
høre (-te)	. . . .	hear 65
høre til	. . . .	belong to, be amongst 131
høres (-tes)	. . .	sound 103
høst c.	. . . .	autumn 138
høy .	. . . .	high 113, 128
høyre	. . . .	right 70
hånd c., pl. hender	. .	hand 50
håp n.; -e (-et)	. .	hope 101
hår n.	. . . .	hair 119(a)

I

i	. . . .	in, into 53, 230
i det siste	. . .	lately 179
i stedet	. . .	instead, page 168
især	. . . .	especially 157
idé c.	. . . .	idea 47
idet (conj.)	. . .	as 260
idrett c.	. . . .	sport 197
idiót c.	. . . .	idiot 186
igjén	. . . .	again; left 70, 206 note
igjénnom	. . .	through 228
ikke	. . . .	not 64, 90
ikke desto mindre	.	none the less
ille	. . . .	badly 144
imídlertid	. . .	however 148
indre	. . . .	inner 125(5)
ingen, intet, pl. ingen		no, not any, nobody 207
ingenting	. . .	nothing 207
inn i; inn(e)	. . .	into; in, adv. 155
innhente (-et)	. .	catch up with 158
innstille (-te)	. . .	cancel, stop
inntil	. . . .	see til
inntrykk n.	. . .	impression, page 125
instru'ment n.	. .	instrument
interessant	. . .	interesting 35
interésse c.	. . .	interest 68
interessert	. . .	interested, pages 52 and 148

J

ja	. . . .	yes 93
jage (-et)	. . .	chase 64(b)
jakke f.	. . . .	coat 75
január	. . . .	January 138
jeger c.	. . . .	hunter, sportsman 79(b)
jo	. . . .	yes (after negative) 93–94
jo—désto	. . .	the—the 128
jo—dess	. . .	the—the 128
jo—jo	. . .	the—the 128
jord [jo:r] c.	. . .	earth 244
juble (-et)	. . .	cheer 121

knapp c. . . .	button 244
kne n., pl. knær .	knee 52(1)
knekke (-te) (v. intr.) .	crack 244
kniv c. . . .	knife, page 113
komme (irr. v.) .	come 60, 85 (7)
kone f. . . .	wife 59
konge c. . . .	king 45, 68, 123
kongedømme n. .	kingdom
kontór n. . .	office 274
konversasjón c. .	conversation
kopp c. . . .	cup 219
kort; n. . . .	short 11; card, page 110
kose (-te) seg .	be comfortable
koselig . . .	cosy 75
koste (-et) . .	cost 64(a)
krabbe (-et) . .	crawl 200
kraft c.; pl. krefter .	strength, power 50
kraftig . . .	powerful, -ly 285, page 187
krage c. . . .	collar 274
krig c. . . .	war, page 41
'krígersk . .	warlike 118(c), 129(1)(a)
krone c. . . .	crown 274
krónprins c. . .	Crown Prince
kry	proud 120
krype (irr. v.) .	creep 79(2)
ku f.; pl. kyr or kuer	cow 50(b)
kulde c. . . .	cold 65, 138
kull n. . . .	coal
kunde c. . . .	customer 107
kvart(er) n. . .	quarter 138
kveld c. . . .	evening 87
kvele (kvalte, kvalt) .	choke 68
kvikk . . .	quick
kvinne c. . . .	woman 45
kyst c. . . .	coast 131
kåt	wanton, wild 119(b)

L

la (irr. v.) . .	let 83(6), 176(6)
lage (-et) . .	make 64(b), 106
laks c. . . .	salmon 131
land n.; -e (-et) .	country, land 48, 128
lang, adv. langt .	long; far 85(g), 125(3)
langs . . .	along 79(b)
langsom . . .	slow 125(1)
lat . . .	lazy 119(b)
lav	low
le (irr. v.) . .	laugh 84
lede (-et) . .	lead 106, 284
lege c. . . .	doctor 251
legge (la, lagt) .	lay, put 68

leke (-te) . . . . play (about children) 66
lem n. . . . . limb 52(2)
lenge . . . . long; a long time 144
lengst . . . . largest 125(3), farthest 144
lese (-te) . . . . read 65, page 170
lete (-te) etter . . . look for, search for 222(2)
lett . . . . easy; light 70, 95
leve (-de) . . . live 69
levére (-te) . . . deliver 65
ligge (irr. v.) . . . lie 70, 82(3)
like (-te) . . . . like 65
like før . . . . just before, page 148
'like ved . . . . just by, page 148
likeså . . . . as 267
 kikeså—som . . as—as; quite—as 267
likevel . . . . nevertheless, yet, still 106, 157
linje c. . . . . line 157
liten n., lite; def. lille, vesle; pl.
 små . . . . little 117, 125(4)
litt, adj., adv. . . . a little 128
liv . . . . life 115 (a) (3)
 livlig . . . . lively
 livløs . . . . lifeless 200
lomme f. . . . . pocket 70, 80(c)
lommetørkle n. . . handkerchief
love [ˇlɔːvə] . . . promise 69
luft c. . . . . air 70, 75
lukte (-et) . . . smell, sniff 200
lus f., pl. . . . . louse 51
lyd c. . . . . sound
lykke c. . . . . happiness, luck, success 8
 lykkelig . . . . happy, -ily 106, 125(1), 143
 lykkes (lyktes, lykkes) . succeed 105
lys n.; adj. . . . light; fair, bright 87, 131
lyve, (irr. v.) . . . tell a lie 75
lære (-te) . . . learn; teach 65
 lærerinne c. . . . school-mistress 284
 lærer c. . . . . teacher 45, 50(d)
løfte n. . . . . promise 79(b)
løpe (irr. v.) . . . run 85(7)
lørdag . . . . Saturday 138
låse (-te) . . . . lock 107, 260
låne (-te) . . . . borrow; lend 65, 186

M

mai . . . . . May 121, 138
man, indef. pron. . . one 102, 202
mándag . . . . Monday 138
mange . . . . many 53, 65
mann c., pl. menn . . man 50
mark f. . . . . field 43

mark c.	. . .	worm, page 147
mars c.	. . .	March 138
marsj c.	. . .	march 121
marsjére (-te)	. .	march 121
mast c.	. . .	mast 268
mat c.	. . .	food 106
materiále n.	. .	material, page 121
med .	. . .	with 75, 234
med étt	. . .	suddenly
meget	. . .	very 70, 87
melk c.	. . .	milk 205, 219
mellom	. .	between 235
mellomst	. .	in the middle 127
men .	. . .	but 53, 64, 256
mene (-te) .	. .	mean, think 67, 73
mening c. .	. .	meaning, sense 207
menneske n.; pl. -r	.	human being, person; pl. people 131
mens	. . .	while 75, 138, 260
mer, mest .	. .	more, most 129
merke n.; (-et)	.	mark; notice 64(a)
merkelig .	. .	strange 107
mest, see mer		
méster c. .	. .	master 95
míddag c. .	. .	dinner, midday 107, 215
middel n. .	. .	means; remedy 49
midt på, i .	. .	in the middle of 115(a)(3)
midtre, den-	. .	the middle one 125(5)
mil f.	. . .	about 6 English miles 51
mindre	. . .	smaller; less; minor 125(4), 131
minne n.; (-te)	.	memory; remind 105, 239(5)
minst	. . .	least, at least 139
minútt n. .	. .	minute 138
mislykkes, see lykkes .	.	fail
mislykket	. .	unsuccessful
miste (-et)	. .	lose 64(a)
modérne .	. .	modern 91, 120
modig	. . .	brave 268
mor c.; pl. mødre	.	mother 50(c)
more (-te, -et) seg	.	enjoy oneself 180
morgen [ˇmɔːrn̩]	.	morning 68
i morgen	.	to-morrow 230(6)
morsom [ˇmɔʃʃɔm]	.	jolly, amusing 179, 188
mot	. . .	against, towards 65, 121, 236
mot n.	. . .	courage 268
mótor c.; pl. motórer .	.	motor 49
mulig	. . .	possible
munne (-et) ut i	.	flow into 131
múnter	. . .	gay 121, 215
múnterhet c. .	.	gaiety 121
musíkk c.	. .	music 65
musikálsk; músiker c.	.	musical; musician 70

nytte c. . . . . benefit, use 215
nær . . . . . near 127
  nærhet c. . . . neighbourhood 244
nød c. . . . . need, distress, page 128
nødt, være n. til . . have to
nøkkel c. . . . . key 156(2a)
nøtt f. . . . . nut 244
nøyaktig . . . exact(ly) 139
nøye (adj., adv.) . . careful, -ly; exact, -ly 200
nå . . . . . now 70
nå (-dde) . . . reach 75
nål f. . . . . needle 244
når (conj., adv.) . . when, at what time 88, 259

O

offisér c. . . . . officer
ofte . . . . . often 75(a), 145
og [ɔː] . . . . and 5, 256
også [ɔssɔ] . . . also, too, as well 87
október . . . . October 138
om . . . . . about; of 65; if 139; in 237
  om og om igjen . . over and over again
omkríng . . . . about 237(5)
område n. . . . . area 131
omtrént . . . . almost, nearly, about 131
ond . . . . . bad, evil 125(4)
ónkel c. . . . . uncle 229
ónsdag . . . . Wednesday 138
opp, oppe . . . up 65, 155
óppdage (-et) . . . discover, detect 106, 139
óppfordre (-et) . . encourage 247(3)
oppførsel c. . . . behaviour
ord n. [oːr] . . . word 75, 113
ordentlig ['oˈɳʈli] . . properly 95
ordne . . . . arrange, fix 176
over . . . . . across, over 75, 131, 238
overált . . . . everywhere 121, 157
overmåte . . . . extremely, exceedingly 147
overórdentlig . . . extraordinarily 147
overraske (-et) . . . surprise 176
ovn c. . . . . stove 128

P

pakke c.; (-et) . . . parcel, pack 274
papír n. . . . . paper
par n. . . . . couple, pair 118(b)
park c. . . . . park 115
partí n. . . . . party, consignment
pasiént c. . . . . patient 145
passasjér c. . . . passenger 131
  assasjérbåt c. . . liner, page 79

peis c.	fireplace, grating 182, 274
pen	nice, pretty 3, 131
penge c. = pengestykke n. .	coin
penger (pl.) . . .	money, pages 31 and 131
penn c.	pen 3, 64
perle c.	pearl 121
piáno n.	piano, page 33
pike c. ' . . .	girl 45
pil f.	arrow
pinne c.	peg 244
plage c.; (-et) . . .	torment
plass c.	place; seat; square 268
pleie (-de)	be in the habit of 70
plutselig	suddenly 148
poesí c.	poetry 131
polití n.	police, page 107
politíkonstabel c. . .	policeman
post c.	post
postkasse c. . . .	letter-box 256
potét c.	potato 119(a)
prate (-et)	chat
preke (-te)	preach
preken c.	sermon 182
presang c. . . .	gift, present 268
presís	punctual; sharp 138
prest c.	parson 182, 274
prinsèsse c. . . .	princess 106, 140
pris c.	price, page 72
proféssor c.; pl. professórer .	professor 49(2)
prosént c. . . .	per cent 141
prøve (-de) . . .	test, try 63, 69, 128
punkt [poŋ(k)t] n. . .	point 52(2)
pust c.	breath, page 128
puste (-et)	breathe
pute f.	pillow
pynte (-et)	decorate
på	on, at 68, 239
påstå (irr. v.) . . .	maintain 176(4)

R

radio c.	radio, page 149
ramle (-et) ned . .	tumble down 244
rand c; pl. rénder . .	edge, border 50
ransake (-te) . . .	ransack, search, page 128
rar	strange 4, 179, page 189
rask	quick 118(c)
redd	afraid 92, 118(d)
redde (et)	save 64, 106
redsel ['retsel] c. . .	fright 59
regel c.	rule 49

regne ['reinə] (-et, -te)	.	rain 108(c); do sums
regning c. . .	.	bill 176
reise (-te) . .	.	travel, go 65; 75, 90
rekke (rakte, rakt)	.	hand, pass 68
ren; rent (adv.) .	.	clean; quite, page 185
renne (irr. v.) .	.	flow, run 131
rent, see ren		
rente c. . .	.	interest (in the bank)
rentefot c. .	.	rate of interest 141
restaurant [restu'raŋ] c.	.	restaurant 35, page 106
rett, adj., adv.; c.	.	right; straight 70; dish; court
rette på . .	.	put right 268
ri(de) (irr. v.) .	.	ride 87
rik . .	.	rich 81(d), 122
rik på .	.	rich in 131
rike n. . .	.	kingdom, realm 115(g)
riktig . .	.	correct 75
ringe (-te) . .	.	ring, phone 179
ro (-dde) . .	.	row 71, 250
rolle c. . .	.	rôle, part 66
rolig . .	.	quiet, page 189
rom n. . .	.	room 48
roman c. . .	.	novel 106
rope (-te) . .	.	shout 65
rose (-te) . .	.	praise 97
rose c. . .	.	rose 244
rote (-et) . .	.	ransack, search
rund, adj.; -t prep.	.	round 237(5)
rússer c., russisk	.	Russian
rusle (-et) . .	.	jog, slouch 200
rygg c. . .	.	back, page 121
ryggsekk c. . .	.	rucksack
rykte n. . .	.	reputation
rød . .	.	red 113, 119(b)
rødkinnet . .	.	rosy-cheeked
røk c., -e (-te)	.	smoke 68, 98(a)
rør n. . .	.	receiver (telephone)
røre (-te) reflex. r- seg	.	touch; move 182
rå . .	.	raw, brutal 119(a)
råd n. . .	.	piece of advice 68

S

sak c. . .	.	cause, matter
sal c. . .	.	spacious room
salt n. . .	.	salt 108(a)
samle (-et) .	.	collect 75
sámmen . .	.	together 192
samtale c. . .	.	conversation 215
sang c. . .	.	song 121, 244
sanger c. . .	.	male singer 70, 244
sann . .	.	true 75
sannelig . .	.	really, indeed 70, 91

sánnhet c. .	.	.	.	truth 68
sannsýnlig	.	.	.	likely 108(a)
sau c.	.	.	.	sheep 186
se (irr. v.) .	.	.	.	see, look 82(5)
se på	.	.	.	look at 121
seier c.	.	.	.	victory
seile (-te) .	.	.	.	sail
sekk c.	.	.	.	sack, bag 246
sekretǽr c.	.	.	.	secretary
sekúnd n.	.	.	.	second 138
selge (solgte, solgt)	.	.	.	sell 68
selskap n. .	.	.	.	party, page 121
selv .	.	.	.	self 191
sen; sent, adv. of time	.	.	slow; late 75
seng f.	.	.	.	bed 75
sent, see sen				
sentrál	.	.	.	central
septémber .	.	.	.	September 138
setning c. .	.	.	.	sentence, clause 70
sette (satte, satt)	.	.	.	place, put 68
si (sier, sa, sagt)	.	.	.	say, tell 68
siden	.	.	.	since 261; later 148
síkker	.	.	.	safe, sure 125(2)
síkkert .	.	.	.	surely 131
sikte n.; (-et)	.	.	.	aim
sild f.	.	.	.	herring 51
sint .	.	.	.	angry 244
sist; til- .	.	.	.	last 127; at last 148, 155
sitát n.	.	.	.	quotation
sitére (-te)	.	.	.	quote 65
sitte (irr. v.)	.	.	.	sit, pages 146 and 149
sjanse [ˇʃaŋsə] c.	.	.	chance, pages 50 and 115
sjø c.	.	.	.	sea 48
sjøfarende	.	.	.	seafaring 131
sjøfart c.	.	.	.	shipping 131
sjømann c.	.	.	.	seaman 250
sjåfør c.	.	.	.	driver 176
skade c. (-et)	.	.	.	harm 68
skaffe (-et) .	.	.	.	provide 64
skal, skulle	.	.	.	shall, should 162
skam c.	.	.	.	shame 197
skap (b.) .	.	.	.	cupboard, page 170
ski f.; pl.—	.	.	.	ski 51
skildre	.	.	.	describe 197
skille n.; (-te)	.	.	.	division; separate, part 65(c), page 186
skinne (-te)	.	.	.	shine
skip n.	.	.	.	ship 113
skitten	.	.	.	dirty 186
skje (-dde)	.	.	.	happen 71, 197
skje c.	.	.	.	spoon 47
skjell n.	.	.	.	shell, page 42

skjelve (irr. v.)	. . .	shiver, tremble
skjorte f.	. . .	shirt 25, page 185
skjære (irr. v.)	. . .	cut 81
skjønne (-te)	. . .	understand, page 33
skjønt (conj.)	. . .	(al)though 264
sko c.; pl. sko(r)	. . .	shoe 68, 87, 113
skog c.	. . .	wood, forest 53
skole c.	. . .	school 239(2)
skrekk c.	. . .	terror, fright
skrekkelig	. . .	terrible, -ly 147
skrekkslagen	. .	terror-stricken
skrike (irr. v.)	. . .	cry, scream 78(1)
skrive (irr. v,)	. . .	write 78(1)
skryte (irr. v.)	. . .	boast, page 185
skudd n.	. . .	shot 159
skuddår n.	. . .	leap-year 138
skuespill n.	. . .	play 157
skuffe (-et)	. . .	disappoint 75
skute f.	. . .	ship, craft 268
skygge c.	. . .	shade, shadow
skynde (-te) seg .	. .	hurry 95, 266
skyte (irr. v.)	. . .	shoot 79(2)
skyve (irr. v.)	. .	push
slag n.	. . .	blow; kind, sort 156(3); battle 244
slik, slikt, slike –	. .	such; thus; like that 190
slik som	. . .	such as 138
slippe (irr. v.)	. . .	drop; let go
slips n.	. . .	tie, page 185
slit n.	. . .	toil, hard work, page 121
slokke (-te)	. . .	extinguish 87
slott n.	. . .	castle 106, 121
slu	. . .	cunning 120
slutt c.; slutte (-et)	. .	end, finish 274
slyngel c.	. . .	rascal 186
slå (irr. v.) .	. . .	strike, beat 84
slåss (irr. v.)	. . .	fight 104
smak c.; smake (-te)	. .	taste 206
smal	. . .	narrow 131
smed [sme:] c.	. . .	smith 244
smelle (-te); (irr. v.)	. .	slam; crack
smette (irr. v.)	. . .	slip 200
smie f.	. . .	smithy 244
smil n.; smile (-te)	. .	smile 7, 65(a)
smør n.	. . .	butter 68
smøre (smurte, smurt)	. .	grease, smear 68
snakke (-et)	. . .	talk, chat 64(a)
snar; snart (adv.)	. .	quick; soon 73, 148
snes n.	. . .	score 141
snipp c.	. . .	collar of shirt 186
snu (-dde) .	. . .	turn 71
snuse (-te)	. . .	sniff, snuff 200

snute c. . . . . snout, nose, page 128
snø c.; (-dde) . . . . snow 108(c)
sol c. . . . . sun 157
soldát c. . . . . soldier 91(page 52)
solíd . . . . solid 118(d)
som (rel. pron.) . . . who, which, that 74, 199
somme tider . . . sometimes, page 92
sommer c. . . . . summer 75
sove (irr. v.) . . . sleep 84(7)
spare (-te) . . . . save, spare 65
spennende . . . exciting 120,206
spille (-te) . . . play (games, etc.) 66, pages 52 and 53
spise (-te) . . . . eat 65, 90
sprekke (irr. v.) . . break, burst
springe (irr. v.) . . . run; jump
språk n. . . . . language 75
spøk c. . . . . joke
spøke (-te) . . . joke
spørre (spurte, spurt) . ask, inquire 68
spørsmål n. . . . question 247
spå (-dde) . . . prophesy 71
sta . . . . stubborn 120
stakkars . . . . poor (in exclamations) 120
stasjón c. . . . station 65
sted [ste:(d)] n. . . place 131, 52(2)
   i stedet . . . instead, page 168
stein c. . . . . stone 64
   steinet . . . stony 129(1)(b)
sterk. . . . . strong 5
stige c.; (irr. v.) . . ladder; arise, increase
stikke (irr. v.) . . . pierce, stab; put 80(3), 107
stille . . . . quiet 120, 122, 131
stiv . . . . stiff 95
stjele (irr. v.) . . . steal 81(4), 107
stjerne c. . . . . star 197
stokk c. . . . . stick 234
stol c. . . . . chair 68, 87
stole (-te) på . . . rely upon 239(5)
stolt . . . . proud
stolthet . . . pride 186, page 187
stoppe (-et) . . . stop 60, 63(1)
stor . . . . big 68
storm c. . . . . storm 85(9)
strekke (strakte, strakt) . stretch 68
straff c.; straffe (-et) . . punishment; punish 106
straks . . . . immediately 131
streife (-et) . . . roam
streve (-de) . . . strive, try hard 68
stri . . . . persistent; swift-flowing 131
stråle c.; (-te) . . . beam, shine
   strålende . . . glorious

strø (-dde)	. . .	strew 71
strømpe f.	. .	stocking 75, 87
student c. .	. .	student 65
stue f.	. .	sitting-room 244
stund c.	. .	time, while 107
stundom	. .	sometimes, page 92
stygg	. .	ugly, bad 116(1)
stykke n. .	. .	piece; distance 131
stø .	. .	steady 119(a)
støy c.	. .	noise page 125
stå (irr. v.)	. .	stand 84
sukk n.; sukke (-et)	. .	sigh
súkker n. .	. .	sugar 108(a)
sulten	. .	hungry 88, 116(2)
sund; rive—	. .	asunder, to pieces 244; tear—
sunn	. .	healthy 203
suppe c.	. .	soup 107
svak	. .	weak
svar n.	. .	answer 118(b)
svare (-te); -til	. .	answer; correspond to 75
svart	. .	black 118(a)
svensk	. .	Swedish 131
svenske c. .	. .	Swede 131
sverd [sværd] n.	. .	sword
Sverige	. .	Sweden 131, 189
sveve (-de, -et) .	. .	float, glide 69
svær	. .	big 274
svært	. .	very 70, 107
svømme (-te)	. .	swim 64, 250
syd, sør	. .	south 121, 126
syk .	. .	sick 82(e), 121(b)
synd c.; det er—	. .	sin; pity, it is a—
synes (syntes, synes) .	.	think, find 73, 103
synge (irr. v.)	. .	sing 76(1)
synke (irr. v.)	. .	sink
synsbedrag n.	. .	optical illusion, page 121
sølv [søll] n.	. .	silver 33
søndag	. .	Sunday 138
sønn c.	. .	son 78(a), 117
søt .	. .	sweet 73, 93, 119(b)
søster c.	. .	sister 50(c)
særdéles	. .	exceptionally
særlig	. .	especially 121
så .	. .	so, thus; then 121, 148
så—som	. .	as—as 87, 95
således	. .	so, thus, in this way 151

T

ta (irr. v.) .	. .	take 83(6)
tak n.	. .	roof, ceiling 70, 244
tak n.	. .	grasp; effort

takk c. . . . . thanks 157
tale c; (-te) . . . speech; speak 6
tang f.; pl. tenger . . pliers, tongs 50
tann c.; pl. ténner . . tooth 50
  tannlege c. ., . . dentist 145
tante c. . . . . aunt
tape (-te) . . . . lose 65
tápper . . . . brave 125(2)
tau n. . . . . rope 268
teater [te'a:tər] n. pl.— . theatre 49, 91
te c. . . . . tea, page 52
tegn [tein] n. . . . sign 200
telefón c. . . . telephone 35, 172
  telefonére (-te) . . telephone 287
telle (talte, talt) . . count 68
temmelig . . . . rather, quite 147
tenke (-te) . . . think 67, 73
tid c. . . . . time 138
tidlig [ˇti:li] . . . early 64, 131
til; . . . . to, till 53, 59, 240; one more
  til slutt . . . at last, in the end 70, 75
tilbáke . . . . back 237(4)
tilfreds [til'frets] . . . contented 118(e)
tilstand c. . . . condition 186
time c. . . . . hour 121, 138
tine (-te) . . . . melt, page 121
ting c.; pl.— . . . thing 51
tirsdag . . . . Tuesday 138
tog [tɔ:g] n. . . . train, procession 95, 121
tom . . . . empty 287
tomt c. . . . . site 129(2)
tone c. . . . . tune, sound 121
tore (tør, torde, tort) . . dare 70, 176(4)
torg, torv n. . . . market
topp c. . . . . top 260
tórsdag . . . . Thursday 138
trapp f. . . . . staircase 274
trassig . . . . obstinate
trável, ha det—t . . busy, be busy 116(2), 125(2)
tre n.; pl. trær . . . tree 51(1), 113, 115
treffe (irr. v.) . . . meet 91(1)
trekke (irr. v.) . . . pull
trenge (-te) . . . need
trenges . . . . be necessary 103
trett (av) . . . . tired (of) 135
trette c. . . . . quarrel 131
trives (irr. v.) . . . be comfortable 105
tro (-dde) . . . . believe, think 71, 73
troll n. . . . . troll, ogre 274
trykke (-et) . . . print 274
tung . . . . heavy 125(3), 244

tur c.	tour, trip, walk 85(g)
turíst c.	tourist 131
tvil c.	doubt 192
tvile (-te) på	doubt 186, 192
tvilsom	doubtful 128
tydelig	clearly, distinctly 73
tysk	German
týsker c.	German 131
Týskland n.	Germany
tyv c.	thief 79(b)
tøm c.	rein
tømme (-te)	empty 40, 287
tørst c.; adj.	thirst; thirsty 128
tå f.; pl. tær	toe 50(b)
tåpelig	silly 95

U

uforsiktig	careless 95
ugjerning c.	crime, evil deed 106
uke c.	week 138
ukjent	unknown 131
ull c., ùllen	wool, woollen 129(1)(c)
ulv c.	wolf 68
ulykke c.	accident 75
under	under, below, during 87, 131, 241
undertíden	occasionally 148
underrette (-et)	inform 176
undre (-et) seg over (= un-dres)	wonder at 103
ung	young 125(3)
unngå (irr. v.)	avoid 87
unnskyld!	excuse me! 278
unntágen	except 272
ur n.	watch 188
uskadd	safe 268
ut, ute	out 155
ut av	out of
utenat	by heart, page 38, 204(b)
utenfor	outside 243
utenlandsk	foreign 131
utlandet	abroad 65
i utlandet	abroad
til utlandet	abroad 65
utlending c.	foreigner, page 183
utmerket	splendid, grand 179
utsikt c.	view, prospect 131
usedvanlig	unusually 147

V

vaie (-et)	(of flag), wave, fly 131
vákker	pretty 75, 116(2)

vandre (-et)	.	.	wander
vane c.	.	.	habit
vanlig	.	.	usual, -ly 107
vann n.	.	.	water; lake 64, 79(*b*)
vanskelig, -het	.	.	difficult, -y 131
vant til	.	.	accustomed to 274
vare (-te)	.	.	last 138, 145
varme c.	.	.	fire; heat, page 106
vaske (-et)	.	.	wash 4
ved	.	.	at, by, near 244
ved c.	.	.	wood (for fuel)
vegg c.	.	.	wall
vei c.	.	.	road, way 14
vekk	.	.	away, page 194
vekke (-te)	.	.	wake, arouse 68
vel	.	.	well 144
veldig	.	.	great; terrible; exceedingly 75, 131, 147
velge (valgte, valgt)	.	.	elect, choose 68, 176
velkjent	.	.	well-known 131
vende.(-te)	.	.	turn, face 244
venn c.	.	.	friend 53, 75
venne (-te) seg til	.	.	accustom oneself to 173
vénstre	.	.	left 70
vente (-et)	.	.	wait, expect 64
verden ['værdn] c.	.	.	world, earth 115(1), 131
verdenshav n.	.	.	ocean
verdi [vær'di:] c.	.	.	value, worth
verdsette	.	.	value, estimate, page 168
verdt [vær't] c.	.	.	worth 129(2)
verk n.	.	.	work 52(2)
verre, verst	.	.	worse, worst 145
vers n.	.	.	verse 27, page 150
'vesen n.	.	.	nature 129(3)
vesentlig.	.	.	mainly, page 185
veske f.	.	.	bag 57(2)
vesle, den—(=lille)	.	.	the little 115
vest	.	.	west 126
vestenfor	.	.	to the west of
videre	.	.	further, on 215
vil, ville	.	.	will, would 75, 116(1), 162
vin c.	.	.	wine, page 106
vind c.	.	.	wind 75
vindu n.	.	.	window 113
vinne (irr. v.)	.	.	win 87
vinnende	.	.	charming 129(3)
vínter c.	.	.	winter 49
virkelig	.	.	really 197
virksom	.	.	active 125(1)
vis	.	.	wise, page 168
vise (-te)	.	.	show 65

visst, adv.	. . .	apparently 156(5)
visstnok	. .	it is true, no doubt 149
vite (vet, visste, visst)		know (a fact) 67, 92
vond, gjøre—t	. .	bad 125(4); hurt, pain 125(4)
vær n.	. . .	weather 121
være (irr. v.)	. .	be 60
værelse n. .	. .	room 48
våge (-et) .	. .	dare, risk 64(b), 158
våken	. .	awake 85(g), 129(1)(c)
våkne (-et)	. .	awake 64, 87
vår c.	. . .	spring 75

Y

ypperlig	. . .	splendid, grand 95
ýpperst	. . .	supreme 127
ytre .	. . .	outer 125(5)

Æ

ære c.	. . .	honour
ærlig	. . .	honest 24, 28
ærlig talt	. .	honestly 145
ærlighet c.	. .	honesty

Ø

øde .	. . .	desolate 120
ødelegge	. . .	spoil, destroy 257
øks f.	. . .	axe
øl n. .	. . .	beer 87
ønske n.; (-et)	. .	wish, want 244
øre n.	. . .	ear, page 128
øre c.	. . .	smallest Norwegian coin 51, 70
ørn c.	. . .	eagle 70
ørret c.	. . .	trout 176
øst .	. . .	east 126
øve (-de) .	. .	practise 69
øvelse c..	. .	practice 95, page 86
øvre .	. . .	upper 125(5)
øy f.	. . .	island 75
øye n.	. . .	eye 52(1)
øyeblikk n.	. .	moment 176

Å

åker, formerly: aker c.	.	field 49, 59
åpen	. . .	open 113
åpne (-et)	. .	open
år n.	. . .	year 98(a)
årstid c.	. . .	season 138
årsak c.	. . .	reason 179
ås c. .	. . .	hill, ridge, page 183

Vocabulary

English – Norwegian

A

about	.	.	.	om, omkríng, omtrént, ca. 65, 139, 237
abroad	.	.	.	til utlandet, utenlands
accompany		.	.	følge (fulgte, fulgt) 68
accustom (oneself) to		.	venne (-te) seg til
accustomed to	.	.	vant til 173, 274
across	.	.	.	over 75, 131, 238
action	.	.	.	handling c., page 186
active	.	.	.	virksom 125(1)
address	.	.	.	adrésse c. 70
admire	.	.	.	beúndre (-et) 131
advice	.	.	.	råd n. 68
aerodrome	.	.	flýplass c. 85(g)
afraid	.	.	.	redd 92, 118(d)
afresh	.	.	.	på ny
after	.	.	.	etter 87, 22
afterwards	.	.	etterpå 75
again	.	.	.	igjen, på ny 70, 206 note
against	.	.	.	mot 65, 121, 236
agree on	.	.	avtale (-te); bli enig om 274
agreement	.	.	avtale c.
aim	.	.	.	sikte (-et); n.
air	.	.	.	luft c. 70, 75
all	.	.	.	all, alt, alle 212
allied	.	.	.	alliért, p. p. of alliére
almost	.	.	.	nesten, omtrént 70
alone	.	.	.	alène 87
along	.	.	.	langs 79(b)
already	.	.	.	allerède 75
also	.	.	.	ógså 87
although	.	.	skjønt conj. 264
American	.	.	.	amerikáner c. 50(d); amerikánsk 285
amusing	.	.	.	morsom 179, 188
and	.	.	.	og, 5, 256
angel	.	.	.	engel c.
angry	.	.	.	sint 244
animal	.	.	.	dyr n. 48
answer	.	.	.	svar n.; svare (-te) 75, 118(b)
any, anybody	.	.	noen, noe, noen 204
applaud	.	.	.	klappe (-et)
apple	.	.	.	eple c. 55
April	.	.	.	apríl 138
area	.	.	.	område n. 131
arise	.	.	.	stige (irr. v.)
arm	.	.	.	arm c. 53, 78(a)
army	.	.	.	armé c., hær c.

arouse	.	.	.	vekke (-te) 68
arrange; -ment	.	.	avtale (-te); c.
arrogance	.	.	hovmod n. 274
arrow	.	.	pil f.
as	.	.	.	idét 260, da 261, ettersom 261, (like) som 267
as—as	.	.	.	likeså—som, så—som 267
as far as	.	.	helt til 131
as if	.	.	.	som om 267
ask	.	.	.	spørre (spurte, spurt) 68; be 82
at	.	.	.	ved 244; i 230(2); på 239(2)
at last	.	.	.	endelig, til sist
attack	.	.	.	àngrep n.; ángripe (irr. v., see gripe)
attempt	.	.	.	forsøk n.; forsøke (-te) 246
August	.	.	.	augúst 138
aunt	.	.	.	tante c.
author	.	.	.	forfátter c. 159
autumn	.	.	.	høst c. 138
awake	.	.	.	våkne (-et); våken (adj.) 64, 87
away	.	.	.	bort, borte, vekk 155
axe	.	.	.	øks f.

B

back	.	.	.	rygg c., page 121; tilbáke 237(4)
bad	.	.	.	dårlig, ille, vond, stygg 144
bag	.	.	.	veske f. 57(2)
baker	.	.	.	baker c. 50(d)
balcony	.	.	.	altán c. 121
ball	.	.	.	ball c.; ball n, i.e. dance 104
band	.	.	.	musíkk-korps n. 121
bank	.	.	.	bank c. 206
barbarian	.	.	.	barbárisk 129(1)(a)
bath	.	.	.	bad n. 75
bathe	.	.	.	bade (-et); bad n. 14(b)
bathroom	.	.	.	bad n. 75, 203
battle	.	.	.	slag n. 244
be	.	.	.	være (irr. v.) 60
beam	.	.	.	stråle (-te); c.
bear	.	.	.	bjørn c., page 128
beast	.	.	.	dyr n. 48
beat	.	.	.	slå (irr. v.) 84
beautiful	.	.	.	pen, vakker 75, 116(2)
because	.	.	.	fordí 261
become	.	.	.	bli (irr. v.) 78, 96
bed	.	.	.	seng f. 75
beer	.	.	.	øl n. 87
before	.	.	.	før 227, 260
beg	.	.	.	be (irr. v.) 82(5)
begin	.	.	.	begýnne (-te) 34
behaviour	.	.	.	oppførsel c.
behind	.	.	.	bak 125(5)

button	. . . .	knapp c. 244
buy	. . . .	kjøpe (-te) 65
by	. . . .	ved 244
by the way	. . .	forrésten

C

café	. . . .	kafé c. 292
cake	. . .	kake c. 43, 65
call; be called	. .	kalle (-te) 65(c), 87; hete 90
can, could	. .	kan, kunne 64, 176(1)
cancel	. . .	avlyse (-te); innstille (-te) 95
capital	. . .	hovedstad c.; pl. -steder 90
captain	. . .	kaptéin c. 268
capture	. . .	fange (-et) 107
car	. . . .	bil c. 57, 64
care to	. . .	gidde (irr. v.) 103
careful (-ly)	. .	forsíktig, nøye 128, 200
careless	. . .	úforsiktig 95
carry	. . .	bære (irr. v.) 274
castle	. . .	slott n. 106, 121
cat	. . . .	katt c. 101
catch	. . .	fange (-et) 107
cause	. . .	sak c.
cease	. . .	ende (-te)
central	. . .	sentrál
certainly	. . .	visst 156(5)
chair	. . .	stol c. 68, 87
chance	. . .	sjanse c., pages 50 and 115
chapter	. . .	kapítel n.
charming	. . .	vinnende 129(3)
chat	. . . .	prat c.; -e (-et)
cheap	. . .	billig 125(1)
cheek	. . .	kinn n. 52(2)
cheer	. . .	juble (-et) 121
cheerful	. . .	frimódig 268
child	. . .	barn n. 52(1)
childhood	. . .	barndom c. 105
choke	. . .	kvele (kvalte, kvalt) 68
choose	. . .	velge (valgte, valgt) 68, 176
Christmas	. . .	jul c. 121(b)
church	. . .	kirke c. 19
cinema	. . .	kíno c. 254(c)
citizen	. . .	borger c. 118(e)
class	. . .	klasse c. 128
clean	. . .	ren, page 185
clever	. . .	flink 128, 271
climate	. . .	klíma n. 119(a)
climb	. . .	klatre (-et); klyve (irr. v.) 268
climbing	. . .	klatring c., page 121
clock	. . .	klokke f. 65, 186
cloth	. . .	duk c. 68

clothe	.	.	.	. kle (-dde) 75, 121
clothes	.	.	.	. klær 52(1), 121
coal .	.	.	.	. kull n.
coast	.	.	.	. kyst c. 131
coat .	.	.	.	. frakk c. 186
coffee	.	.	.	. kaffe c. 157
coin .	.	.	.	. penge c.; pengestykke n.
cold .	.	.	.	. kald; kulde c.; forkjølelse c. 65, 73, 138
collar	.	.	.	. krage c. 274; snipp c. 186
collect	.	.	.	. samle (-et) 75
colour	.	.	.	. farge c.; (-et) 57, 121
colourful	.	.	.	. fargerik 121
come	.	.	.	. komme (irr. v.) 60, 85(7)
comfortable, be—	.	.	. trives (irr. v.); ha det bra 105
common	.	.	.	. félles 120
completely	.	.	.	. aldéles, helt 157
comrade	.	.	.	. kamerát c. 200
concern	.	.	.	. gjelde (irr. v.) 131, 157
condition	.	.	.	. tilstand c. 186
consequently	.	.	.	. áltså 139
consist of	.	.	.	. bístå av in 219
contented .	.	.	.	fornøyd, tilfréds 118(e), 268
continue	.	.	.	. fórtsette (-satte, -satt) 70
conversation	.	.	.	. konversasjón c.; samtale c. 215
corner	.	.	.	. hjørne n. 68
correct	.	.	.	. riktig 75
correspond to	.	.	. svare (-te) til 75
cost .	.	.	.	. koste (-et) 64(a)
costume	.	.	.	. drakt c. 121
count	.	.	.	. telle (talte, talt) 68
country	.	.	.	. land n. 48, 128
couple, a—of	.	.	. par n.; et— 118(b)
courage	.	.	.	. mot n. 268
courageous	.	.	.	. modig 268
course	.	.	.	. gang c. 70
of course	.	.	.	. natúrligvis 95
cow .	.	.	.	. ku f.; pl. kyr or kuer 50(b)
crack	.	.	.	. knekke 244; smelle, see irr. v.
craft	.	.	.	. skute f. 268
crash	.	.	.	. brake (-et) 244
crawl	.	.	.	. krabbe (-et) 200
creep	.	.	.	. krype (irr. v.) 79(2)
crime	.	.	.	. ugjerning c. 106
crown	.	.	.	. krone c. 274
Crown Prince	.	.	. krónprins c.
cry .	.	.	.	. skrike (irr. v.) 78(1)
cunning	.	.	.	. slu 120
cup .	.	.	.	. kopp c. 219
cupboard .	.	.	.	skap n., page 170
curve	.	.	.	. bue c.; (-et) 121

| cut | . | . | . | . | hugge (-de) |
| cut off | . | . | . | . | ávskjære (irr. v.) 159 |

D

daily	.	.	.	.	daglig, dagligdags 70, 118(e)
damage	.	.	.	.	skade c.; (-et) 68
damned	.	.	.	.	fordømt
Dane	.	.	.	.	danske c. 131
danger; -ous	.	.	.	fare c. 200; farlig 268, 285
dare	.	.	.	.	våge (-et, -de), tore 64(b), 158, 176(4)
dark	.	.	.	.	mørk 113
darkness	.	.	.	.	mørke n. 176(4)
daughter	.	.	.	.	datter c.; pl. døtre 50(c)
dawn	.	.	.	.	daggry n.
day	.	.	.	.	dag c. 70
dead	.	.	.	.	død 119(b)
deal with	.	.	.	.	behándle (-et)
dear	.	.	.	.	ávholdt, kjær; dyr 19, 121; pages 72 and 76
death	.	.	.	.	død c. 106
December	.	.	.	.	desémber 138
decide	.	.	.	.	bestemme (-te), page 187
deep	.	.	.	.	dyp 131
delicious	.	.	.	.	deilig, page 121
delight	.	.	.	.	fest c. 121
deliver	.	.	.	.	levére (-te) 65
dentist	.	.	.	.	tannlege c. 145
depart	.	.	.	.	dra (irr. v.) 83(6)
depend on	.	.	.	.	beró (-dde) på 71
descent	.	.	.	.	nédstigning c., page 121
desolate	.	.	.	.	øde 120
destroy	.	.	.	.	ødelegge (-la, -lagt) 257
detail	.	.	.	.	detálj c. 131
detect	.	.	.	.	óppdage (-et) 106, 139
deuce, devil	.	.	.	.	fanden 244
different	.	.	.	.	forskjéllig, page 121
difficult, -y	.	.	.	.	vanskelig, -het 131
dig	.	.	.	.	grave (-de or irr. v.)
dinner	.	.	.	.	míddag c. 107, 215
dirty	.	.	.	.	skitten 186
disappear	.	.	.	.	forsvínne (irr. v.) 268
discover	.	.	.	.	óppdage (-et) 106, 139
discuss	.	.	.	.	diskutére (-te) 274
distance	.	.	.	.	avstand c. 244
at a distance	.	.	.	på avstand
divan	.	.	.	.	diván c. 95
divide	.	.	.	.	dele (-te) 65, 176
do	.	.	.	.	gjøre (gjør, gjorde, gjort) 68
doctor	.	.	.	.	lege c. 251

dog . . . . . hund c. 59, 78(a), 115(c)
door . . . dør c. 9
doubt . . . tvil c.; tvile (-te) på 186, 192
down . . . ned 125(5), 155
dozen . . . dusín n. 141
drag . . . dra (irr. v.) 83(6)
draw . . . dra (irr. v.) 83(6)
dream . . . drøm n.; drømme (-te) 65(c)
dress . . . drakt c.; kle (-dde) 75, 121
drink . . . drikke (irr. v.) 80(3)
drip . . . dryppe (-et) 259(2)
drive . . . kjøre (-te) 64
drop . . . slippe, falle (irr. v.)
duck . . . and f.; pl. énder 50
during . . . under 87, 131, 241
dwarf . . . dverg c. 274

E

each . . . hver 65, 131, 213
eagle . . . ørn c. 70
ear . . . øre n., page 128
earlier . . . før 227, 260
early . . . tidlig 64, 131
earth . . . jord c. 244
easy . . . lett 70, 95
eat . . . spise (-te) 65, 90
edge . . . rand c.; pl. rénder 50
educated . . . dannet
egg . . . egg n. 68
either—or . . . enten—eller 256
elder, eldest . . . eldre, eldst 128, 131
ember . . . glo f.; pl. glør 50(b)
emperor . . . keiser c.
empty . . . tom; tømme (-te) 40, 287
encourage . . . óppfordre (-et) 247(3)
end . . . ende c.; (-te); slutt c. 274
enemy . . . fiende c. 106
engaged (to be married) . forlóvet 215
English . . . éngelsk 53, page 121
Englishman . . . éngelskmann c. 53, 131
enjoy oneself . . . more (-et, -te) seg 180
enough . . . nok 157
enterprising . . . foretaksom, page 138
entirely . . . fullstendig 147
error . . . feil c. 51, 274
especially . . . i sær, særlig 121, 157
even . . . endog
evening . . . aften c.; kveld c. 87
every . . . hver, alle 65, 111, 131, 213
everybody . . . enhver, alle 213
everyday . . . dagligdags 118(e)

everything	.	.	.	alt 212
every time	.	.	.	hver gang, page 79
everywhere	.	.	.	overált 121, 157
exactly	.	.	.	akkurát, néttopp, nøye 148, 157, 200
example; for—(e.g.)	.	.	eksémpel n.; for—(f.eks) 49, 131
exceedingly	.	.	.	overmåte, veldig 147
excellent	.	.	.	bra, útmerket 120, 179
except	.	.	.	unntágen 242
excuse me!	.	.	.	unnskyld! 278
exercise	.	.	.	gymnastíkk c. 203
expensive	.	.	.	dyr, pages 72 and 76
experience	.	.	.	erfáring c. 156(1)
extraordinary	.	.	.	overórdentlig 147
extremely	.	.	.	overmåte 147

F

face	.	.	.	ansikt n. 121
factory	.	.	.	fabríkk c. 131
fair	.	.	.	lys 87, 131
fairy-tale	.	.	.	eventyr n. 68
fall	.	.	.	fall n.; falle (irr. v.)
famous	.	.	.	berømt, page 183
far	.	.	.	lang, langt (adv.) 85(g), 125(3)
farm	.	.	.	gård c. 29
farmer	.	.	.	bonde c.; pl. bønder 50, 68
farther	.	.	.	bortre 125(5)
farthest	.	.	.	bortest 125(5), lengst 144
father	.	.	.	far c.; pl. fedre 50(c)
fear	.	.	.	frykt c. 129(3)
fearless	.	.	.	frimódig 268
February	.	.	.	február 138
feel	.	.	.	føle (-te); kjenne (-te) 65, 103
fellow	.	.	.	fyr c.; kar 274
fence	.	.	.	gjerde n. 79(2)
fetch	.	.	.	hente(-et)
few	.	.	.	få 125(3)
field	.	.	.	mark f. 43, (ploughed) åker, aker c. 37, 49
fight	.	.	.	kjempe (-et); slåss (irr. v.) 104
film	.	.	.	film c. 113
find	.	.	.	finne (irr. v.) 80(3)
fine	.	.	.	bra 120
finger	.	.	.	finger c. 49, 81(d)
finish	.	.	.	slutt c. 224; slutte (-t)
fire	.	.	.	avfyre (-te) 159; varme c. 176
firm (-ly)	.	.	.	bestémt
first	.	.	.	først 75, 127
fish	.	.	.	fisk c. 48
fishing-rod	.	.	.	fiskestang f.
fishing trip	.	.	.	fisketur c. 143
fjord	.	.	.	fjord c. 131

flag . . . . . flagg n. 121
flow . . . . . renne (irr. v.) 131
flow into . . . . munne (-et) ut i 131
flower . . . . blomst c. 65
fly . . . . . fly, flyge (irr. v.), page 147
follow . . . . følge (fulgte, fulgt) 68
fond of . . . . glad i 70
fool . . . . . narr c.; tosk c.
foot . . . . . fot c.; pl. føtter 50(a), 51
for . . . . . for 223
foreign (-er) . . . fremmed 118(d) c.; utenlandsk
                   131; utlending c., page 183
foremost . . . . forrest, fremst 127
forest . . . . skog c. 53
forget . . . . glemme (-te) 65(c)
form . . . . . klasse c. 128
forward . . . . fram/frem 125(5), 155
free . . . . . fri 103, 112, 119(a)
freeze . . . . fryse (irr. v.) 79(2)
fresh . . . . . fersk 118(b)
Friday . . . . frédag 138
friend . . . . venn c. 53, 75
fright . . . . . rédsel c. 59
frightened . . . . bange 120
from . . . . . fra 226
from where . . . hvórfra
frontier . . . . grense c. 131
fruit . . . . . frukt c.
furniture; piece of— . . pl. møbler; sg. møbel n. 118(e)
further . . . . videre 215

G

gaiety . . . . múnterhet c. 121
gay . . . . . múnter 121, 215
generally . . . . i alminnelighet
genius . . . . gení n.
gentleman . . . herre c. 5
get . . . . . bli (irr. v.) 78, 96; få 85, 176(5)
German . . . . tysk; týsker c. 131
Germany . . . . Týskland n.
gift . . . . . gave c. 65
girl . . . . . pike c. 45
give . . . . . gi (irr. v.) 82(5)
glass . . . . . glass n. 80
glitter . . . . glitre (-et) 274
glorious . . . . strålende
gloriously . . . . glimrende 216
go . . . . . gå (irr. v.) 85(7); dra (irr. v.) 83(6);
                   reise (-te) 65
goblin . . . . nisse c., page 170
good . . . . . bra, god 120
good-bye . . . . adjø, farvél n. 277

golden	.	.	.	gyllen 129(1)(c)
grand	.	.	.	útmerket 179
grasp	.	.	.	tak n.
grease	.	.	.	smøre (smurte, smurt) 68
great	.	.	.	stor 68
greet	.	.	.	hilse (-te) 121
grey .	.	.	.	grå 119(a)
grow	.	.	.	: gro 71
guide	.	.	.	fører, leder c., page 121
gymnastics	.	.	.	gymnastíkk c. 203

H

hair .	.	.	.	hår n. 119(a)
half .	.	.	.	halv, halvdel c.; halvpart c. 33, 140
halfmoon .	.	.	.	halvmåne c. 140
halfway	.	.	.	halvveis 140
hammer	.	.	.	hammer c. 244
hand	.	.	.	hånd c.; pl. hender 50; rekke (rakte, rakt) 68
handkerchief	.	.	.	lommetørkle n.
hang	.	.	.	henge (-te) (irr. v.)
happen	.	.	.	hende (-te) 40; skje (-dde) 71
happy (-ily)	.	.	.	lykkelig 106, 143
harbour	.	.	.	havn c. 121, 131
hard	.	.	.	hard 29, 70
hardly	.	.	.	neppe 152
harm	.	.	.	skade c.; (-et)68
hat .	.	.	.	hatt c., page 33
have	.	.	.	ha (hadde, hatt) 53
head .	.	.	.	hode n., page 170
healthy	.	.	.	sunn 203
hear .	.	.	.	høre (-te) 65
heart	.	.	.	hjerte n.
hearty	.	.	.	hjertelig 157
heat .	.	.	.	varme c., page 106
heaven	.	.	.	himmel c. 119(a)
heavy	.	.	.	tung 125(3), 244
help .	.	.	.	hjelp c. 244(2); -e (irr. v.) 80(3)
hen .	.	.	.	høne f. 43
here .	.	.	.	her, hit 5, 155
hero .	.	.	.	helt c. 106
heroic novel	.	.	.	helteromán c. 106
herring	.	.	.	sild f. 51
hide .	.	.	.	gjemme (-te) 65(c)
high .	.	.	.	høy 113, 128
hill .	.	.	.	bakke c.; ås c. 131
hilly .	.	.	.	bakket 129(1)(a)
hind .	.	.	.	bakre 125(5)
hither	.	.	.	hit 155
hold .	.	.	.	holde (irr. v.) 85(7)

hole	.	.	.	hull n. 244
holiday	.	.	.	férie c. 75
home	.	.	.	hjem n. 121
at home		.	.	hjemme 155
homeland		.	.	hjemland n. 128
homeward		.	.	hjémover, page 42
hope	.	.	.	håp n., page 156; -e (-et) 101
horse	.	.	.	hest c. 186
hotel	.	.	.	hotéll n. 35
hot-tempered		.	.	hissig 131
hour	.	.	.	time c. 121, 138
house	.	.	.	hus n. 43
hover	.	.	.	sveve (-de, -et) 69
how	.	.	.	hvórdan 88, 128; hvor 88
however	.	.	.	forrésten, imídlertid 148
humour	.	.	.	humør n. 121, 188
humorous		.	.	humorístisk, page 125
hundred	.	.	.	hundre n. 68
hungry	.	.	.	sulten 88, 116(2)
hunter	.	.	.	jeger c. 79(b)
hurry	.	.	.	skynde (-te) seg 95, 266
hysterical	.	.	.	hystérisk 129(1)(a)

I

idea	.	.	.	idé 47; anelse c. 91, 207
idiot	.	.	.	idiót c. 186
if	.	.	.	hvis, dersom, om 261 186
immediately		.	.	straks 131
impression		.	.	inntrykk n, page 125
in; into		.	.	i; inn (ut) i 53, 230
in front of		.	.	fóran 65, 224
in order to		.	.	for å 87
increase	.	.	.	stige (irr. v.)
indeed	.	.	.	sannelig 70, 91
industrious		.	.	flittig 271
inform	.	.	.	underrette (-et) 176
ink	.	.	.	blekk n. 108(b)
instead	.	.	.	i stedet, page 168
instrument	.	.	instru´ment n.
interest	.	.	.	interésse c. 68
interrupt	.	.	.	ávbryte (irr. v.) 159
island	.	.	.	øy f. 75

J

January	.	.	.	január 138
jog	.	.	.	rusle (-et) 200
joke	.	.	.	spøk c.; -e (-te)
jolly	.	.	.	morsom 179, 188
joy	.	.	.	glede c. 65, 121
July	.	.	.	júli 138
jump	.	.	.	hoppe (-et)

June	.	.	.	.	júni 138
just	.	.	.	.	nettopp 148; bare 157

K

keep	.	.	.	.	holde (irr. v.) 85(7)
key	.	.	.	.	nøkkel c. 156(2a)
kill	.	.	.	.	drepe (-te) 106, 107
kilo; -metre	.	.	.	kílo n.; -meter c. 51
kind	.	.	.	.	slag n.
king	.	.	.	.	konge c. 45, 68, 123
kingdom	.	.	.	.	kongedømme n.
knee	.	.	.	.	kne n.; pl. knær 52(1)
knife	.	.	.	.	kniv c., page 113
know	.	.	.	.	kjenne (-te); vite (vet, visste, visst) 67

L

ladder	.	.	.	.	stige c.
lady	.	.	.	.	dame c. 57(2), 121
lake	.	.	.	.	vann n. 64, 79(b)
language	.	.	.	.	språk n. 75
last; at—	.	.	.	.	vare (-te) 138, 145; sist 127; til slutt, page 44
late	.	.	.	.	sen, sent (adv.) 75
lately	.	.	.	.	nylig, page 92; i det siste 179
later	.	.	.	.	siden, senere 148, 261
laugh	.	.	.	.	le (irr. v.) 84
lazy	.	.	.	.	doven, lat 119(b)
lay	.	.	.	.	legge (la, lagt) 68
lead	.	.	.	.	føre (-te), lede (-et) 106, 284
leader	.	.	.	.	fører c., page 121
leap-year	.	.	.	.	skuddår n. 138
learn	.	.	.	.	lære (-te) 65
least	.	.	.	.	minst 139
at least	.	.	.	minst
left	.	.	.	.	vénstre 70
leg	.	.	.	.	ben n., page 25
lend	.	.	.	.	låne (-te) 65, 186
let	.	.	.	.	la (irr. v.) 83(6), 176(6)
letter; -box	.	.	.	brev n. 64, 112; postkasse c. 256
lie	.	.	.	.	ligge (irr. v.) 70, 82(3)
lie, i.e. tell a lie	.	.	lyve, lyge (irr. v.) 75
life	.	.	.	.	liv n. 115(a)(3)
lifeless	.	.	.	.	livløs 200
light	.	.	.	.	lys (n., adj.); lett 70, 95
like	.	.	.	.	like (-te) 65
likely	.	.	.	.	sannsýnlig 108(a)
limb	.	.	.	.	lem n. 52(2)
line	.	.	.	.	linje c. 157
liner	.	.	.	.	passasjérbåt c. n., page 79

little . . . . liten n., lite; def. lille or vesle; pl. små 117, 125(4)
a little . . . . litt 128
live . . . . bo (-dde), leve (-de) 60
lively . . . . livlig
lock . . . . låse (-te) 107, 260
long . . . . lang 85(g), 125(3); lenge (adv.) 144
look (at) . . . . se (på) 82(5), 121
look for . . . . lete (-te) etter 222(2)
lose . . . . miste (-et) 64(a)
louse . . . . lus f.; pl.— 51
love . . . . elske (-et) 118
low . . . . lav
lower . . . . nedre 125(5)
luck . . . . lykke c. 8
lucky . . . . heldig 91
lure . . . . narre (-et) 106

M

main road . . . . hovedvei c. 274
maintain . . . . påstå (irr. v.) 176(4)
make . . . . lage (-et), gjøre 64(b), 106
man . . . . mann c.; pl. menn; menneske n. 50
manage . . . . greie (-de) 69, klare (-te) 274
manner . . . . måte c. 115(a), 250
many . . . . mange 52, 65
map . . . . kart n. 52(3)
March . . . . mars 138
march . . . . marsj c.; marsjére (-te) 121
mark . . . . blink c.; merke n.; (-et)
married . . . . gift, page 135
marry . . . . gifte (-et) seg med 91(1)
mast . . . . mast c. 268
master . . . . méster c. 95
match . . . . fýrstikk c. 141
material . . . . materiále n., page 121
matter . . . . sak c.
May . . . . mai 138
mean . . . . bety (-dde) 71; mene (-te) 73
meaning . . . . mening c. 207
means . . . . middel n. 49
meat . . . . kjøtt n. 206
meet . . . . møte (-te); treffe (irr. v.) 65, 95
meeting . . . . møte n. 65, 95
melt . . . . tine (-te), page 121
memory . . . . minne n. 274
mention . . . . nevne (-te) 179
merry . . . . glad, múnter 121, 215
midday . . . . middag c. 107, 215
mile . . . . mil f. = 6 English miles 51
milk . . . . melk c. 205, 219

minister . . . . prest c. 182, 274
minute . . . . minútt n. 138
miserable . . . . eléndig
mistake . . . . feil n., pl.— 51, 274
modern . . . . modérne 91, 120
moment . . . . øyeblikk n. 176
Monday . . . . mándag 138
money . . . . penger pl., pages 31 and 131
month . . . . måned c. 115(d), 138
moon . . . . måne c., page 184
more, most . . . . mer, mest 129: flere, flest 75
morning . . . . morgen c. 68
mother . . . . mor c.; pl. mødre 50(c)
motor . . . . mótor c. 49
mountain . . . . fjell n. 113
mountaineer . . . fjellmann c., page 121
mountain range . . fjellkjede c., page 121
move . . . . røre (-te) seg 182; flytte (-et)
Mr. . . . . . herr 59
Mrs. . . . . . fru 176
much . . . . mye 124, 125(4)
music . . . . musíkk c. 65
musical . . . . musikálsk 70
musician . . . . músiker c.

N

name . . . . navn n. 46, 138
narrow . . . . smal 131
nation . . . . nasjón c. 131
National Anthem . . nasjonálsang c. 121
national costume . . nasjonáldrakt c. 121
National Day . . . nasjonáldag c. 121
natural (-ly) . . . natúrlig, -vis 95
nature . . . . vésen n. 129(3)
near . . . . . nær, ved 127
nearly . . . . omtrént 131
neck . . . . hals c. 121
need . . . . behøve (de); trenge (-te) 69
needle . . . . nål f. 244
Negro . . . . néger c. 140
neighbour . . . . nabo c. 58, 143
neighbourhood . . nærhet c. 244
neither—nor . . . hverken—eller
never . . . . aldri, pages 42 and 92
nevertheless . . . likevel 106, 157
new . . . . . ny 119(a)
news . . . . nýhet c. 68, 244
newspaper . . . . avís c. 65
next . . . . . nest 127
nice . . . . pen 3, 131
night . . . . natt f.; pl. netter 50, 70

no	ingen, intet, ingen 207; nei 53
nobody	ingen 207
noise	støy c., page 125
none	ingen, intet, ingen 207
north	nord 121, 126
(The) North Sea . .	Nordsjøen
northwards . . .	nórdover 131
Norway	Norge 53
Norwegian . . .	nórdmann c. 50; norsk 27, 54, 118(c)
nose	nese c.; snute c., page 128
not	ikke 64, 90
nothing	ingenting 207
notice	merke n. 64(a); legge—til, —(-et)
November . . .	novémber 138
novel	román c. 106
now and again . .	av og til 91
nut	nøtt f. 244

O

obstinate	trassig
occasion	anlédning c. 121
occasionally . . .	av og til 91
ocean	vérdenshav n.
October	október 138
of	av 219, om 237
offer	by (irr. v.), page 187
office	kontór n. 274
officer	offisér c.
often	ofte 75(a), 145
ogre	troll n. 274
old, older, oldest .	gammel, eldre, eldst 116(2), 125(4)
oldfashioned . .	gammeldags 118(d)
on	på 239
only	bare 53, 64, 262, (adj.) eneste 133
open	åpen; åpne (-et) 113
other	annen, annet, andre 135, 208
otherwise	éllers 154
ought to	bør, burde, see 176(3)
out	ut, ute, see 155
out of	ut av
outer	ytre 125(5)
overtake	innhente (-et) 158
own	eie (-de) 244; egen (adj.) 117

P

pair	par n. 118(b)
paper	papír n.
park	park c. 115
parson	prest c. 182, 274
part	del c. 140
part	skille (-te) 65(c); skilles 103

party	. . . .	selskap n., page 121
pass	. . . .	rekke (rakte, rakt) 68
passenger	. . .	passasjér c. 131
patch	. . .	bot f.; pl. bøter 50
patient	. . .	pasiént c. 145
pavement	. . .	fortau n.
pay .	. . . .	betåle (-te) 70, 99
peak	. . .	topp c. 260
pearl	. . .	perle c. 121
peep	. . .	kikke (-et) 215
peg .	. . . .	pinne c. 244
pen .	. . . .	penn c. 3, 64
people	. . .	folk n.; mennesker n. pl. 100
per cent	. . .	prosént c. 141
performance	. .	forestilling c.
perhaps	. . .	kanskje 128, 244
persistent	. .	stri 131
person	. . .	person c. 27, menneske n.
physician .	. .	lege c. 251
piano	. . .	piáno n., page 33
picture	. . .	bilde n. 73, page 135
piece	. . .	stykke n. 131
pierce	. . .	stikke (irr. v.) 80(3), 107
pig .	. . . .	gris c. 124(b), 186
pillow	. . .	pute f.
pilot	. . .	flyger c.
place	. . .	plass c.; sted n. 268
plane	. . .	fly n. 84(f)
play .	. . . .	leke (-te); spille (-te) 66; skuespill n. 157
pleasant	. . .	deilig, page 121
pliers	. . .	tang f.; pl. ténger 50
pocket	. . .	lomme f. 70, 80(c)
poem	. . .	dikt n. 70, 88
poet .	. . .	dikter c. 215(3)
poetry	. . .	poesí c. 131
point	. . .	punkt n. 52(2)
police	. . .	polití n, page 107
policeman .	. .	politíkonstabel c.
polite (-ly)	. .	høflig
pond	. . .	dam c. 48
poor	. . .	fattig; stakkars (in exclamations) 70, 120
population	. .	befólkning c. 140
possible	. . .	mulig
post .	. . .	post c.
potato	. . .	potét c. 119(a)
potter	. . .	rusle (-et) 200
power	. . .	kraft c., pl. krefter 50
powerful (-ly)	. .	kraftig 285, page 187
practice	. . .	øvelse c. 95, page 86

practise . . . . øve (-de) 69
praise . . . . rose (-te) 97
prefer . . . . foretrekke (irr. v.) 121, 182
preferably . . . heller, helst 145
pretty . . . . vakker 75, 116(2)
price . . . . pris c. 121
pride . . . . stólthet c. 186, page 187
princess . . . . prinsèsse c. 106, 140
print . . . . trykke (-et) 274
prison . . . . féngsel n. 284
prisoner . . . . fange c.
probably . . . . antakelig 171, 293
procession . . . tog n. 121
professor . . . . proféssor c. 49(2)
promise . . . . løfte n.; love (-te) 69, 79(b)
proper (-ly) . . . órdentlig 95
prophesy . . . . spå (-dde) 71
prospect . . . . utsikt c., page 79
proud . . . . kry, stolt 120
provide . . . . skaffe (-et) 64
prudent . . . . klok 274
pull . . . . trekke (irr. v.)
punctual, ... presís 138
punish . . . . straffe (-et) 106
punishment . . . straff c.
pupil . . . . elév c., page 38
push . . . . skyve (irr. v.)
put . . . . stikke (irr. v.); legge (la, lagt) 80(3), 107

Q

quay . . . . kai c. 131
quarrel . . . . trette c.; (-et) 131
quick . . . . kvikk, rask, snar 118(c)
quickly . . . . fort 145
quiet . . . . rolig, stille 120, page 189
quite . . . . fullsténdig; ganske, temmelig 147
quote . . . . sitére (-te) 65
quotation . . . . sitát n.

R

radio . . . . radio c., page 149
rain . . . . regn n.; regne (-et, -te) 108(c)
ransack . . . . ransake (-et), page 128
rascal . . . . kjeltring c.; slýngel c. 186
rate of interest . . rentefot c. 141
rather . . . . heller, helst 145; temmelig 147
raw . . . . rå 119(a)
reach . . . . nå (-dde) 75
read . . . . lese (-te) 65, page 170
ready . . . . ferdig 118(b), 244

really . . . . virkelig, rent, sannelig 70, 91, 197
realm . . . . rike n. 115(g)
reason . . . . grunn c., årsak c. 179
receive . . . . få (irr. v.) 75, 76(5)
receiver . . . . rør n.
recently . . . . néttopp, nylig, nyss 139, 148
recognise . . . . kjenne (-te) igjen 67(1), 91
red . . . . rød 113, 119(b)
rein . . . . tøm c.
relate . . . . fortélle (-talte, -talt) 68
rely upon . . . . stole (-te) på 239(5)
remark . . . . bemerkning c.; bemérke (-et) 139
remedy . . . . míddel n. 49
remember . . . . huske (-et) 64(a), page 128
remind . . . . minne (-te) 105, 239(5)
reputation . . . . rykte n.
reside . . . . bo (-dde) 60
rest . . . . hvil c.; hvile (-te), page 121
restaurant . . . . restauránt c. 35, page 106
rich . . . . rik 81(d), 122
ride . . . . ri(de) (irr. v.) 87
ridge . . . . ås c., page 183
rifle . . . . gevær n. 34
right . . . . høyre; rett 70
ring . . . . ringe (-te) 179
river . . . . elv f., pages 44 and 78
road . . . . vei c. 14
roam . . . . streife (-et)
roof . . . . tak n. 70, 244
room . . . . værelse n., rom 48
rope . . . . tau n. 268
rose . . . . rose c. 244
round . . . . rund, rundt, adv.; prep. 237(5)
row . . . . ro (-dde) 71, 250
rucksack . . . . ryggsekk c.
run . . . . løpe (irr. v.), springe (irr. v.) 85(7)
rush . . . . fare (irr. v.)
Russian . . . . rússer c.; rússisk

S

sack . . . . sekk c. 246
safe . . . . sikker, uskadd 125(2)
sail . . . . seile (-te)
salmon . . . . laks c. 131
salt . . . . salt n. 108(a)
Saturday . . . . lørdag 138
save . . . . redde (-et); spare (-te) 64, 106
say . . . . si (sier, sa, sagt) 68
scarcely . . . . neppe 152
school; —mistress . . skole c. 239(2); lærerinne c. 284
score . . . . snes n. 141

scream	.	.	.	skrike (irr. v.) 78(1)
sea	.	.	.	hav n., sjø c. 48, 131
seafaring	.	.	.	sjøfarende 131
search	.	.	.	lete etter (-te), rote (-et)
season	.	.	.	årstid c. 138
seat	.	.	.	plass c. 268
second	.	.	.	sekúnd n. 138
secretary	.	.	.	sekretær c.
see	.	.	.	se (irr. v.) 82(5)
seize	.	.	.	gripe (irr. v.) 87
self	.	.	.	selv 191
sell	.	.	.	selge (solgte, solgt) 68
September	.	.	.	septémber 138
serious	.	.	.	alvórlig 176
sermon	.	.	.	preken c. 182
set	.	.	.	sette 68
several	.	.	.	flére 75
sexton	.	.	.	klokker c., page 168
shade, shadow	.	.	.	skygge c.
shall, should	.	.	.	skal, skulle 162
shame	.	.	.	skam c. 197
shape	.	.	.	danne (-et); form c.
share	.	.	.	dele (-te); del c. 65, 176
sharp	.	.	.	skarp; presís 138
sheep	.	.	.	sau c. 186
shell	.	.	.	skjell n., page 42
shine	.	.	.	stråle (-te), skinne (-te)
ship	.	.	.	skip n.; skute f. 113, 268
shipping	.	.	.	sjøfart c. 131
shiver	.	.	.	skjelve (irr. v.)
shoe	.	.	.	sko c. 68, 87, 113
shoot	.	.	.	skyte (irr. v.) 79(2)
shop	.	.	.	butíkk c. 65
shot	.	.	.	skudd n. 159
shout	.	.	.	rope (-te) 65
show	.	.	.	vise (-te) 65
shower	.	.	.	dusj c. 203
sigh	.	.	.	sukk n.; sukke (-et)
sign	.	.	.	tegn n. 200
silly	.	.	.	tåpelig 95
silver	.	.	.	sølv n. 33
sin	.	.	.	synd c.
since	.	.	.	siden 148, 261
sing	.	.	.	synge (irr. v.) 76(I)
singer	.	.	.	sanger 70, 244
sink	.	.	.	synke (irr. v.)
sister	.	.	.	søster c. 50(c)
sit	.	.	.	sitte (irr. v.), pages 146 and 149
site	.	.	.	tomt c. 129(2)
sitting-room	.	.	.	stue f. 244
ski	.	.	.	ski f. 51
sky	.	.	.	himmel c. 119(a)

sleep	.	.	.	.	sove (irr. v.) 84(7)
slip .	.	.	.	.	gli (irr. v.); smette (irr. v.) 200
slow .	.	.	.	.	langsom, sen 75, 125(1)
small	.	.	.	.	see little
smell	.	.	.	.	lukte (-et) 200
smile	.	.	.	.	smile (-te) 65(a); smil n. 7
smith	.	.	.	.	smed c. 244
smithy	.	.	.	.	smie f. 244
sniff .	.	.	.	.	lukte (-et); snuse (-te) 200
snout	.	.	.	.	snute c., page 128
snow	.	.	.	.	snø c.; (-dde) 108(c)
so .	.	.	.	.	så, således 121, 148
sober	.	.	.	.	edru 120
soldier	.	.	.	.	soldát c. 91
solid	.	.	.	.	solíd 118(d)
some	.	.	.	.	noen, noe, noen 204
somebody	.	.	.		noen 204
something	.	.	.		noe 204
sometimes	.	.	.		somme tider, stundom, page 92
son .	.	.	.	.	sønn c. 78(a), 117
song	.	.	.	.	sang c. 121, 244
soon .	.	.	.	.	snar, snart (adv.) 73, 148
sort .	.	.	.	.	slag n.
sound	.	.	.	.	høres (-tes); lyd c. 103
south	.	.	.	.	sør, syd 121, 126
spare	.	.	.	.	spare (-te) 65
speak	.	.	.	.	tale (-te) 6
speech	.	.	.	.	tale c.
speed	.	.	.	.	fart c. 75, 103, 131
splendid, -ly	.	.	.		útmerket, glimrende 179
spoil	.	.	.	.	ødelegge (-la, -lagt) 257
spring	.	.	.	.	vår c. 75
spruce	.	.	.	.	gran f., page 183
square	.	.	.	.	plass c. 268
squirrel	.	.	.	.	ekorn n., c. 268
stab	.	.	.	.	stikke (irr. v.) 80(3), 107
staircase	.	.	.	.	trapp f. 274
stand	.	.	.	.	stå (irr. v.) 84
station	.	.	.	.	stasjón c. 65
steady	.	.	.	.	stø 119(a)
steal	.	.	.	.	stjele (irr. v.) 81(4), 107
stick	.	.	.	.	stokk c. 234
stiff .	.	.	.	.	stiv 95
still (adv.)	.	.	.	.	(al)likevel, enda, ennå 106, 157
stone	.	.	.	.	stein c. 64
stony	.	.	.	.	steinet 129(1)(b)
stop .	.	.	.	.	stoppe (-et) 60, 63(1)
storm	.	.	.	.	storm c.; (-et) 85(9)
story	.	.	.	.	histórie c. 106, 131
stove	.	.	.	.	ovn c. 128
straight	.	.	.	.	rett 170
strange	.	.	.	.	rar 4, 170, page 180

street . . . . gate f. 48, 57
strength . . . kraft c.; pl. krefter 50
strenuous . . . . ánstrengende, page 121
stretch . . . . strekke (strakte, strakt) 68
strew . . . . strø (-dde) 71
strike . . . . slå (irr. v.) 84
strive . . . . streve (-de) 68
stubborn . . . . sta 120
student . . . . studént c. 65
stupid . . . . dum 121
succeed . . . . lykkes (lyktes, lykkes) 105
success . . . . lykke c. 8
such (as) . . . . slik (som) 138
suddenly . . . . med étt, plutselig 148
sugar . .. . súkker n. 108(a)
summer . . . . sommer c. 75
sun . . . . sol c. 157
Sunday . . . . søndag 138
supreme . . . . ypperst 127
sure, -ly . . . . síkker, -t 125(2)
surprise . . . . overraske (-et) 176; forbause (-et)
Swede . . . . svenske c. 131
Swedish . . . . svensk 131
sweet . . . . søt 73, 93, 119(b)
sword . . . . sverd n.

T

table . . . . bord n. 68
take . . . . . ta (irr. v.); føre (-te) 106
talk . . . . . snakke (-et) 64(a)
taste . . . . smak c.; smake (-te) 206
taxi . . . . . drosje c. 70
tea . . . . . te c., page 52
teach . . . . lære (-te) 65
teacher . . . . lærer c. 45, 50(d)
tear up . . . . rive (irr. v.) sund
telephone . . . . telefón c. 35, 172; telefonére (-te) 287
tell . . . . si, fortélle (-talte, talt) 68
tell about . . . . fortelle om 237
terrible, -ly . . . . forférdelig, skrekkelig 147
terror . . . . skrekk c.
till, see until
than . . . . enn 123
thanks . . . . takk c. 157
that (conj.) . . . . at 257
the—the . . . . jo—jo; jo—dess; jo—desto 128
theatre . . . . teáter n. 49, 91
then . . . . da, déngang, så, dérpå 108(b), 148
there . . . . der 5, 65
therefore . . . . dérfor 87
thief . . . . tyv c. 79(b)

think . . . . tenke (-te), tro (-dde), synes (-tes) 73
thing . . . . ting e.; pl.— 51
thirst, -y . . . . tørst c., adj. 128
though . . . . skjønt conj. 264; dog adv.
throat . . . . hals c. 121
through . . . . gjénnom 228
Thursday . . . . tórsdag 138
thus . . . . . således, slik 151, 190
tie . . . . . binde (irr. v.) 95
time . . . . . gang c. 70; tid c. 138; stund c. 107
tired (of) . . . . trett (av) 135
to . . . . . til 240
today . . . . i dag 230(6)
together . . . . sámmen 192
toil . . . . . slit n., page 121
to-morrow . . . . i morgen 230(6)
tongs . . . . tang f.; pl. ténger 50
too . . . . . (ált)for 147; også 87
tooth . . . . tann n.; pl. ténner 50
top . . . . . topp c. 260
torment . . . . plage c.; (-et)
touch . . . . røre (-te) 182
tourist . . . . turíst c. 131
town . . . . by c. 48
train . . . . tog n. 121
traitor . . . . forræder c. 106
tram . . . . trikk c.
travel . . . . fare (irr. v.); reise (-te) 65, 75, 90
tree . . . . . tre n.; pl. trær 51(1), 113, 115
tremble . . . . skjelve (irr. v.)
trip . . . . . tur c. 85(g)
troll . . . . . troll n. 274
trout . . . . ørret c. 176
true . . . . . sann 75
truth . . . . sánnhet c. 68
try . . . . . prøve(-de),forsøke(-te) 63,69,128, 246
    try hard . . . . streve (irr. v.) 68
Tuesday . . . . tírsdag 138
tumble . . . . ramle (-et) 244
tune . . . . tone c. 121
turn . . . . . snu (-dde); vende (-te); reflex. — seg
                71, 244

U

ugly . . . . . stygg 116(I)
uncle . . . . ónkel c. 229
understand . . . forstå (irr. v.), skjønne (-te), page 33
unfamiliar . . . . fremmed 118(d)
unfortunately . . dessvérre 91(1)
until, till (conj.) . . (inn)til 233
up . . . . . opp, oppe 155

window	. . . .	vindu n. 113
wine	. . . .	vin c., page 106
winter	. . . .	vinter c. 49
wise .	. . . .	vis, klok 274
wish	. . . .	ønske n.; (-et) 244
with	. . . .	med 75, 234
wolf .	. . . .	ulv c. 68
woman	. . . .	kvinne c. 45
wonder	. . . .	under n.; undre (-et); reflex. — seg 103
wood	. . . .	skog c. 53; ved c., i.e. fuel
world	. . . .	vérden c. 115(1), 131
word	. . . .	ord n. 75, 113
work	. . . .	àrbeid n. 118(a); arbéide (-et) 65; verk n. 52(2)
worker	. . . .	arbéider c.
worm	. . . .	mark c., page 147
worst	. . . .	verst 145
worth	. . . .	verdí c.; verdt 129(2)
write	. . . .	skrive (irr. v.) 78(1)
wrong	. . . .	gal 143; feil (adj., adv.) 51, 274

Y

year .	. . . .	år n. 98(a)
this , last	. .	i år; i fjor 230(6)
yes .	. . . .	ja; jo (after negation) 93-94
yet .	. . . .	(al)likevel, dog, enda, ennå 106, 157

SWEDISH

R. J. McCLEAN

This book provides a complete and practical course in Swedish, designed primarily for those learning through private study but also of real value for all students.

Pronunciation, grammar and syntax are fully explained, and a basic vocabulary is introduced. Each chapter contains exercises, a key to which is given at the back of the book, and the text also includes a two-way vocabulary and an alphabetical list of contents.

'The difficult Swedish sound system is dealt with scientifically, with great thoroughness, and there is an equally exhaustive presentation of the grammar . . . certainly an outstanding work.'

THE HIGHER EDUCATIONAL JOURNAL

TEACH YOURSELF BOOKS

FINNISH

ARTHUR H. WHITNEY

A lively and practical course in Finnish from which the student will emerge with a sound grasp of the language.

This course has been divided into twenty lessons, each dealing with the key points in the construction, use and grammar of modern Finnish. Exercises are to be found at the end of each lesson and also included in the text are several reading passages from modern Finnish writings.

TEACH YOURSELF BOOKS

ICELANDIC

A. J. T. GLENDENING

A planned, comprehensive course in Icelandic, invaluable both to the absolute beginner and to the student of Icelandic culture and its literature.

This book provides a thorough and detailed course in Icelandic. The student is taken through a series of lessons which provide a complete grounding in pronunciation, grammar and vocabulary. Exercises are included to cover each stage in the course and the aim is to provide a practical series of lessons by which the student can smoothly progress, on his own if necessary, to a sound working knowledge of Icelandic.

TEACH YOURSELF BOOKS

DANISH

H. A. KOEFOED

This book offers a clear and comprehensive guide to everyday conversational Danish for readers with no previous experience of the language.

Pronunciation, grammar and vocabulary are fully covered, and the text includes numerous exercises and examples—some of them taken direct from Danish literature—chosen to illustrate the different styles in use today and to introduce the reader to the life and culture of modern Denmark.

TEACH YOURSELF BOOKS